MW00764694

Building Self-Esteem with Koala-Roo Can-Do

Laura Fendel

Illustrated by
Beverly Ecker

Scott, Foresman and Company
Glenview, Illinois London

A GOOD YEAR BOOK® **Good Year Books**

are available for preschool through grade 12 and for every basic curriculum subject plus many enrichment areas. For more Good Year Books, contact your local bookseller or educational dealer. For a complete catalog with information about other Good Year Books, please write:

Good Year Books
Department GYB
1900 East Lake Avenue
Glenview, Illinois 60025

5678910 – EBI – 9291

ISBN 0-673-38080-7

Building Self-Esteem with Koala-Roo Can-Do

For:
All Can-Do Kids...
especially,
Julia & You!
Love, B.E.
For: Bev Larrabee
&
Becky Adams
Can-Do Thinkers
Love, L.F.

Preface

If we provide opportunities for children to succeed, we enhance their self-esteem. Children who gain in their sense of self-worth are more capable of realizing their potential.

Contained in this book are dozens of ideas that you can adapt to your specific needs and to many kinds of children. All the ideas are based on Koala-Roo Can-Do and his positive self-esteem program. Various sections of the book may be helpful to you at different times and with different students. Many of the activities interrelate and are cross-referenced within the text. Many of the reproducibles are flexible enough for you to modify as your creativity suggests.

If you would like, take a moment to send me your suggestions, questions, or reports of success. I welcome the opportunity to conduct in-service workshops to train teachers or group leaders in the use of these positive techniques. Please write to:

Laura Fendel
c/o Good Year Books
1900 East Lake Avenue
Glenview, Illinois 60025

Acknowledgments

Thanks to George Fendel, Charline Lake, Albert Menashe, Bette Lynn Menashe, Bev Baril, Sandi Beavers, Nancy Leiker, Joanne Aldrich, Carol Gross, Sandy Seres, Robin Lawson, Pat Kehoe, Diana Kerman, Holly Spearing, Lynn Black Moss, Loren Black, Janet Holstein, Barry Menashe, Michael Grinder, and Sonja Morton. A special thank-you to my supporting fan club—Marc, Aliza, and Reyna.

Contents

Introduction		**1**
Meet Koala-Roo Can-Do		1
Recipe for a Can-Do Classroom		2
Fostering an I-Can-Do-It Attitude		2
Positive Teacher Talk		4
How Koala-Roo Can-Do Got His Name	(21)*	7

1

Setting Up Your Can-Do Classroom		**17**
Introduction		17
How to Use the Materials		17
Can-Do Compliment Slips	(17)	25
Can-Do Buttons	(18)	26
Can-Do Name Tags	(18)	27
Super Reader Logo	(18)	28
Koala-Roo Can-Do Door Logo	(18)	29
Koala-Roo Assignment Sheet	(18)	30
Can-Do Deliveroo	(18)	31
Be Proud Poster	(18)	32
Doing Your Best Poster	(18)	33
Say "I Can" Poster	(18)	34
Koala-Roo Can-Do Reader Poster	(18)	35
Can-Do Placard Holder	(18)	36
Placard	(18)	37
Room Job Chart	(20)	38
Stand-up Can-Do	(20)	39
The Name Game	(21)	42
I Am Special	(21)	43
Absentee Pouch	(21)	44
A Tree for All Seasons	(21)	45
Can-Do Can	(21)	46
Can-Do Door Decor	(22)	51
Can-Do Chances	(22)	57
Can-Do Caps	(23)	58

***(Page on which reproducible material is discussed)**

Can-Do Ears	(23)*	59
Can-Do Clip Art 1–3	(23)	60
Can-Do Border 1–7	(23)	63
Koala-Roo Can-Do Pencil Tops	(23)	70
Introductory Letter Home	(23)	71
Parent Involvement Letter Home	(23)	72
Careers and Hobbies Letter Home	(23)	73
Kid of the Week Letter Home	(23)	74
Show-and-Tell Letter Home	(23)	75
Questionnaire Letter Home	(23)	76
Sticker Board Letter Home	(24)	77
My Sticker Board	(24)	78
Can-Do Curriculum Review	(24)	79
How to Draw Koala-Roo Can-Do	(24)	80
Getting Started Checklist	(24)	81
You Are Special	(24)	82

2

Success Management for Individual Children		**83**
Introduction		83
How to Use the Materials		83
Can-Do Assignments Tally	(83)	87
Can-Do 1-2-3 Tally	(83)	88
Can-Do Hand Raiser Tally	(83)	88
Can-Do Habit Changer Tally	(83)	89
Can-Do Hop-a-roo Tally	(83)	90
Observable Problem Behaviors	(84)	91
Focus Sheet	(84)	92
Things I Like	(84)	93
Ideas for Individual Reinforcers	(84)	94
Planning Sheet	(84)	95
Setting Expectations	(85)	96
Can-Do Contract	(85)	97
Child's Success Record	(85)	98
Overview Assessment	(85)	99
Teacher Effectiveness Sheet	(85)	100
Teacher Effectiveness Checklist	(86)	101
Child's Self-Evaluation 1–4	(86)	102
Colossal Kid Award	(86)	105
Can-Do Awards 1–7	(86)	106
Can-Do Blue Ribbons	(86)	113
Can-Do Gram	(86)	114
Good News Note	(86)	114

3

Success Management for Small Groups		**115**
Introduction		115
How to Use the Materials		115
Ideas for Group Reinforcers	(115)	118
Goal and Reward Sheet	(116)	119
Apple Compliment Grid	(115)	120

***(Page on which reproducible material is discussed)**

Backpack Compliment Grid	(115)*	121
Balloon Compliment Grid	(115)	122
Bucket Compliment Grid	(115)	123
Gingerbread House Compliment Grid	(115)	124
Heart-Flower Compliment Grid	(115)	125
Ice Cream Compliment Grid	(115)	126
Igloo Compliment Grid	(115)	127
Kite Compliment Grid	(115)	128
Knapsack Compliment Grid	(115)	129
Leaf Compliment Grid	(115)	130
Pumpkin Compliment Grid	(115)	131
Spaceship Compliment Grid	(115)	132
Turkey Compliment Grid	(115)	133
Umbrella Compliment Grid	(115)	134
Balloon Detailed Compliment Grid 1	(117)	135
Balloon Detailed Compliment Grid 2	(117)	136
Bouquet Detailed Compliment Grid	(117)	137
Can-Do-Fly Detailed Compliment Grid	(117)	138

4

Can-Do in the Curriculum		**139**
Reading		139
Introduction		139
How to Use the Materials		140
Book Record Sheet	(140)	142
Favorite Book Awards with Pouch	(140)	143
Can-Do Reading Shoes	(140)	144
Reading Apple Barrel	(140)	145
Apples	(140)	146
Koala-Roo Reading Tree	(140)	147
Pouch Book Report	(140)	148
Dear Can-Do Book Report	(140)	149
Color Code for Can-Do Reading	(140)	150
Can-Do Reading Tickets	(140)	151
Koala-Roo Can-Do Bookmarks	(141)	152
Math		153
Introduction		153
How to Use the Materials		153
Can-Do Group Tally Sheet	(153)	158
Individual Can-Do Counting	(154)	159
Group Can-Do Counting	(154)	160
Can-Do Backpack Bingo Board	(155)	161
Can-Do Coins and Can-Dollars	(155)	162
Valentine Post Office Flyer	(155)	163
Valentine Employment Form	(156)	164
Valentine Postal Worker Schedule	(156)	165
Valentine Graph	(156)	166
Fifty-Valentine Pattern Sheet	(156)	167
Valentine Postal Worker Checks	(157)	168
Valentine Math Report	(157)	169
I "Chews" You Valentine	(157)	170

***(Page on which reproducible material is discussed)**

Language Arts		171
Introduction		171
How to Use the Materials		171
Can-Do Chronicle	(171)*	173
Ideas for Show-and-Tell	(171)	174
Can-Do Birthday Card	(171)	175
Can-Do Giving Card	(171)	176
Can-Do Note Card	(171)	177
Can-Do Thanksgiving Card	(171)	178
Can-Do Triangle Card	(171)	179
Koala-Roo Finger Puppets	(172)	180

5

Celebrations of Success		**181**
Introduction		181
How to Use the Materials		181
Invitation for Magnificent Monday	(182)	186
Invitation for Tea Party Tuesday	(182)	187
Invitation for Wonderful Wednesday	(182)	188
Invitation for Thoughtful Thursday	(182)	189
Invitation for Fabulous Friday	(183)	190
Invitation for Koala-Roo Can-Do's Birthday	(183)	191
Invitation for Grandparents' Day	(183)	192
Invitation for Parents' Career Day	(183)	193
Invitation for a Fall Festival	(183)	194
Invitation for a Book Bash	(184)	195
Invitation for Success in All Seasons	(184)	196
Invitation for Games Galore	(184)	197
Invitation for a Spring Fling	(185)	198
Invitation for a Summer Circus Celebration	(185)	199
Can-Do Recipe Book Cover	(181)	200
Recipe for a Popcorn Picnic	(182)	200
Recipe for a Colossal Cookie	(182)	201
Recipe for Bravo Garbanzo Dip	(182)	201
Recipe for Terrific Tofu Dip	(182)	202
Recipe for Koala-Roo Malted Milk	(182)	202
Recipe for Dessert Pizza	(183)	203
Recipe for Koala Cake 1 and 2	(183)	203
Recipe for Koala Apple Crispy	(183)	204
Recipe for Koala Frozen Yogurt	(184)	205
Recipe for Chocolate Soup à la Can-Do	(184)	205
Recipe for Peanut Butter Hors d'Oeuvres	(184)	206
Recipe for Koala Cooler	(185)	206
Suggested Reading		**207**
Books about Self-Esteem		207
Cookbooks: Ideas for Themes		220
Books for Teachers		221
Index		**222**

***(Page on which reproducible material is discussed)**

Introduction

Meet Koala-Roo Can-Do

A koala-roo is an invented animal, a cross between a koala bear and a kangaroo. Koala-Roo Can-Do is our hero's full name, but he answers to just Koala-Roo or just Can-Do as well. I often call him Can-Do in this book's activities in order to link self-confidence—an I-can-do-it attitude—with the activities, in the minds of the children who participate.

Introduce Koala-Roo Can-Do to the children in your class or group by reading them the story **How Koala-Roo Can-Do Got His Name** (page 7). Duplicate the story and hand it out first, if you like. (See page 21 for more on how to use the story.)

You can use the Koala-Roo Can-Do activities in this book with children ages five through eight or nine. The book is packed with flexible activities that you can easily adapt to suit the specific academic or social needs of your children. Classroom teachers, teacher aides, librarians, p.e. teachers, music teachers, special education teachers, and special duty teachers will find direct applications for these activities with small groups, entire classes, or individual children in the classroom, in the cafeteria, or on the playground. Day-care providers, bus drivers, youth group leaders, counselors, parents, and others working with children can also find a variety of ideas to adapt to particular needs and settings. Select the activities or programs that will help your children become more successful, and praise, praise, praise the positive behaviors you observe.

Koala-Roo Can-Do will hop his way into your heart, and he will become your class mascot in lessons in success. Throughout the activities is woven his message: "You can do anything if you try. You can do it. I can do it. I did it!" The activities help children focus on areas that need improvement and then practice new skills or behaviors positively. They encourage us as teachers to sharpen our skills in giving compliments to help children learn and grow. If you use the activities, emphasize the positive when you talk to your class, and consistently give compliments, you will help your students reach their learning potential, and you will build and reinforce their self-esteem.

How many of us recall bitter moments in our childhood when someone put us down privately or in public! Harsh criticism usually makes us want to hide, not try harder. We react far better, of course, to praise, which builds our self-esteem—our belief in our own capabilities. This is not to say that we as adults should not correct children. We must teach, guide, and train them. My challenge to you is to try your own Can-Do experiment for at least a month and observe the results of positive teacher talk and these exciting, fun ideas in your classroom or setting. You will grow as an individual and as a professional. Your students will delight in their success and feel good about themselves. You will find that teaching, guiding, and training your students is easier than before, but your greatest reward will be seeing the children simply flourish.

Recipe for a Can-Do Classroom

Ingredients

One classful children, each talented and unique

One teacher, a positive communicator, supplied with tools for bringing out the potential and talent in each child

One classroom where constant praise prevails and persistence is fostered

Directions

1. Place the children in an environment where the atmosphere promotes friendship and where growth can flourish.
2. Add clear rules and routines.
3. Blend in a careful measure of incentives and rewards.
4. Add in abundance:
   Tons of love and excitement for learning
   A variety of creative ways to solve problems
5. Fold in heaping armfuls of fun and laughter in a room where discovery is encouraged.
6. Add a sprinkling of high expectations that are attainable.
7. Add dashes of realistic and fair consequences.
8. Simmer continuously and consistently for the entire school year.

Fostering an I-Can-Do-It Attitude

Self-Image

Self-image or self-concept is how we see or think of ourselves. A child's own behavior, especially verbal behavior, often gives clues as to the child's self-image. Self-defeating statements like "I can't do that," "Oh, well, I don't want to," "Why try? I'm not good at that anyway," and "She's better than I am" all reflect a poor self-image.

A child's self-image is based in large part on the child's impressions of what other people think of the child. It is also, intriguingly, based in part on the self-esteem displayed by the child's own role models. As teachers, we can help children replace self-defeating thoughts and statements with self-affirming ones by modeling positive talk about ourselves. We can express our thoughts out loud, for instance, as we are giving a demonstration of how to do something. We can talk ourselves through difficulties and give ourselves some praise when we do well.

More important, though, is the impression we give each child of what we think of him or her. We never have a class of children with the same skills and the same experiences. We evaluate individual skills to determine what to teach and how to teach. We make judgments about maturity of behavior and quickness of intellect. If we are going to help all our students learn as well as they can, though, we must make sure our judgments about individuals do not keep us from expressing our confidence that every one of them **can** do well, **can** learn a new concept, **can** master a new skill.

Positive talk to the class as a whole affects individuals, too. If the teacher projects a belief that the class is going to succeed, the upbeat message affects every student. Children strive to meet great expectations if they believe in themselves and are motivated by people who believe in them.

It isn't just what you say that lets a student know your expectations. Nonverbal communication can send powerful messages of reassurance or disapproval. One way or another, your image of a child gets communicated, and the child feels liked or disliked, accepted or rejected.

If you are working with a child whose behavior seems not at all appealing, you need somehow to find something special about the child that you can admire. When you do see progress in the child, it is vital that you change your image of the child.

A Case Study

I had a little girl in my class whom I will call Randy. Randy was eight years old, but she acted younger. She seemed to have pine needles in her pants: she could never sit still when she was in her seat, which wasn't often. She sucked her finger continuously. She whined and talked baby talk. She was always getting underfoot wanting to help me and trying to anticipate what I would do next. I couldn't pass out papers without her wanting to do it for me. She would clean up after me without asking or even telling me. I wanted to like her, but it was hard. I just didn't find her likable; she was a considerable nuisance to me. I couldn't figure out what to do first to help her. The difficult situation went on.

Then, several weeks into the school year, I asked the children to bring all kinds of junk jewelry, trinkets, spools, buttons, and odds and ends to use in a counting and sorting project. Randy brought in a small bucket full of buttons that her grandmother had given her. She was proud to donate it to the class. I was not only overjoyed to receive these treasures to add to the collection but also relieved to find an opportunity, finally, to praise something Randy had done. I also saw that I could incorporate the button collection into a plan for success.

Randy and I worked out the plan. My proposal was that if Randy stayed in her seat during our study times that day, the class could take guesses as to how many buttons were in the bucket. At the end of the next day, she could count them. I told Randy that I knew it was hard for her to sit for long periods of time, but that I knew she was grown-up enough to do it if she worked at it. We talked about all of the times during the day she would have to be in her seat, and it seemed like a lot to her. We compromised and decided that when she finished an assignment, she could leave her seat. We taped a blank tally sheet on her desk. I drew a line down the middle. On one side I wrote "yes" and on the other "no." I would give her points on the yes side when she was in her seat during the correct times. I would give points on the no side when she was out of her seat at inappropriate times. If she had more yes points than no points at the end of the day, the class could take guesses at how many buttons were in her bucket.

Randy was successful, and she loved the positive attention she received. We made a chart for Randy's button collection, and for the next several weeks we did all kinds of classifying and graphing lessons with the collection.

The day the buttons came to school, I phoned Randy's mother to set up a conference for the next afternoon. Randy's mother described the same behavior at home as I was observing at school except that at home Randy demanded attention all the time, not just most of it. During the course of our conversation, the mother mentioned an incident at the dinner table and said something about Randy sitting in a high chair. Keep in mind that Randy was eight years old at the time. The mother said the high chair helped Randy reach the table. Now I began to understand Randy's behavior. She was still using a baby's chair, and her family unintentionally was encouraging infantile behavior. Randy was being treated like a baby and, as a result, was acting like a baby. She was living up to the expectations set for her. I strongly suggested that Randy sit at the table in a regular chair and be expected in other ways to act her age.

It was many months before Randy learned to shed her infantile behavior and begin to act like an eight-year-old. I had to make her believe that she was older than she had considered herself to be and could act like a second grader. I was consistent. I didn't listen to her when she talked baby talk. I looked at her with approval when she talked normally. When she acted grown-up in other ways, I let her know it. She so desperately wanted to please me and gain my approval that she managed to live up to my high expectations. She was then able to do grown-up jobs for me and be my assistant teacher.

I met with Randy's parents many times. We talked and made plans together to reinforce each other. It was a difficult year for this little girl, but she came a long way in a short time. It had taken eight years to form infantile habits. In one school year, her immature patterns of behavior became appropriate ones. As she began to make changes, I had to view her in a new way. If I had held on to my old impressions of her, she could have made no progress. When a child makes significant changes, you as a teacher must change your view of that child. Your image of the child, communicated verbally and nonverbally, affects the self-image the child is developing and consequently the child's ability to learn and grow.

You cannot force a child to change behavior. You can change your behavior in a way that causes the child to change his or her response. Positive reinforcement is one way to help a child change behavior and improve his or her self-concept.

Self-esteem develops in childhood and is the basis for success throughout life. Let's help our students be the best they can be.

Positive Teacher Talk

If you praise the children who behave most productively in your classroom, you will find that other children in the class begin to do better in order to gain such praise for themselves. Try lavishing praise on the class and individuals whenever you have the least occasion. Feel free to compliment several children at a time. Look for on-task behaviors or any small improvement in children who are having a difficult time in your class. It is most important to praise such children; they need extra reinforcement in order to change. Try saying things like these:

- "Allen, you were listening so well. What a good idea."
- "I like the way Beth is concentrating."
- "Tiffany, I am so proud of you. You came on time."
- "This row (or table) is working as a team. They are all super workers." (Name what they are doing that is on-task.)

Set the stage with your expectations in a positive way:

- "We need to complete three things in the next hour: our spelling, our handwriting, and the map. I know we can do it by concentrating quietly. I need everyone to help. We **can** do it."

After you set the stage, as soon as the group is at work, look for children who are meeting your expectations, and praise them. Notice the child who is off-task. Praise several people around him or her. Review the expectations by restating them:

- "I like the way Josh is following directions." (Restate the expectation.)
- "You read so smoothly."
- "Jenny is doing her best work today."
- "When David raises his hand, it makes me so happy."

During each lesson, focus on one item. For example, during an English lesson you might say:

- "While you are completing this, I'm going to be looking for all those people who are using good spacing in their handwriting. I will stamp each paper that has the work done correctly and with good spacing."

As you circulate around the room, hold up a paper and make a specific compliment:

- "Look at Sue's work. What fine handwriting."
- "Lisa, show us how to do that."

Here are more ideas. I'm sure you could add to the list:

- "Table 3 is doing a great job. Super!"
- "I'm looking to see who is cleaning up. Dan is doing a great job helping."
- "Fantastic! You have the right idea."
- "I knew you could do it."
- "That's your best work."
- "I'm so proud of you."
- "You're improving."
- "That's better than yesterday."
- "Pat came in so quietly."
- "Cindy has her name on her paper already. What beautiful handwriting."

Reinforce with a Purpose

1. Set expectations and explain them.
2. Give praise consistently to the class and to individuals.
3. Be specific when giving praise.
4. Focus on appropriate behaviors.

Ways to Say or Write "Good Job"

1. This is special!
2. You are special!
3. That's very grown-up of you!
4. Swell!
5. Bravo!
6. Dandy!
7. We could try that!
8. Cool idea!
9. Super!
10. All right!
11. Right on!
12. Classy!
13. Sure!
14. You got it!
15. Nifty!
16. That's the best!
17. Terrific!
18. Wonderful!
19. Fabulous idea!
20. I knew you could do it!
21. I'm proud of you!
22. Be proud!
23. Clever!
24. Way to go!
25. V.I.P.—that's you!
26. You are tops!
27. Outstanding!
28. Splendiferous!
29. Awesome!
30. Great!
31. What a gem!
32. That's grand!
33. You did it!
34. Fantastic!
35. That's clever!
36. That's neat!
37. Spiffy!
38. You're getting it!
39. You came up with that yourself!
40. That's sensational!
41. Exceptional!
42. First class!
43. Primo work!
44. Superb!
45. A-1!
46. Top-notch!
47. That's electric!
48. What high energy you've put out!
49. You're blooming!
50. You're bursting with ideas today!
51. Magnificent!
52. Splendid!
53. Glow with pride; you made it!
54. Fine as fine can be!
55. Perfect!
56. You're getting there!
57. Wow! You've reached a mountain peak!
58. You're getting to be an expert at this!

Ways to Promote Self-Esteem

1. When you as an adult make a mistake, serve as a role model by saying something like "I made a mistake, but I know I'm still an okay person."
2. Praise appropriate behavior.
3. Provide honest and specific praise.
4. Provide activities that guarantee success.
5. Give students useful jobs that make them feel important and competent.
6. Talk to children about their world. Show concern and interest.
7. Bring the outside world into the classroom with news or hobbies. Use the activity to make your students feel a part of the larger world.
8. Have children write about experiences they've had.
9. Have children tell a story about an experience. Tape each story as it is told.
10. Give notes of recognition as awards.
11. Praise small steps: mastery takes time.
12. Explain expectations and consequences clearly.
13. Encourage parents to visit, observe, and help in the classroom or to share their jobs or hobbies.
14. When you can, give students choices as to what they will learn or when they will complete a particular project.
15. Provide excitement and discovery in learning.
16. Encourage children to solve conflicts with peers by talking about their problems and telling each other how they feel.
17. Encourage grandparents to visit the school. Invite them to share a hobby, talk about a job, or tell a story about their life.
18. Eat lunch with a small group of children or an individual child.
19. Allow kids to be kids. Understand the interests of their age level. Talk to them about the latest toys, television shows, clubs, sports, classes, and lessons with which they are involved.
20. Be sensitive to a variety of life-styles and family forms when referring to families in class discussions.
21. Be supportive of parents. Teach them alternative ways to be positive with their children.
22. Have your principal show positive recognition to a child who reaches a goal. They could have lunch, ice cream, or hot chocolate together.
23. Celebrate birthdays or unbirthdays with special recognition.

24. Have children who are shy or uncomfortable in a large group share objects or experiences in a small group.
25. Allow children who demonstrate that they can manage their own behavior for a short period of time to go to lunch or be dismissed on their own.
26. Promote kids helping kids and caring for each other.
27. Set expectations that are realistic for individual children.
28. In the morning greet each child at the door, shake hands, make eye contact, and have a short exchange of words.
29. Match up an older child with a younger one (for instance, a sixth grader with a first grader) to work together on an art project or story-writing project.
30. Match up peers to work together on a project. Praise and teach cooperation.
31. On a consistent basis have another teacher also give praise to a particular child.
32. Provide art projects in which you teach only the skills and then let the children use their imagination and creativity to choose what they will produce.
33. During creative activities provide nonjudgmental praise.
34. Teach children how to solve problems.
35. Teach kids to believe in themselves.
36. Promote self-affirmation. Praise self-compliments, and help children differentiate between self-compliments and boasts.
37. Praise or compliment other teachers, individuals, or classes while your class is present.
38. While your students are present, praise them to other teachers.
39. Respect the uniqueness of each individual in your class.
40. Write one self-esteem objective per day into your plans. Focus on this objective.
41. Read the book *Alexander and the Terrible, Horrible, No Good, Very Bad Day* by Judith Viorst (Atheneum, 1972). Discuss the experiences and feelings that we all have on terrible, horrible, no good, very bad days. Brainstorm ways to cope.
42. Have secret pals in another class, and write notes to them.
43. Share photo albums.
44. Send good wishes for the new year and other such messages to another class.
45. To celebrate another teacher's birthday, have your students make birthday cards as a surprise.
46. Tell individual children something they accomplished that week.
47. Have children write down one thing they learned or accomplished that week.
48. Have a class talent show once a month.
49. Have a hobby show, pet show, stuffed animal show, or art show.
50. Have students write on the topic "something I did for myself."
51. Have children set goals and work toward accomplishing them.
52. Help children grow in confidence of their knowledge of right and wrong.
53. Provide occasions for children to do good deeds for others.
54. Discuss the good feeling we have inside when we do for others. Send appreciation notes to the secretaries, special teachers, custodian, or cooks.
55. Help children understand how you grade them. Explain that grades are only one small part of a description of them. They are good at many things in their lives that you never grade.
56. Teach children **how** to learn. Break down steps in a particular skill such as organizing a desk, finding patterns in a textbook, or following steps in completing an assignment.
57. Help children learn how to express feelings honestly.
58. Teach kids how to praise others: what to look for and what to say.
59. Listen to children. Maintain eye contact and be nonjudgmental.
60. Understand the sense of humor of your class's age level.
61. Have fun with the children. Laugh with them.
62. Praise yourself for trying something new.
63. Smile!

How Koala-Roo Can-Do Got His Name

All the koala-roos hopped high and hung from tree branches for sport. They played games. They had contests. All except Cally. Cally sat sadly and watched. He wished he could hop high enough to be able to hang from the highest branches. But poor Cally wouldn't even try. He was sure he wouldn't make it. At first his friends tried to convince him to do it. "Cally, come on. You can do it!" they yelled.

Then they teased him. "Cally, you're a 'fraidy cat." Pretty soon Cally was so convinced that he couldn't do it that he couldn't even try. He thought that if he missed, the other koala-roos would laugh at him.

Days passed, and Cally was missing all the fun with the other koala-roo kids. They hopped and hung from tree branches and paid no attention to Cally.

Cally did try a few times to hop, but he missed even the lowest branch. So he gave up and just sat and watched the others.

One day Cally was sitting on a large rock wishing he could be like his friends. His Aunt Kanga-Lou came hopping by on her way to pick berries. She stopped to talk with Cally.

"Why do you look so sad?" she asked.

"Gosh, Auntie Kanga-Lou," said Cally, "I want so much to hop and hang like the other koala-roo kids. I've tried, and I can't do it. Won't you please help me? Show me how! I want to do it, too."

"I'm so proud of you, Cally," she said, "because you asked for help. That's the first step. It shows you **want** to learn." Auntie Kanga-Lou gave Cally a big smile. "Come with me," she said, "and we'll go to a quiet part of the forest and practice each day."

Cally went with his aunt every day to a quiet part of the forest. First he learned to hop low jumps. He practiced that many times. Then he practiced higher jumps.

He also practiced exercises that gave his tail strength. He gripped onto tree trunks harder and tighter. After many days, Cally told his Aunt Kanga-Lou, "I want to try to hop and hang from a low branch. I think I can do it now."

Cally took a running hop and barely missed the tree. He tried again. This time he took a great running leap.

His tail wrapped around the branch, and he hung on. He did it! Cally beamed with joy. "I can do it, Auntie Kanga-Lou, I can do it!" he cried.

Cally practiced several more days with his aunt until he could hang on every time.

One day Cally saw the koala-roo kids out hopping and hanging onto trees. He joined right in, hopping and hanging along with them. They were so surprised and so happy for him! They all thumped their tails with glee and yelled, "You can do it!"

When they asked Cally how he had learned to hop and jump so well, he told them about his hard work and practicing. Then he said, "I can do it if I try, and try, and try some more." They were so proud of him that they called him Koala-Roo Can-Do from that day on.

Discussion Questions

1. How did Can-Do feel when he learned how to hop and hang?
2. What was his goal?
3. What did he need to do in order to reach his goal?
4. What were the first steps in learning to hop and hang?
5. Have you ever had an experience like Can-Do when you thought you couldn't do something you really could do?
6. How did he learn to hop and hang?
7. How can you be a Can-Do kid?

Learning something and doing it well are things that don't always come easy. Wanting to do something, however, and practicing and working hard to reach your goal can bring you success.

1

Setting Up Your Can-Do Classroom

Introduction

The following is a collection of Koala-Roo Can-Do activities that enhance the development of self-esteem. You will find some of the activities helpful in classroom organization and others as positive reinforcers for skills you are teaching. In the first part of this chapter are explanations and directions for the materials in the latter part of the chapter. You can duplicate the materials to use with your students. Utilizing Koala-Roo Can-Do visually throughout your classroom and integrating him into the curriculum will help reinforce his message **I can do it if I try!**

How to Use the Materials

Can-Do Compliment Slips

Use Can-Do Compliment Slips (page 25) to reinforce a specific academic skill or behavior with an immediate tangible reward. Duplicate page 25 many times so that each child will earn more than ten compliments over a period of several days or a week.

Example Determine an expectation for a short period of time. You might observe many children needing to focus on the spacing of their handwriting. You say to the class, "This week I'm going to be looking for children who are trying to improve the spacing between words while they are writing." Demonstrate the expected outcome by showing the desired spacing between words. "I'll be handing out Can-Do Compliment Slips when I see you trying hard to improve your handwriting spacing. Save all your compliment slips in your envelope or pocket [you may find pockets for book cards in your library, or you may use envelopes to store the compliment slips]. At the end of each day we'll count all the compliment slips. We'll record our total each day. At the end of the week we'll have a grand total." Then determine a class goal of compliment slips to earn and decide on a reward or celebration at the end of the week or short given time. "If we can earn at least a total of seventy-five compliment slips, then each person may draw a picture with colored chalk on the chalkboard." Remember, you want the students to succeed!

- Distributing many compliment slips is very important in encouraging the desired expectation as well as promoting praise in the classroom.
- You may need to have the students write their initials on each slip.
- When you count the compliment slips you can give the lesson a math focus by having the students estimate how many compliment slips the class has accumulated that day. Or have the children hold up one finger for every ten compliment slips they think the class has earned, stack all the slips in groups of fives, tens, or fifties, or glue them in columns of tens to a large piece of paper.

Can-Do Buttons

You can color (or have the children color) the Can-Do Buttons (page 26) with felt pens. Then you can make them into buttons with a button machine. Use the buttons as immediate reinforcement for specific expectations. For example, you might announce that children who speak in normal tones at lunch may wear a button for the afternoon, or that children who complete their reading assignment may wear a button for the remainder of the day.

You can also surprise a student by giving the student a button to wear for something specific that you noticed he or she was doing well. Perhaps you go up to Dan and quietly whisper in his ear, "Dan, you are doing so well today by remembering to raise your hand to share ideas. You may wear this Can-Do Button for the rest of the day. I'm proud of you."

Immediate reinforcement is important in forming new behaviors.

Can-Do Name Tags

Around the bottom of the koala-roo on each Can-Do Name Tag (page 27), fill in the child's name. Color the tags with markers, and mount one on each desk with a piece of clear contact paper. The contact paper should be slightly larger than the name tag.

You can also use the filled-in name tags as a border on a bulletin board (see, for instance, the Can-Do Kid of the Week bulletin board, described on page 19). These posted name tags can be helpful to substitute teachers, by the way. Cover each name tag with clear contact paper to make the tag more durable.

Super Reader Logo and Koala-Roo Can-Do Door Logo

You can enlarge the Super Reader Logo (page 28) and Koala-Roo Can-Do Door Logo (page 29) to 18 or 24 inches in diameter and use them on a bulletin board or on your classroom door. You can copy them on colored paper or add color with markers. Laminate them or cover them with clear contact paper to add to their durability.

Koala-Roo Assignment Sheet

Use the Koala-Roo Assignment Sheet (page 30) for writing a list of assignments to complete, homework to remember, assignments missed because of absence, or accomplishments of the day or week (head the sheet "Can You Believe We Did All This?").

You can also use the sheet as stationery for letters or notes to go home. You can adapt it for story writing, thank-you notes, or handwriting lessons.

Can-Do Deliveroo

Use the Can-Do Deliveroo (page 31) as note paper throughout the year for communicating with children or parents. Use it for a welcome letter from Koala-Roo Can-Do to each child the very first day of school. In this note write something special that happens in your class that the students can look forward to doing. Distribute these notes at the end of the first day. You can use the Can-Do Deliveroo when you introduce Koala-Roo Can-Do to your class anytime during the school year.

Posters

- **Be Proud Poster**
- **Doing Your Best Poster**
- **Say "I Can" Poster**
- **Koala-Roo Can-Do Reader Poster**

These posters (pages 32–35) all provide positive motivation. Mount one poster a week, and use it as a discussion starter. List the ideas that children share, and then write a class story together.

Discuss a poster. Have the children write their own stories. Bind all the stories together with the poster as the cover. Read the stories to the class, and after several class books are made, place them in a location where children may read them on their own.

Discuss a poster idea. Then divide a large piece of butcher paper into sections, and have each child write and illustrate his or her own story. One sentence underneath each story could accompany it as a summary.

Can-Do Placard Holder and Placard

Mount the Can-Do Placard Holder (page 36) with the Placard (page 37) on a bulletin board or chalkboard. Place the placard in Can-Do's hands (you may wish to enlarge it first). Attach a piece of paper to the placard. On the piece of paper write, "I Did It Today." As you see a child achieve a small success, ask the child to write his or her name on the placard. Tape a new sheet of paper on the placard each day. Use the same slogan, or select another from the following:

Super Listeners
Good Friends
The Get-Along Kids
We Try Hard
Math Go-Getters
We Love Books

Instead of attaching a new sheet of paper each day, you might want to laminate the placard and use erasable pens to write the slogans.

Mottoes Select a motto to post on the placard to use as a discussion or story starter. Discuss the motto with the class or small group, and have the students write their names under the motto as they live up to it. Mottoes might include:

- Be Proud of Yourself
- Say "I Can" and Practice It
- Be The Best You Can Be
- Don't Worry about How Other People Are Doing: Concentrate on Doing Your Best
- Reach to Your Heights
- I Don't Have to Be Perfect: I Can Be the Best I Can Be
- I Am My Best Friend
- Cheer for Yourself—Clap for Small Victories
- Smile When You're Proud

Other Bulletin Board Ideas All sorts of bulletin boards and posted materials can use the Koala-Roo Can-Do theme to promote classroom goals. Let your imagination be your guide. A few suggestions follow.

Can-Do Kid of the Week Bulletin Board Create a Can-Do Kid of the Week bulletin board to feature a different child each week. Have the student bring in photos of himself or herself, family members, and pets. Encourage the child to write a short story about family, hobbies, or other interesting personal facts. Send parents the Kid of the Week Letter Home (page 74) explaining the bulletin board. You can use the Can-Do Placard Holder (page 36) and Placard (page 37) on this bulletin board, and members of the class can each write one sentence telling something they like or admire about the Can-Do Kid of the Week.

Class Rules Chart Choose three to five class rules that you feel are essential in your classroom. Write them on a large piece of paper, and post it. Include a picture of Can-Do. On the chart write:

I am a Can-Do kid. I can . . .

1. Raise my hand to share ideas
2. Work quietly at my seat
3. Leave toys and stuffed animals at home
4. Keep my hands and feet to myself

Word the rules positively: tell children what to do, not what **not** to do.

Print a list of the class rules or expectations, and send them home in a flyer to inform parents.

Can-Do Compliment Bulletin Board A Can-Do Compliment bulletin board can be a permanent bulletin board in your classroom. On it you can display successes by posting compliments given to individuals, groups, and the class.

To create the bulletin board enlarge one Can-Do Button (page 26) and mount it in an upper corner of the bulletin board as a visual logo of Can-Do. On a strip of paper write "Compliment Board." Mount the strip as a title at the top of your bulletin board. If you don't have a free bulletin board, devise one out of a large piece of heavy poster paper and tape it to your chalkboard, a wall, or the inside of your door.

Determine a goal that you want a small group to achieve. For example, you might have one math group that needs to focus on working toward accuracy in computation. Discuss with the group your expectation and **how** they can work on improving their accuracy. Discuss what compliments are.

Select a Compliment Grid (pages 120–138), and duplicate it. Post the Compliment Grid on the Can-Do Compliment bulletin board. Together you and the students agree on a reinforcing reward that they will receive after they earn compliments for achieving the expectation (see Ideas for Group Reinforcers, page 118). Then duplicate the Goal and Reward Sheet (page 119), fill it out, and mount it on the Can-Do Compliment bulletin board. The sheet defines what everyone is focusing on and what the class will earn.

As you see a child in the group achieve more accuracy in the daily work, compliment him or her. Call on that child to go up to the Compliment Grid and color in a space. Give compliments out freely. Praise small achievements. When all the spaces have been colored, then the group has achieved the goal, and the reward is given. Provide the reward as soon as possible. At the beginning of a program like this one, young children must achieve their goal within a short time—a week or less—or they lose interest.

The Compliment Grid can also be used with several groups at one time, all working on the same expectation. Each group has its own Compliment Grid (print the same grid for each group, and write one group name on each grid). Each group earns the reinforcing reward when its grid has been completely colored in with compliments. Everyone is successful! (For a more detailed description, see chapter 3, pages 115–119.)

You can also use the Compliment Grid with the entire class when you want the whole class to work as a team to reach a class expectation. For example, you might want to reinforce one of the following with your class:

Lining up quietly
Working quietly
Playing fairly
Following directions

As you observe the class meeting your expectation, give compliments and call on different children to color a space on the grid. It is important to select one expectation at a time and to give compliments freely to maintain high motivation. Even after the Compliment Grid has been completed, continue giving compliments verbally. This will intermittently reinforce your expectation and the new behavior that has been learned.

Variations On the Can-Do Compliment bulletin board you can mount the Can-Do Placard Holder (page 36) and Placard (page 37), the four posters that provide positive motivation (pages 32–35), Can-Do Blue Ribbons (page 113) with children's names on them for small successes achieved, and Can-Do Awards (pages 106–112) for accomplishments. An alternative is to have the students compliment teachers and staff and write compliment notes to post on the Can-Do Compliment bulletin board (see Can-Do Cards, pages 175–179). Children could also compliment each other and post notes on the Can-Do Compliment bulletin board. Compliments written to parents or family could be posted before they are sent home.

Vary the use of these positive motivation self-esteem programs. Allow several days between the programs so that each one is special and not merely routine.

Room Job Chart

Duplicate the Room Job Chart (page 38), and enlarge it if you want. Write the names of all your students on the left side. Write jobs on separate pieces of construction paper. Laminate the chart and the job labels if you like, or cover them with clear contact paper. Use Holdit Plastic Adhesive or paper clips to attach jobs next to student names.

Stand-up Can-Do

- **Stand-up Can-Do Diagram, Pouch, and Tail**
- **Stand-up Can-Do Body**
- **Stand-up Can-Do Backpack**

You can use the Stand-up Can-Do (pages 39–41) for a variety of language activities. Discuss things your students can do that they couldn't do last year. List accomplishments like:

Riding a bike
Skating
Dressing themselves
Making their own lunches

Have the students write these accomplishments on slips of paper. You might ask them to write a sentence, with a capital and period, about one accomplishment, on each slip of paper. Place these slips in Can-Do's pouch. Then have the students fill out slips with goals they would like to attain. Have the children place these slips in the backpack.

Enlarge the Stand-up Can-Do to use with class activities. You can write messages to the class and put them in the pouch. Language experience ideas (see Pouch Stories, page 171), story ideas, and discussion ideas can be written on slips of paper and put into the pouch to be drawn and then developed into a lesson.

Assembly See the diagram on page 39. Duplicate the pouch and tail (one piece, page 39) and body (page 40) on heavy tag paper. Copy the backpack (page 41) on colored construction paper. Color the pouch, tail, and body if you like. Cut out the pouch, tail, body, and backpack along the solid lines.

The dashed lines are all fold lines. Fold the legs and feet toward you so that Can-Do can stand up. Fold the pouch and tail so that you can glue the flaps on the pouch to the body. The tail fits between Can-Do's legs. Fold the tail on the dotted line so that the sides of the tail rest on the table (the dashed line will show).

See the diagram on page 41. Fold the backpack into a boxlike shape with the top flap facing to the outside. Fit the straps over Can-Do's arms, and glue them in place.

If you use the Stand-Up Can-Do as a construction project in class, you probably want to make one Stand-up Can-Do ahead of time so that you can anticipate the problems your students may encounter.

You can pin a finished Stand-up Can-Do to a bulletin board, tape one to the edge of a chalkboard ledge, or stand one on each child's desk.

How Koala-Roo Can-Do Got His Name

The story **How Koala-Roo Can-Do Got His Name** (pages 7–16) introduces the character Koala-Roo Can-Do. Discussion questions at the end of the story focus on the ways that trying and practicing can bring success.

You can make the story into a booklet to reread in small groups and then share with parents.

After you have read the story to the children, you can review the events in the story and have the children illustrate them. Then you can write one sentence under each picture to summarize.

The Name Game

The Name Game (page 42) can be an exciting game for the first day of school for children who can read or help each other read. The purpose of the game is to let students learn something about each other and discover things in common. It can be helpful for children new to the school as well as children returning. Everyone can become involved, and the first-day jitters are dispelled. The game is useful even if the children know each other and the school year has already begun.

Duplicate copies for each child and one for yourself. Players read the items in each square and find someone who has that quality or who can answer that question. The person who fills the bill then writes his or her signature in the square.

I Am Special

Duplicate the I Am Special sheet (page 43) and have each student fill out a copy. Use the information you collect to learn something new about each child, help you develop a lesson that encourages a child's hobby or interest, or help you determine a reward that a child might be especially interested in earning.

Absentee Pouch

The Absentee Pouch (page 44) is a handy holder for papers and assignments for children who are absent. Glue this page to the top of a 10-by-13-inch manila envelope. Post the envelope in a useful place in your classroom.

A Tree for All Seasons

Use A Tree for All Seasons (page 45) to create a bulletin board (or use the Koala-Roo Reading Tree, page 147, if you prefer). Throughout the school year you can display children's work and ideas on the tree. Enlarge the tree to fit your bulletin board. You can leave the tree there permanently and change the items on it for each season, class project, or lesson.

Here are some ideas for items your students can make to put on A Tree for All Seasons:

- Fall: Hang autumn leaves or Apples (page 146). Compliments could be written on the apples. Hang pumpkins, witches, and turkeys.
- Winter: Hang snowflakes.
- Spring: Use tissue flowers and umbrellas.
- Summer: Use balloons.
- Careers: Hang pictures of people at work.
- *A Treeful of Pigs* by Arnold Lobel (Greenwillow, 1979): Use this book as an idea starter for your bulletin board.
- Wishing Tree: Hang wishes written by each child.
- Family Tree: Children research their families' culture groups and hang appropriate notes, drawings, or mementos.
- Valentine Tree: Hang hearts. Have your students first write compliments on the hearts. Or have them write down answers after they think about the question "What do I like about myself?" or the question "What do I like about my world?"
- Seasons Tree: Hang pictures of different seasons and weather conditions.

Can-Do Can

- **Can-Do Can Body**
- **Can-Do Can Cover and Tail**
- **Can-Do Can Boots, Legs, and Pouch**
- **Can-Do Can Shirt and Shoes**
- **Can-Do Can Accessories**

Use the versatile Can-Do Can (pages 46–50) to hold pencils, Can-Dollars (page 162), Can-Do Coins (page 162), Can-Do Compliment Slips (page

25), Can-Do Chances (page 57), story starters (see Pouch Stories, page 171, for a list of story ideas), or whatever small items your imagination suggests.

Materials You need an empty 12-ounce juice can, card stock or heavy paper, scissors, and crayons or felt pens.

Assembly After you have gathered the materials, duplicate pages 46–50. Color the pieces if you like, and cut them out. Cover the juice can with the Can-Do Can Cover (piece A, page 47), and glue it in place. Glue the Can-Do Can Body (piece C, page 46) over the seam where the cover overlaps.

Bend the ears and shoulders forward a bit. Fold the Can-Do Can Tail (piece B, page 47) along the dashed lines, and glue it to the back of the can. The flaps will be spread apart below the folded tail.

Fold the Can-Do Can Legs and Pouch (piece D, page 48) along the dashed lines so that the legs are folded forward and the bottom flap backward. Glue the bottom flap onto the lower part of the body so that the bottom of the pouch is about half an inch from the bottom of the can.

Spread a line of glue along each folded edge of the pouch. Press the folded edges of the pouch against the body section, leaving the pouch curved open so that it sticks out from the can. Hold the edges in place until they are attached.

Fold over the flaps on the Can-Do Can Boots (page 48), Shirt and Shoes (page 49), and Accessories (page 50). Put them on Can-Do, taping them in place as necessary.

Can-Do Door Decor

- **Can-Do Door Decor Head**
- **Can-Do Door Decor Body**
- **Can-Do Door Decor Arms**
- **Can-Do Door Decor Pouch**
- **Can-Do Door Decor Left Leg**
- **Can-Do Door Decor Right Leg**

Display the Can-Do Door Decor (pages 51–56) on your classroom door. (Use a Can-Do Door Decor Head in the Koala-Roo Can-Do Bookmark mobile, page 141.) The pouch can hold notices if you fold them in half. You can put signs or slogans in Can-Do's hands (see page 19 for motto ideas).

Assembly Reproduce pages 51–56 on heavy paper or tagboard. Color the pieces if you like, and cut them out. Assemble them by pushing brads through the small x's. The brads attaching the arms will be hidden by the bow tie. The legs and pouch are attached to the body with the same set of brads. The pouch will stick out at the waist.

Fold the bottom of the pouch along the dashed line, and glue the flap to the back of the bottom edge of the body.

Can-Do Chances

Can-Do Chances (page 57) are slips of paper you can distribute as motivators. Announce your expectation in advance, saying something like, "I'm going to be looking for children who raise their hands to share ideas today. I will give you a Can-Do Chance slip when I see you raise your hand. Then you can write your name on the chance slip. At the end of the day we'll put all the slips in a container and draw a name." Explain the reward that the student whose name is drawn will receive: perhaps the student will get to do something special with you or receive something special (see Ideas for Individual Reinforcers, page 94).

When you hand out a Can-Do Chance, give a verbal compliment as well. Tell the class before you begin giving out compliments and chance slips that everyone will be a winner because of all the compliments earned. Each chance slip represents a compliment.

At the drawing it is a good idea to have extra items (posters, used paperback books, stickers, and the like) so that several children have a chance at something special. Reinforce that everyone is a winner because everyone earned compliments.

To begin, duplicate many copies of the Can-Do Chances (page 57).

Can-Do Caps and Can-Do Ears

You can use Can-Do Caps (page 58) and Can-Do Ears (page 59) for special occasions like Valentine's Day (the Can-Do Postal Worker cap), birthdays (the Happy Birthday Kid cap), and success celebrations (the Proud Person of the Day cap). Cut a strip of paper 2 inches wide and long enough to go around the child's head. Glue or staple the strip to make a ring to fit on the child's head. Reproduce a Can-Do Cap (page 58), color it, cut it out, and glue it to the front of the strip. Reproduce the ear pattern (page 59), and use it to cut two ears. Attach them to the sides of the band.

Can-Do Clip Art 1–3

You can use the Can-Do Clip Art (pages 60–62) in many ways. Reduce or enlarge the pictures. Cut them out, and make your own tally sheets, awards, and note paper. Use the pictures on notes you write home, flyers, and bulletin boards. Use your imagination.

Can-Do Borders 1–7

Use the Can-Do Borders (pages 63–69) for flyers, instruction sheets, letters, creative writing pages, and story covers. You can use parts of the borders as clip art, too.

Koala-Roo Can-Do Pencil Tops

Use Koala-Roo Can-Do Pencil Tops (page 70) as individual rewards for great work or as something you give to everyone just because you like them.

Copy page 70 several times on sturdy paper. You or another adult must use an X-Acto knife or scissors point to cut slits along the dotted lines and to cut out the inside of the curved tail of the koala-roo who is leaning down. Then you or the students themselves can cut out the pencil tops along the outlines. Students may color their pencil tops as they wish.

Introductory Letter Home

Date and sign the Introductory Letter Home (page 71), and send it to introduce parents to Koala-Roo Can-Do and to explain how he will be used in the classroom to develop self-esteem in your students. Send this letter within a week of your introduction of Koala-Roo Can-Do to your class. You might duplicate your classroom rules to send home along with the letter.

Parent Involvement Letter Home

Date and sign the Parent Involvement Letter Home (page 72), and send it to survey parents so that you can involve them in the classroom.

Careers and Hobbies Letter Home

The Careers and Hobbies Letter Home (page 73) invites parents to visit the classroom to share their hobbies and careers. Date it and sign it before you send it.

Kid of the Week Letter Home

The Kid of the Week Letter Home (page 74) explains the Can-Do Kid of the Week bulletin board (page 19). The letter encourages parents to help their child write a story about himself or herself and find photographs to bring and share.

Date and sign the letter. You must also fill in the date in the body of the letter: specify a date that gives you some time to remind the child who forgets to bring in materials. Attach a piece of construction paper (not too dark a color), and send the letter home.

Show-and-Tell Letter Home

Date and sign the Show-and-Tell Letter Home (page 75), and send it to give parents ideas of how to help their child find things to bring to school. (See Ideas for Show-and-Tell, page 174.)

Questionnaire Letter Home

You might want to send the Questionnaire Letter Home (page 76) close to conference time. Parents know their child far better than you do and in different ways from the ways you know their child. The answers to the questionnaire may give you insight and spark useful dialogue with the parents about your student.

Date and sign the note at the top of the questionnaire before you send the sheet home.

Sticker Board Letter Home

The Sticker Board Letter Home (page 77) describes how parents can use stickers as rewards in a positive motivation program at home to complement programs in the classroom. Date and sign the letter, and attach it to My Sticker Board (see below).

My Sticker Board

Duplicate My Sticker Board (page 78), and glue it to heavy paper. Color the designs. Laminate the board, or cover it with clear contact paper. Punch two holes at the top about three inches apart; make sure the holes are centered. Tie yarn or ribbon through the holes so that the board can hang on a wall. Attach the Sticker Board Letter Home (see above), and send the board home.

Can-Do Curriculum Review

Send the Can-Do Curriculum Review (page 79) home to parents to give them a brief outline of what you are teaching. Duplicate several copies, and place them in a folder. Every month or six weeks, fill out a copy, duplicate it, and send it home to show parents the current curriculum and units you are teaching. Use the blank sections for additional subjects, topics of concern, or artwork by a student.

How to Draw Koala-Roo Can-Do

Use How to Draw Koala-Roo Can-Do (page 80) as an independent activity, a directed lesson with teacher instruction, or a reward one child can earn either for himself or herself or for the entire class. The step-by-step instructions are easy to follow.

Getting Started Checklist

Use the Getting Started Checklist (page 81) in September when you are setting up your classroom for the new school year (or when you begin the Koala-Roo Can-Do activities anytime during the year).

You Are Special

At the end of the school year, duplicate the You Are Special poem (page 82) with the grade level filled in, fill in one child's name on each sheet, and give it to each child with the report card.

Can-Do Kid
Compliment

Can-Do Kid
Compliment

Can-Do Kid
Compliment

Can-Do Kid
Compliment

Can-Do Kid
Compliment

Can-Do Kid
Compliment

I AM
A CAN-DO KID!

I AM
A CAN-DO KID!

I AM
A CAN-DO KID!

I AM
A CAN-DO KID!

I AM
A CAN-DO KID!

I AM
A CAN-DO KID!

I AM
A CAN-DO KID!

I AM
A CAN-DO KID!

I AM
A CAN-DO KID!

I AM
A CAN-DO KID!

Can-Do Kid

Can-Do Kid

Can-Do Kid

Can-Do Kid

Can-Do Kid

Can-Do Kid

Super Reader Logo

Koala-Roo Can-Do Door Logo

Date ________

Dear ________,

____

____

____

____

____

____

Love,

Koala-Roo Can-Do

Special Deliveroo for You!

BE PROUD OF YOURSELF

WHEN "YOU DID IT!"

DON'T WORRY ABOUT HOW OTHER PEOPLE ARE DOING

CONCENTRATE ON DOING YOUR BEST!

SAY "I CAN"

AND PRACTICE IT!

BE A KOALA-ROO CAN-DO READER

READ LOTS OF BOOKS!

Can-Do Placard Holder

Placard

I am a helper...	My job is ...

Stand-up Can-Do Diagram, Pouch, and Tail

Stand-up Can-Do Body

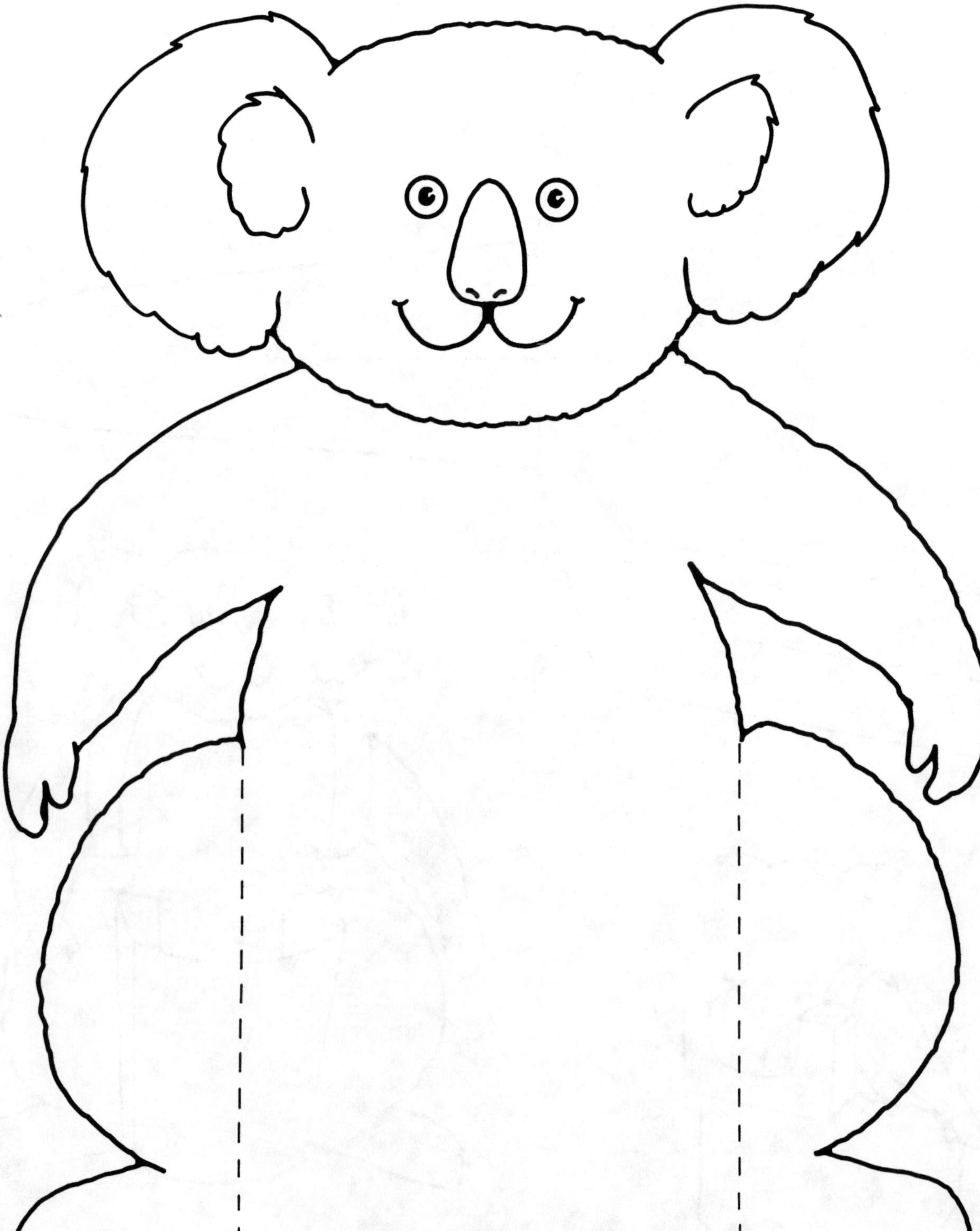

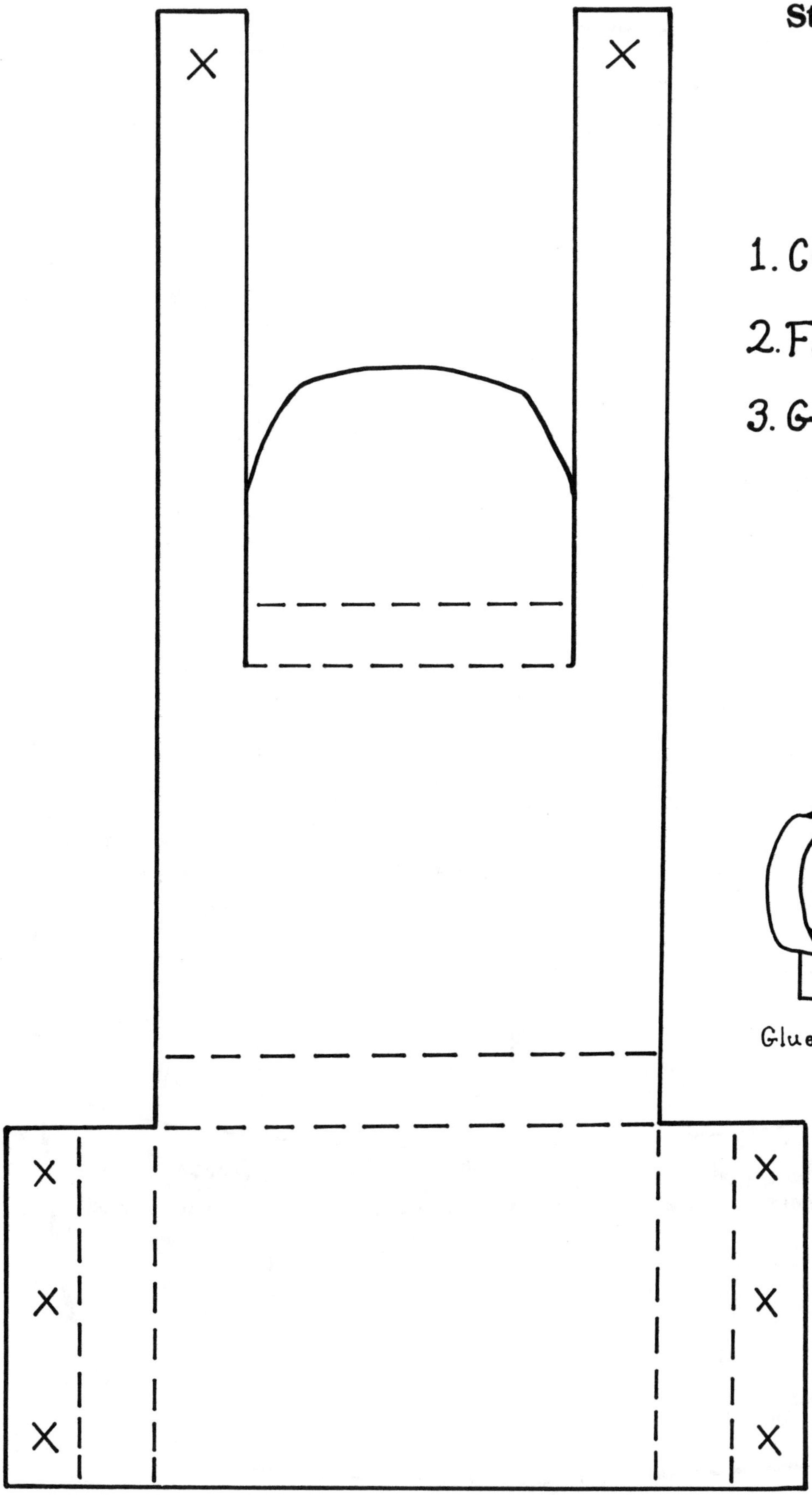

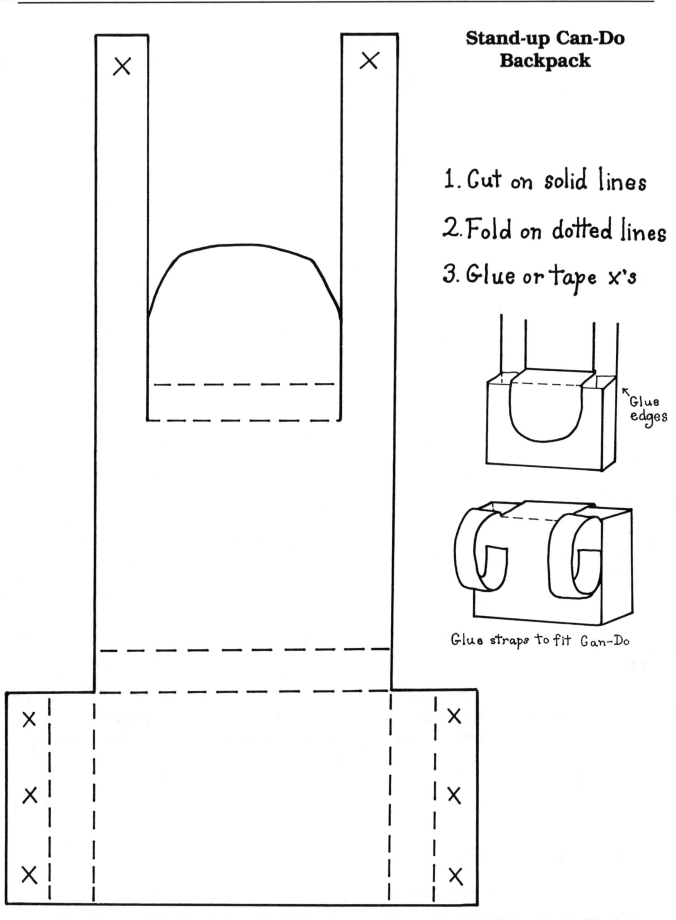

Stand-up Can-Do Backpack

1. Cut on solid lines
2. Fold on dotted lines
3. Glue or tape x's

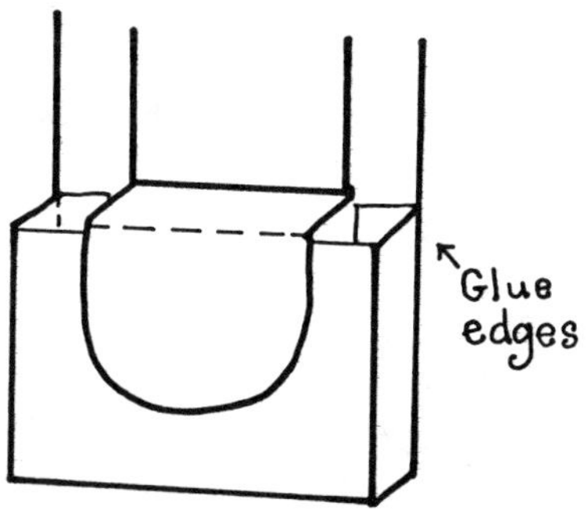

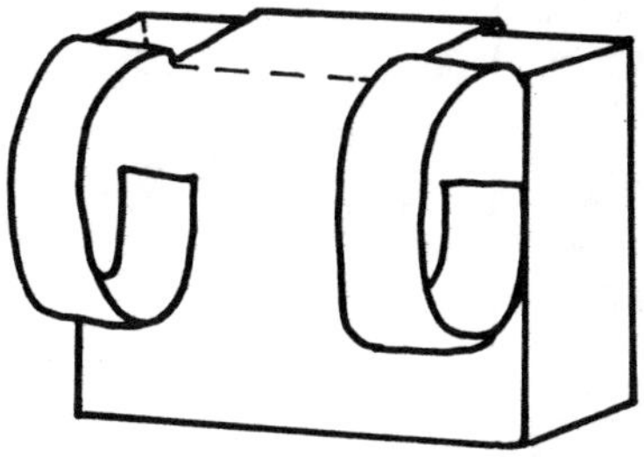

Glue straps to fit Can-Do

THE NAME GAME

Directions:
Find someone who fits each square. Have them write their name in the box.

Who likes to swim	Who has a summer birthday	Who likes to sing	Who does not like chocolate
Who is older than you	Who has a pet cat	Who has curly hair	Who was born outside this state
Who is wearing your favorite color	Who has a baby brother	Who shares a bedroom	Whose favorite subject is math

I Am Special

My name ____________________

My nickname ____________________

What I like to be called in school ____________________

My favorite food ____________________

My favorite TV show ____________________

My best friend ____________________

What I like to do at home ____________________

What I collect ____________________

My favorite toy ____________________

Something I like to do in school ____________________

Something I wish I could do in school ____________________

ABSENTEE POUCH

"GLAD YOU'RE BACK!"

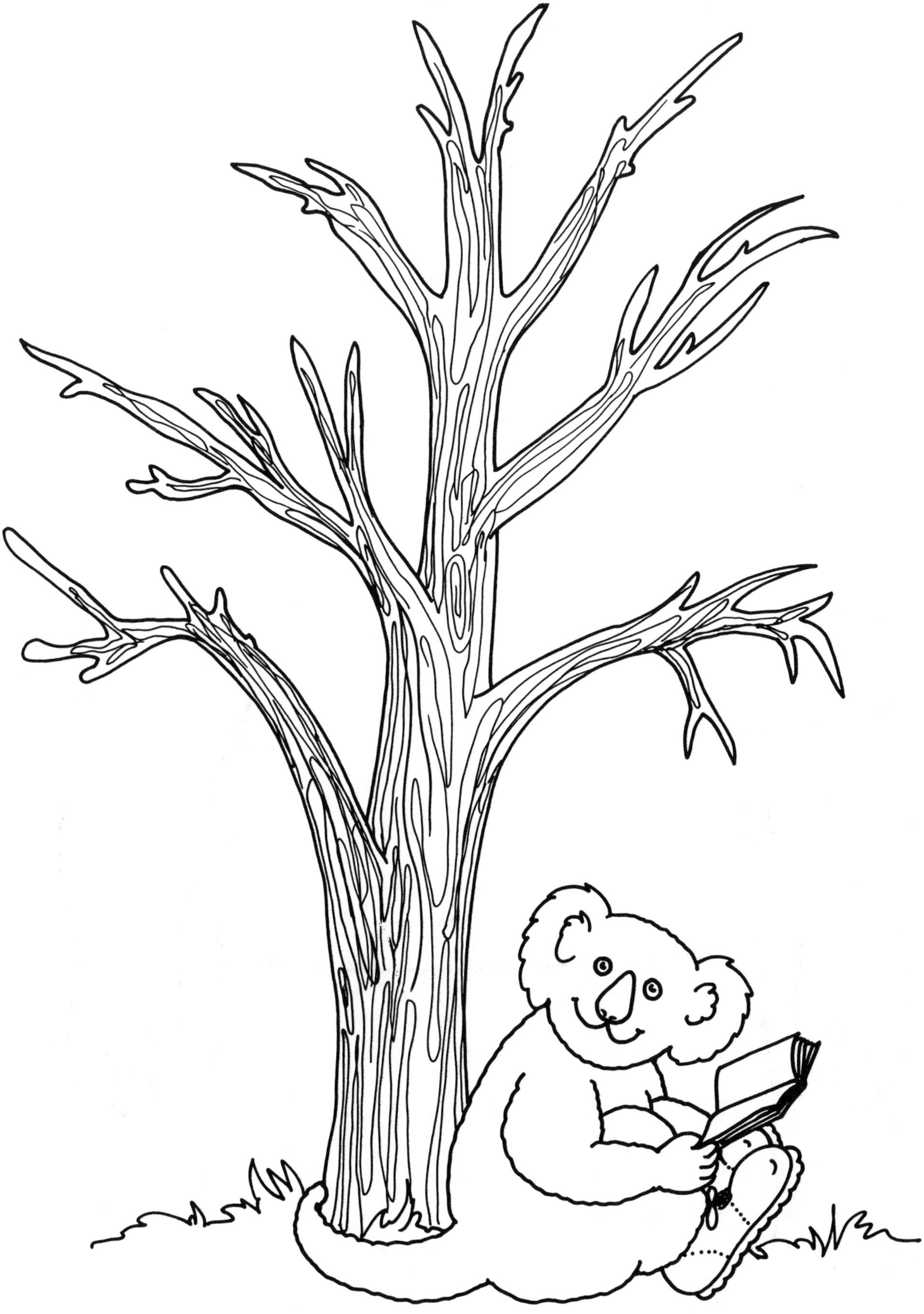

C. Can-Do Can Body

A. Can-Do Can Cover

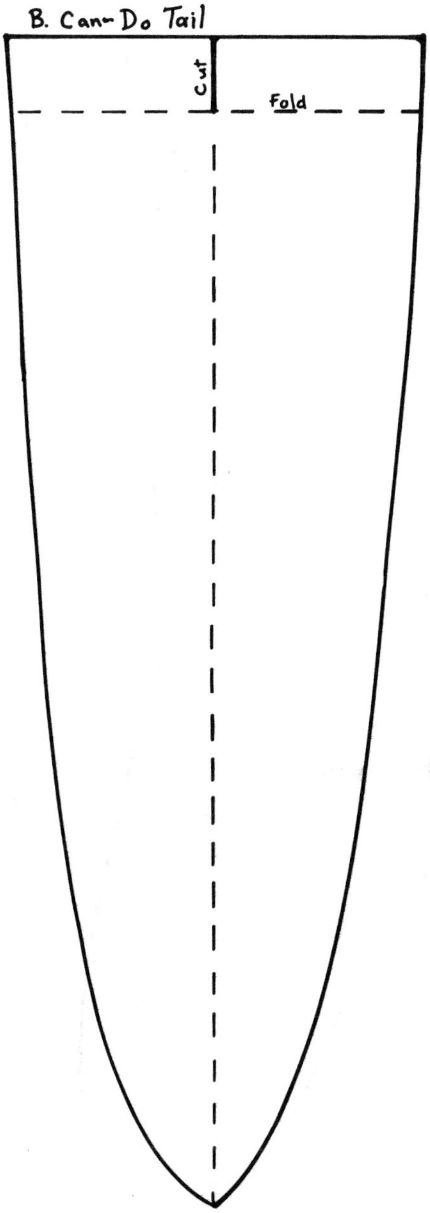
B. Can-Do Tail
Cut
Fold

D. Can-Do Can Legs and Pouch

Can-Do Boots

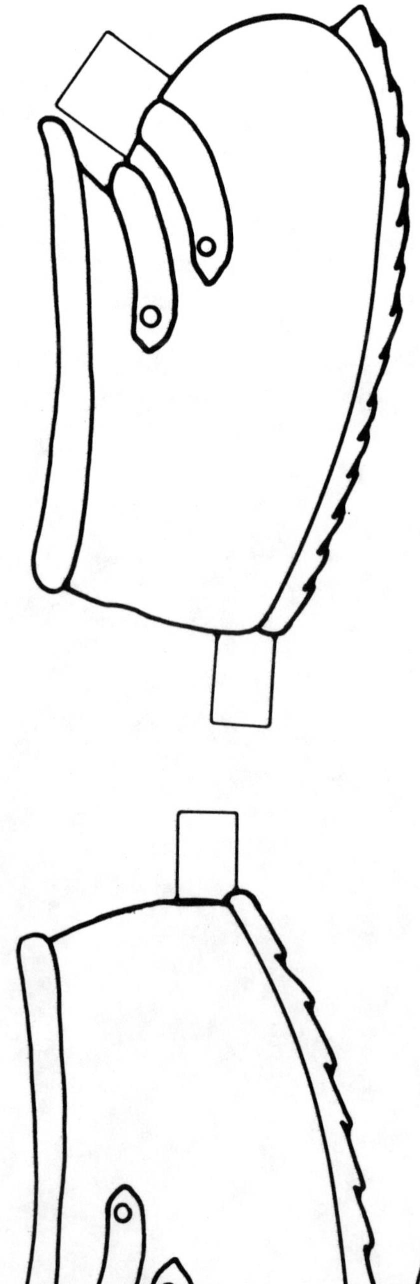

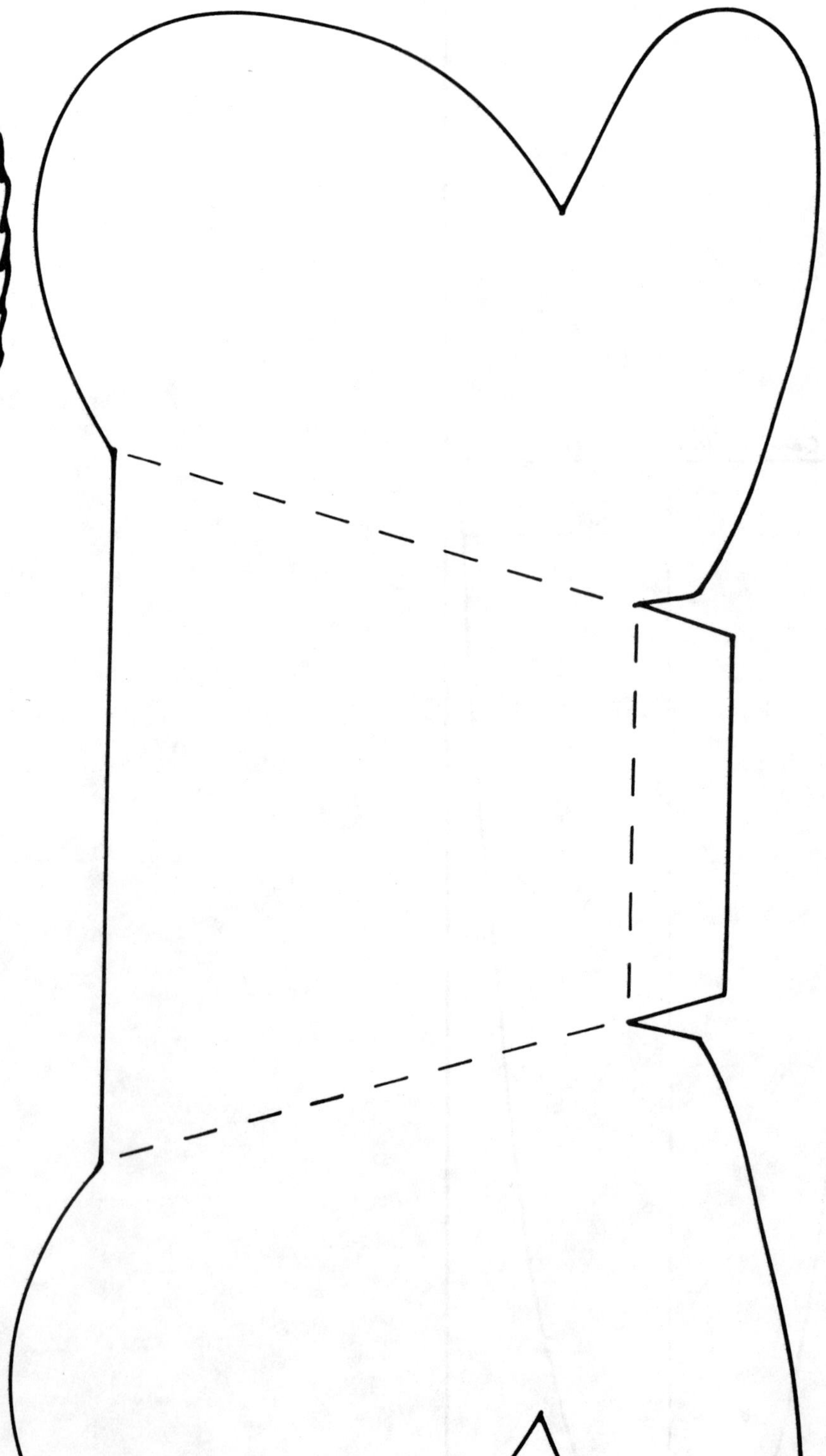

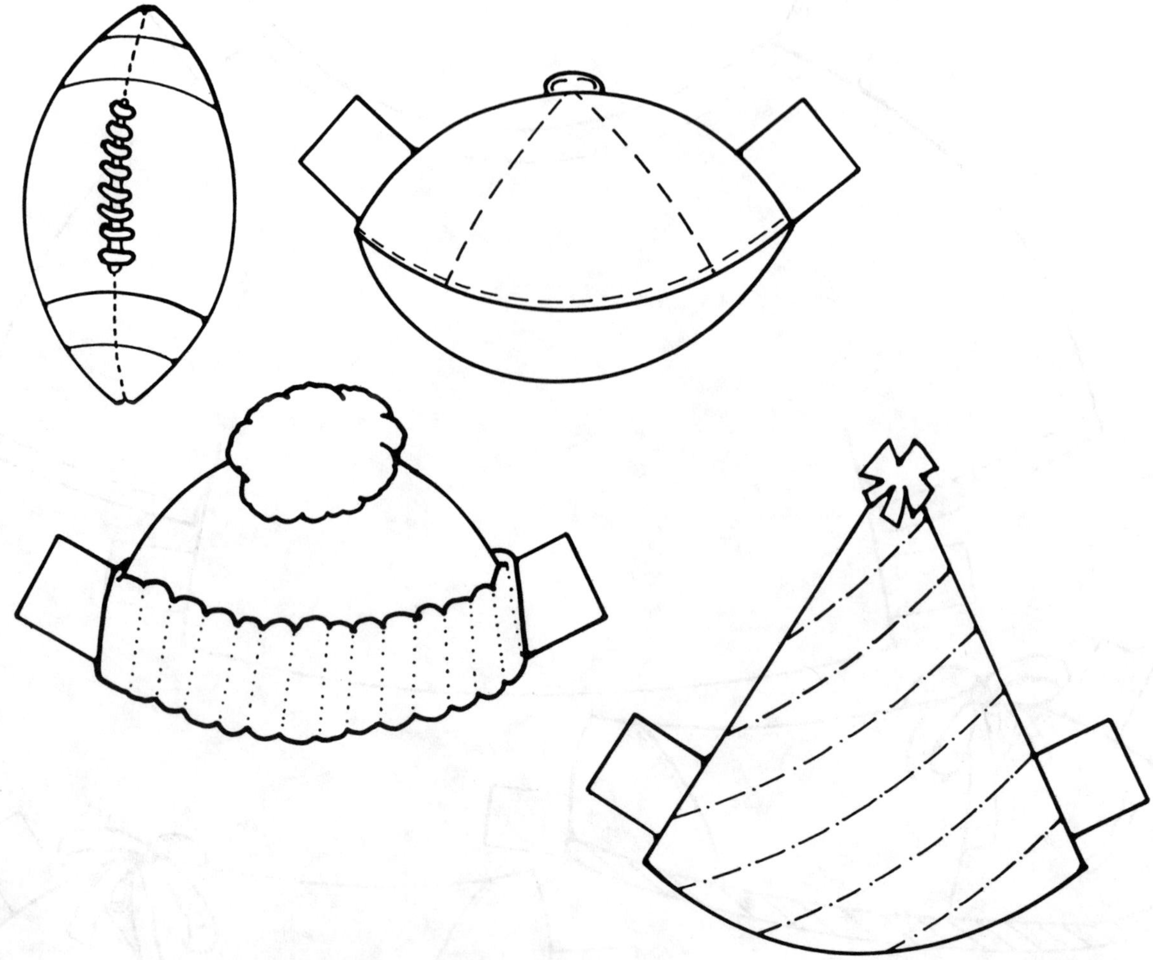
NBA

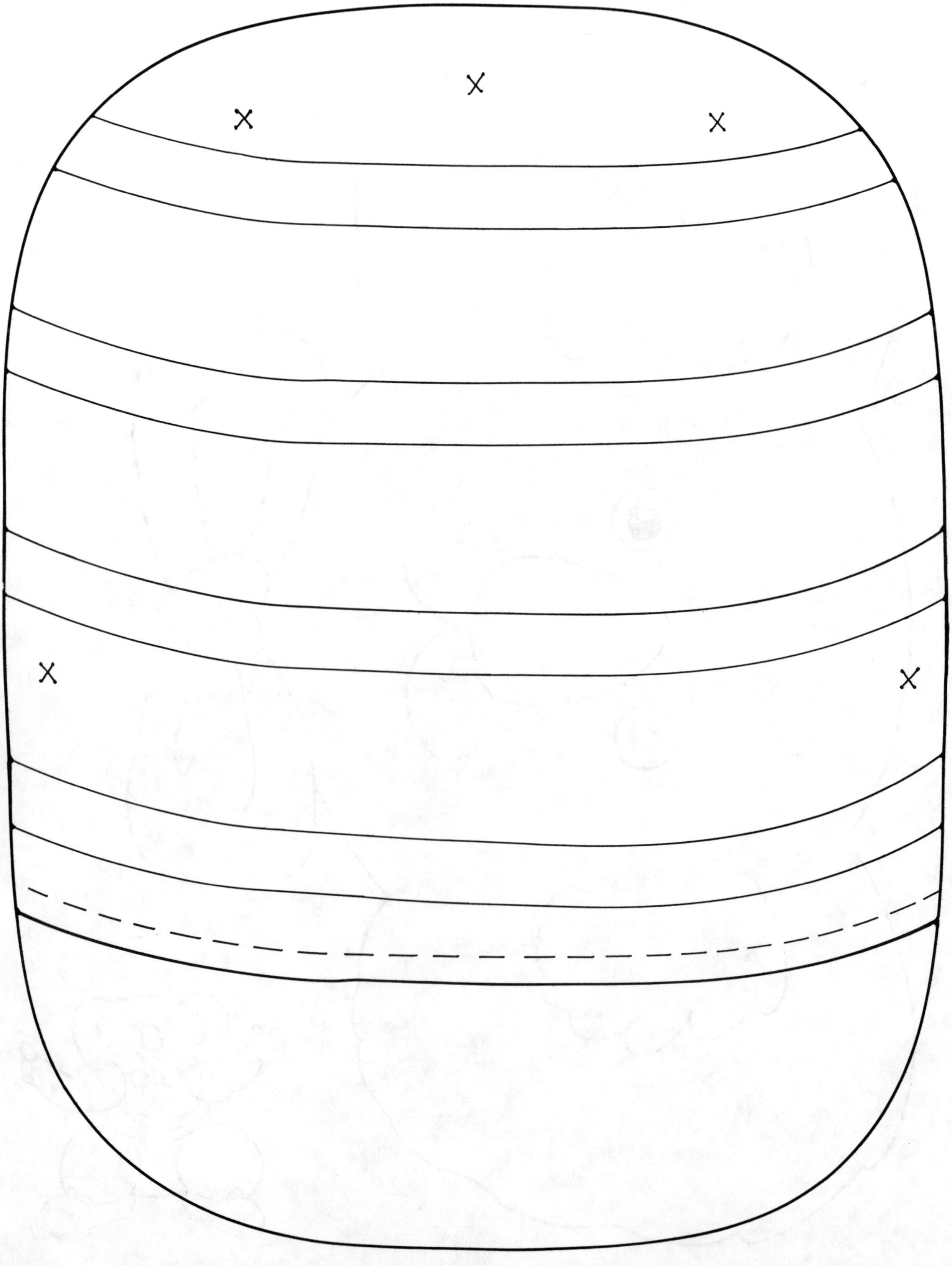

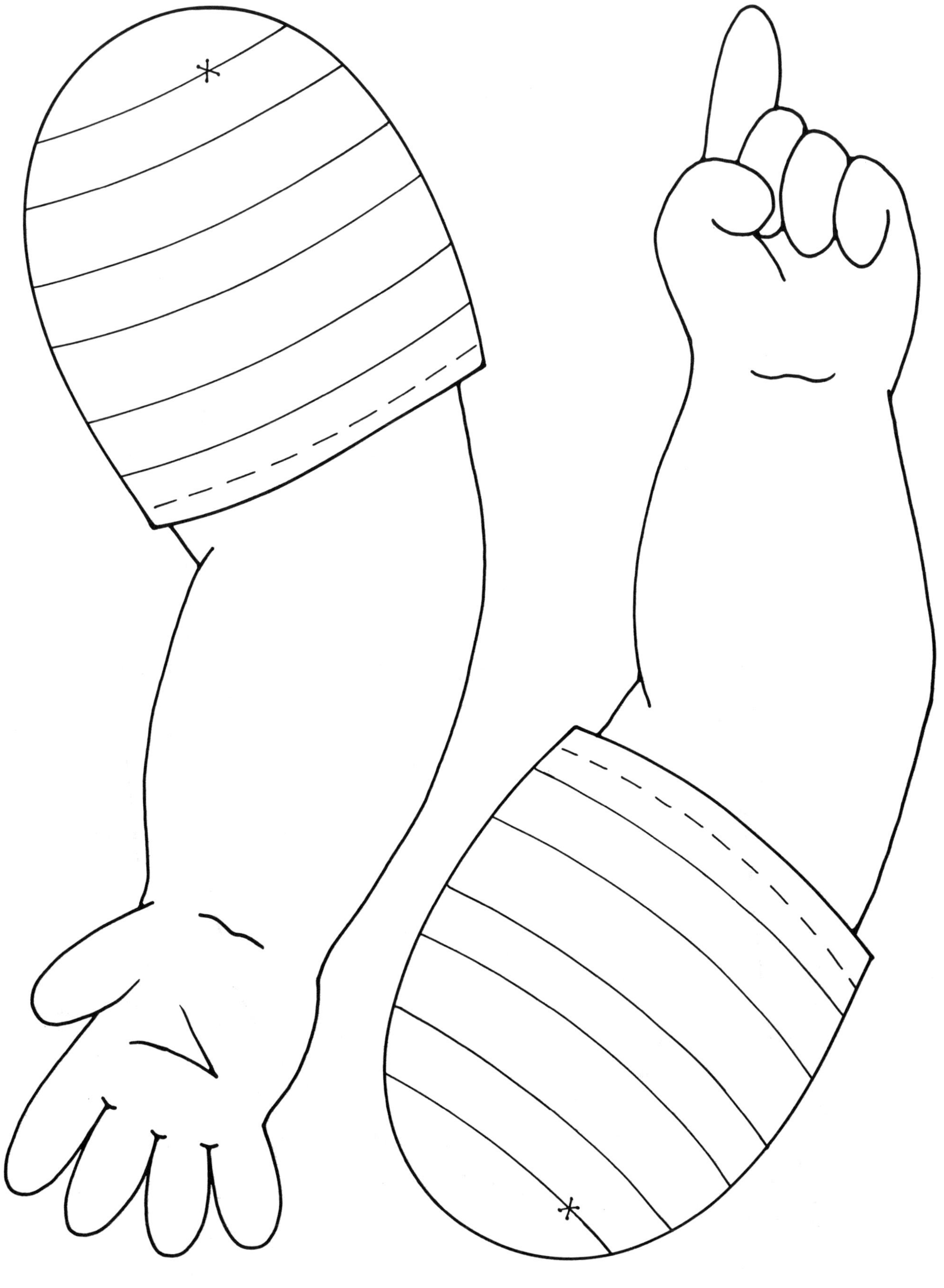

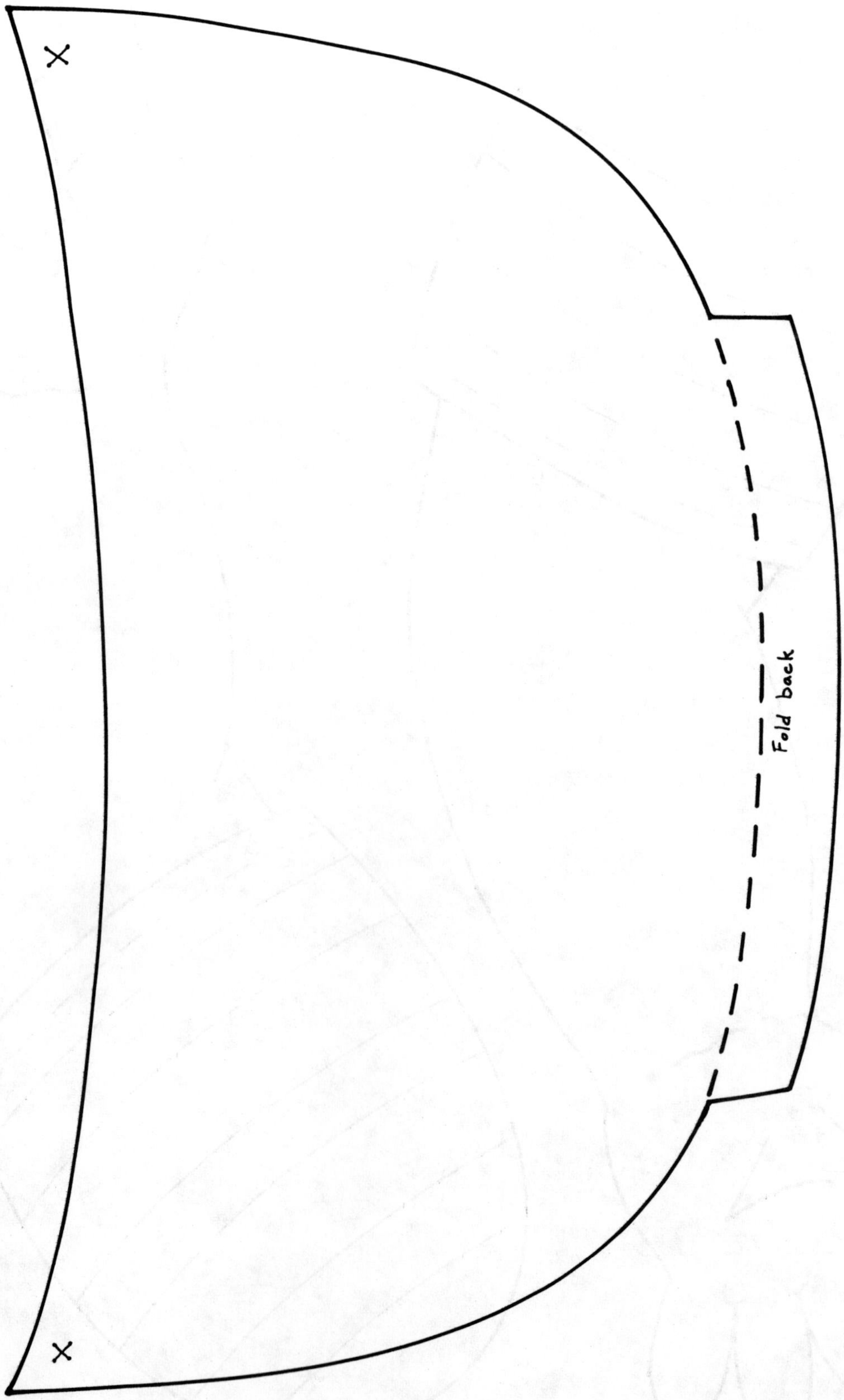
Fold back

X

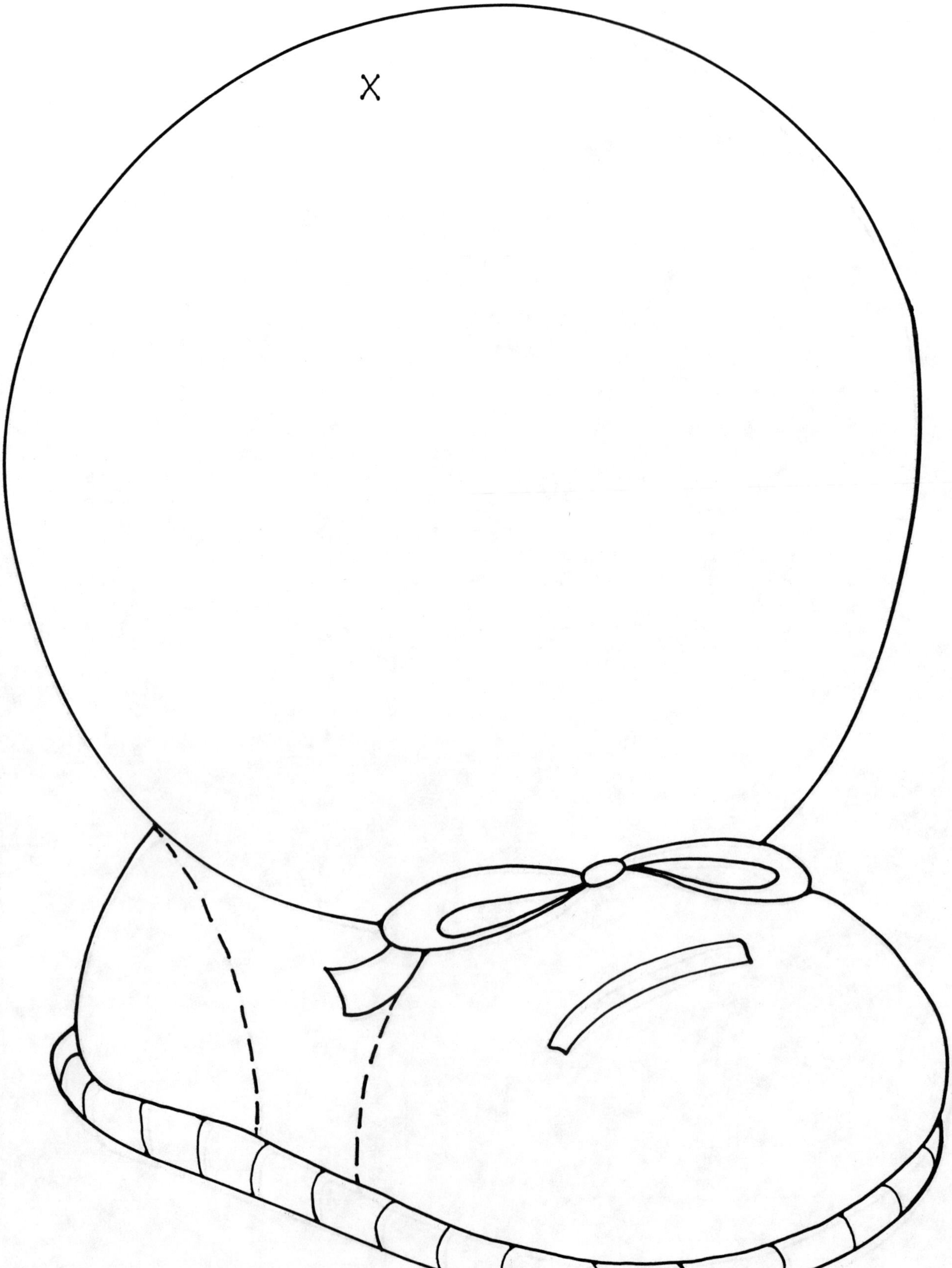
X

Can-Do Chances

YOU DID IT!

Earned a Can-Do Chance

YOU DID IT!

Earned a Can-Do Chance

YOU DID IT!

Earned a Can-Do Chance

YOU DID IT!

Earned a Can-Do Chance

YOU DID IT!

Earned a Can-Do Chance

YOU DID IT!

Earned a Can-Do Chance

YOU DID IT!

Earned a Can-Do Chance

YOU DID IT!

Earned a Can-Do Chance

YOU DID IT!

Earned a Can-Do Chance

YOU DID IT!

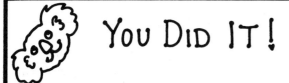

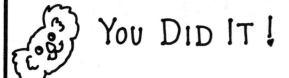

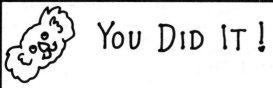

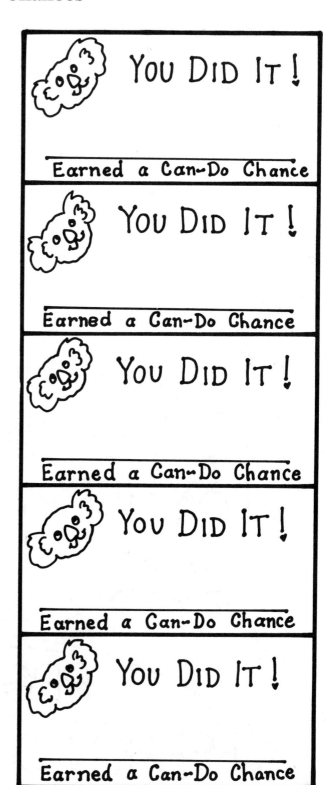

Earned a Can-Do Chance

Can-Do Caps

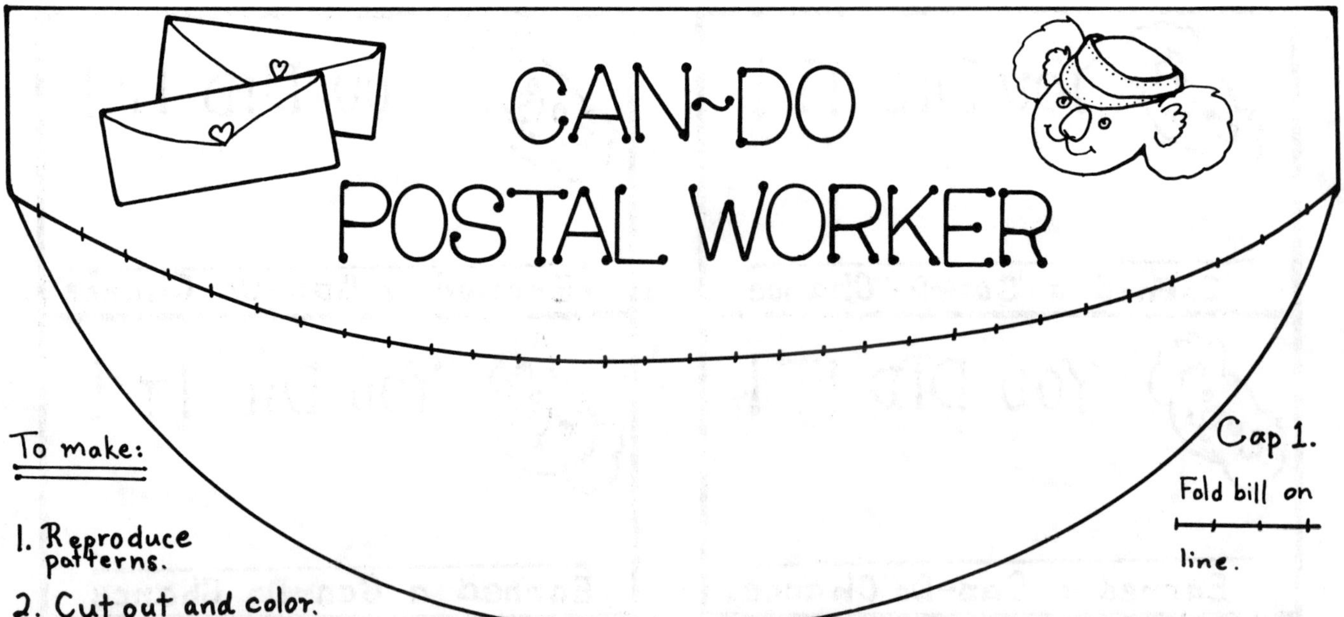

To make:

1. Reproduce patterns.
2. Cut out and color.
3. Staple or glue to front of Can-Do Ears band.

Cap 1. Fold bill on line.

Cap 2. Write age on line.

Cap 3. Write name of student on line.

Can-Do Ears

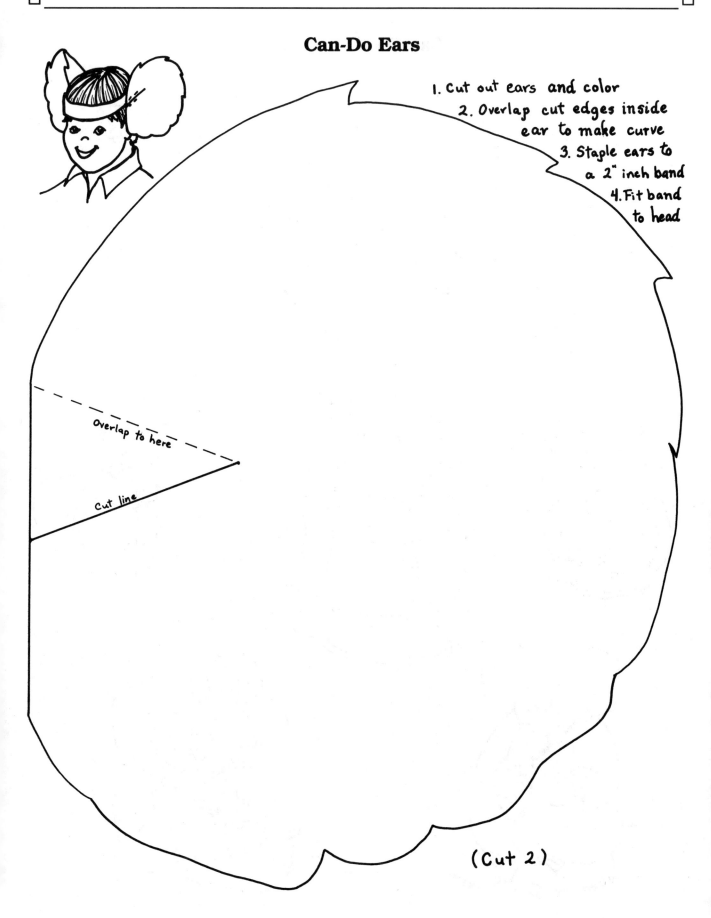

1. Cut out ears and color
2. Overlap cut edges inside ear to make curve
3. Staple ears to a 2" inch band
4. Fit band to head

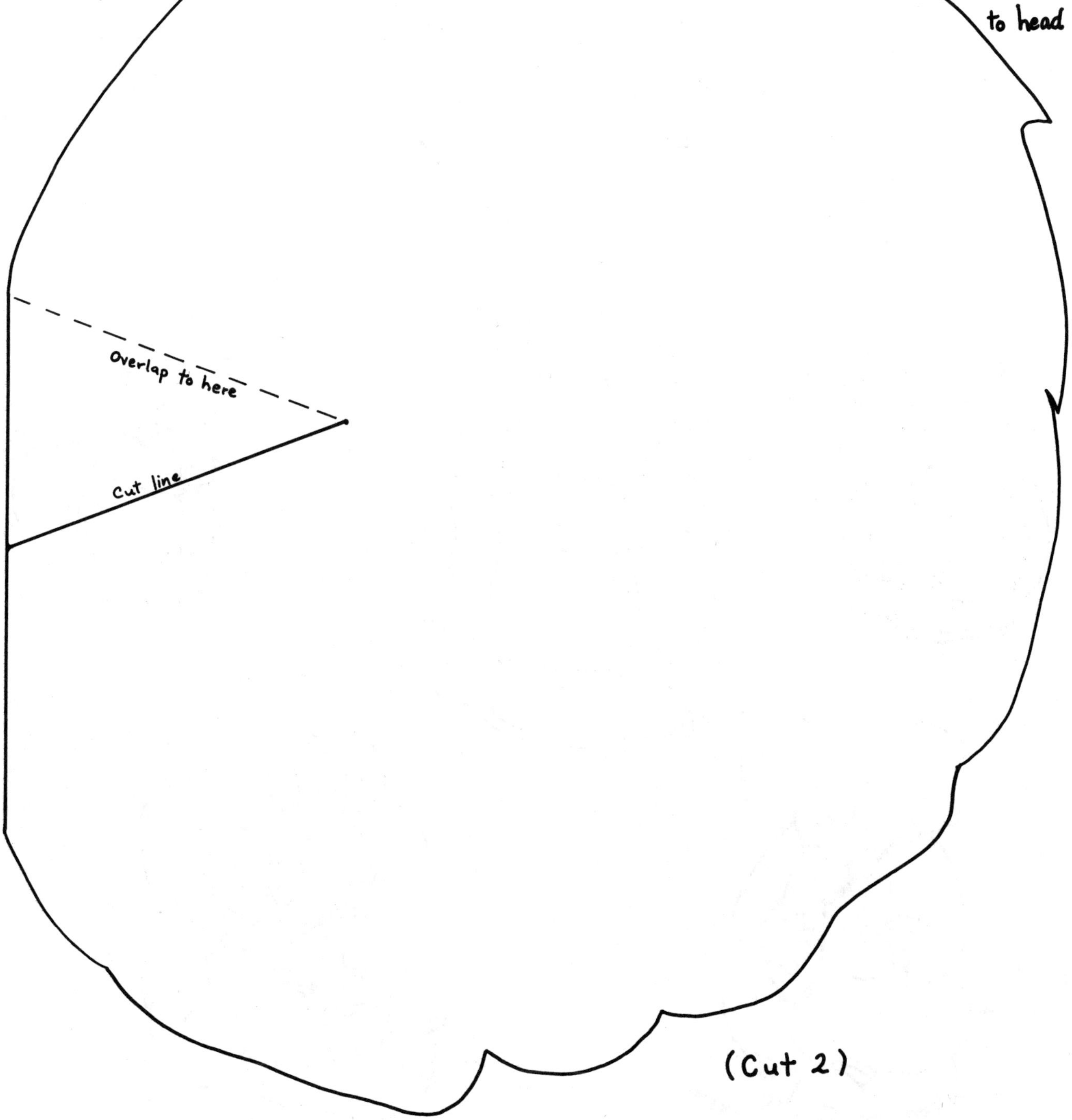

Can-Do Clip Art 1

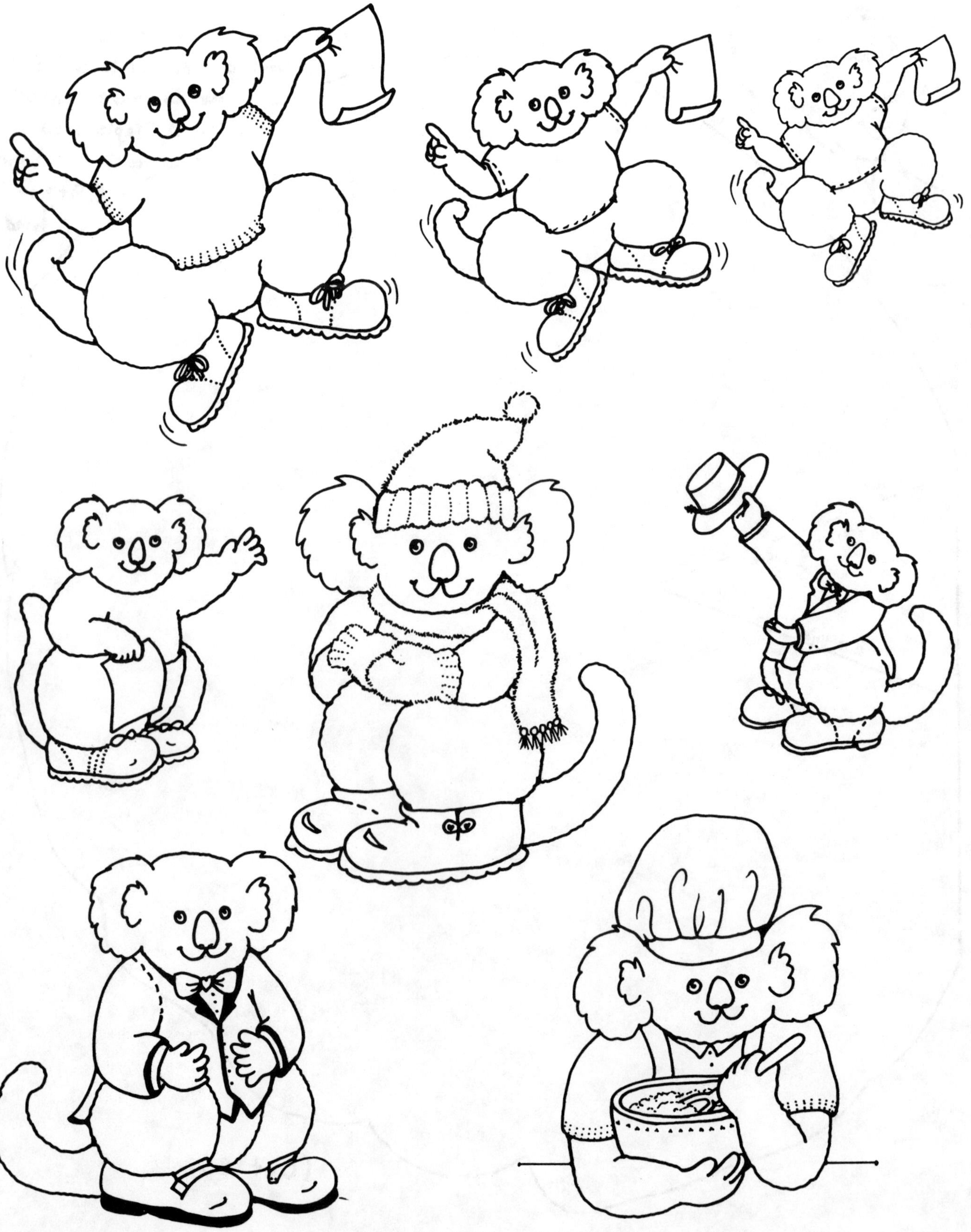

Can-Do Clip Art 2

Can-Do Clip Art 3

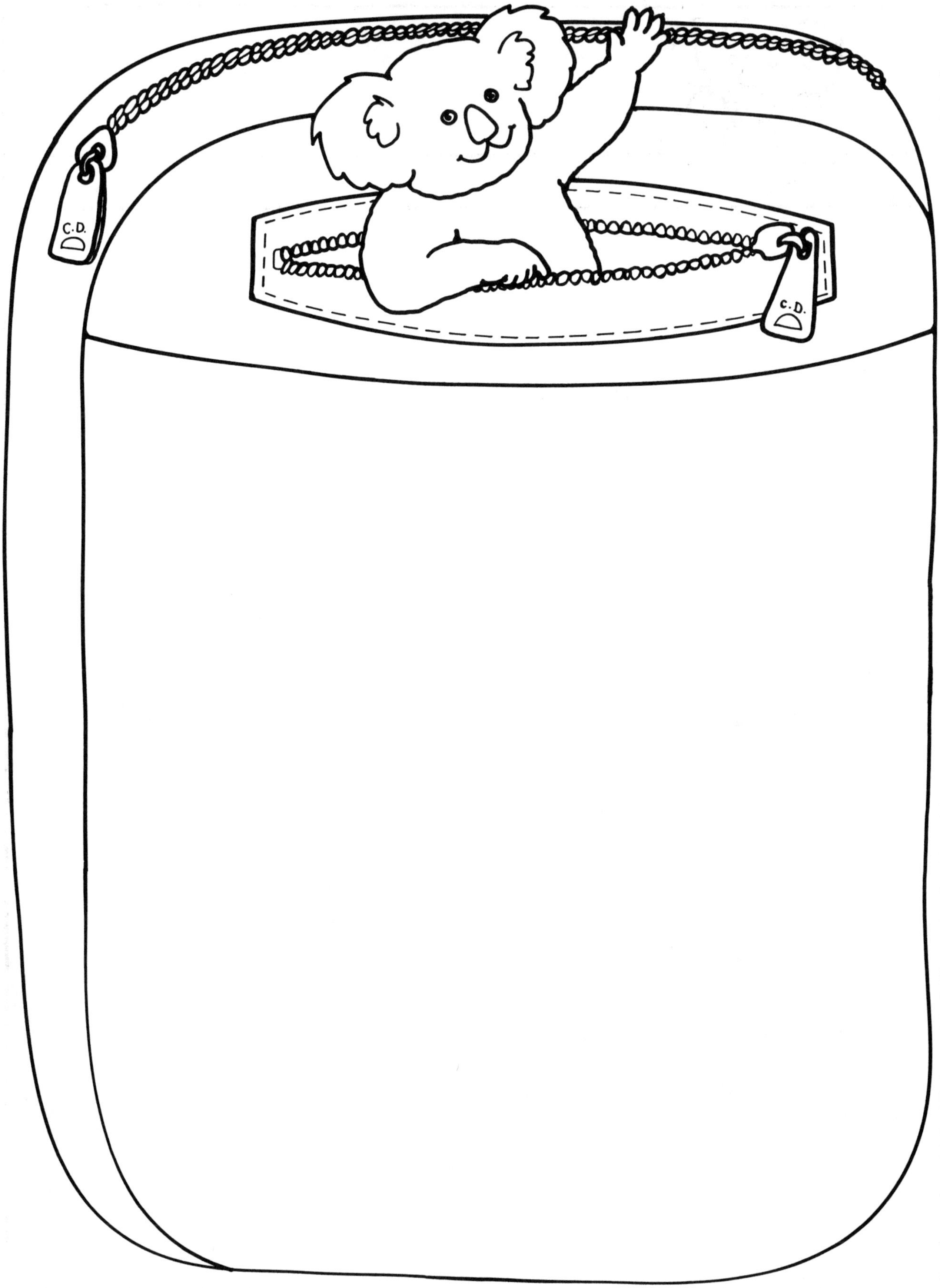
C.D.
C.D.

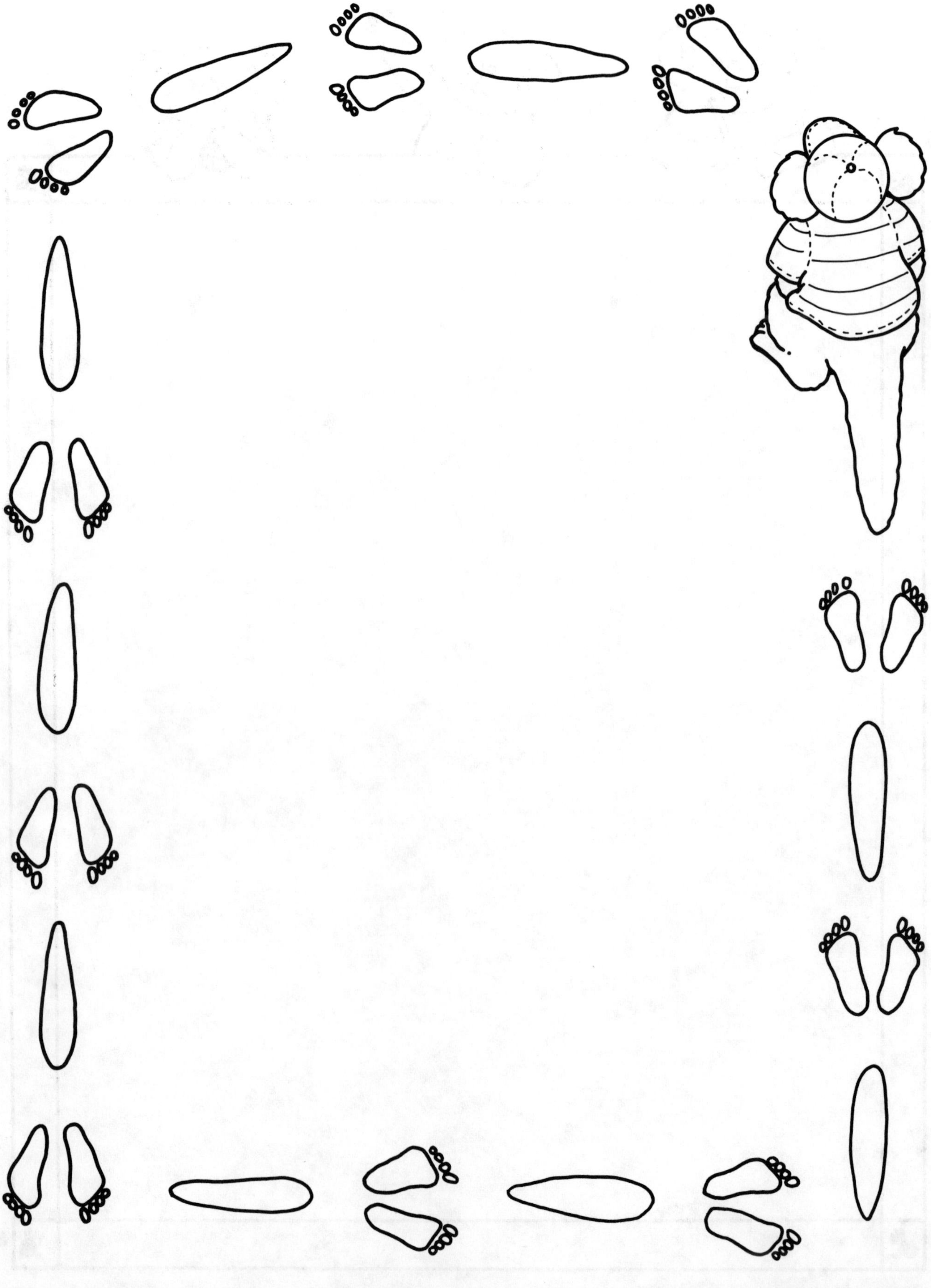

U Can Do It!

Koala-Roo Can-Do Pencil Tops

Introducing Koala-Roo Can-Do

Date:

Dear Parents,

I'd like to introduce Koala-Roo Can-Do, our class mascot. This character has been created to convey the message **I can do it if I try**.

I will be using Koala-Roo Can-Do in many ways to make learning enjoyable. He will help your child follow our classroom guidelines and learn as much as possible. The class, both small groups and individuals, will work toward goals by earning compliments. They will earn compliments by meeting my expectations that they do such things as follow directions, concentrate, share, complete assignments, and respect others.

Koala-Roo Can-Do will be incorporated into the curriculum areas of reading, math, and language arts.

Most important, Koala-Roo Can-Do will be a visible symbol of self-esteem for your child. He will help me encourage your child to believe:

- I am terrific!
- If I try again and again, I can do it!
- I want to be the best I can be!

Please call or stop in to visit if you have a special question or concern. I look forward to your enthusiasm in helping your child achieve his or her goals.

Sincerely,

Parent Involvement Opportunities

Date:

Dear Parents,

I would like to encourage you to become involved in our classroom activities. Please check any of the following roles that interest you, and return this form with your child as soon as possible.

____ **1.** Room mother or father: helping plan special activities and parties

____ **2.** Chaperone for field trips

____ **3.** Guest speaker for our careers unit

____ **4.** Reading or math helper

____ **5.** Teacher aide: typing, duplicating materials, and preparing projects

____ **6.** Art assistant

____ **7.** Other ____________________

Your name ____________________

Your child's name ____________________

Thanks so much for your help!

Sincerely,

Careers and Hobbies

Date:

Dear Parents,

Throughout the year I would like to invite moms and dads to come in to share hobbies or careers with our class. In recent years there has been a focus on jobs and leisure time in education. I hope you can bring your knowledge into the classroom.

- **Hobbies or leisure activities:** You might share objects, slides, samples of things you've made, or collections. You could talk about experiences with clubs or other groups.
- **Jobs or careers:** You might talk about what you do, the skills you need, the education you rely on, what you like and don't like about your work, what you wear while you work, and perhaps interesting fringe benefits. You might show photographs or samples.

Sharing your hobby or career would entail a ten-minute talk and five minutes for questions.

Please fill in the blanks, and return this sheet with your child. I will have a volunteer contact you to arrange the month, day, and time of your visit.

Name ______________________ Job or hobby ________________

Daytime phone ______________ Home phone _________________

Times I could be available ____________________________________

I hope that you can arrange to take the time to share your experience with our class. Your child will be excited and proud, and all the students will see that what they're learning will help them when they grow up.

Sincerely,

Can-Do Kid of the Week

Date:

Dear Parents and Children,

A special bulletin board is set up in our classroom, and each week a different child is encouraged to share snapshots and a personal story. A piece of construction paper is attached. Please use it for your story. The story should be short and written in large print so that it can be read from a distance.

Here are some ideas for the story:

- Write about your family.
- Write about your pets.
- Write about the fun things you like to do.
- Write about a special time, a happy event.

Please bring your story and snapshots to school on the following date:

____

Thank you for helping to make our class a friendly place to be.

Sincerely,

Show-and-Tell

Date:

Dear Parents,

Children enjoy sharing items or stories from home. This activity encourages language development and builds self-confidence. Please monitor what comes to school. The following are some suggestions for sharing:

1. Something unusual
2. Something someone has made for your child
3. Something brand new or special
4. Something with a special story
5. Something touching on nature or science
6. An interesting book
7. Something from another city or country

A doll, stuffed toy, or toy car is acceptable only if you feel it is very special at this particular time to your child.

Thank you for your help.

Sincerely,

Questionnaire

Date:

Dear Parents,

I am getting to know your child more and more each day. You know your child far better than I do. You can help me understand your boy or girl from your point of view by returning this form after you have circled choices and filled in blanks.

Sincerely,

My child's name is ________________________. My child . . .

1. Learns best by   Doing / Seeing / Listening / Other ____________
2. Likes to play mostly   Inside / Outside
3. Likes to be   With one friend / With lots of friends / Alone
4. Is mostly   Friendly / Shy or reserved / Other ____________
5. Would rather be a   Leader / Follower / Other ____________
6. Needs at home   Lots of attention / Average attention / Other ________
7. Needs   Lots of sleep / An average amount of sleep / Other ________
8. Does well in these school areas: Math / Reading / English / Handwriting / P.e. / Music / Study habits / Getting along with others / Following directions
9. Does well in these areas outside school: Sports / Music / Art / Relationships / Other ____________________
10. Likes these activities outside school: ____________________
11. Has difficulty doing ____________________
12. Has these responsibilities at home: ____________________
13. Would like to ____________________ in school this year.

I'd like you to know this about my child: ____________________

My Sticker Board

Date:

Dear Parents,

At school we have been working on teamwork and individual progress. Your child is learning to think about himself or herself in a positive way—to say, "I can do it if I try."

You can use the accompanying sticker board to help your child work toward positive goals at home, too. The goals might include being courteous to other family members, going to bed at a certain time, or doing chores without being reminded. Here's how to get started:

1. Think about what you want to accomplish. Consider your child's capabilities carefully. Ask yourself, "What do I want my child to do that I know my child can do?"

a. ______________________________

b. ______________________________

c. ______________________________

2. Decide on only one goal for a start. Be sure you set an expectation that your child can meet. If your child experiences success, your child will continue to be interested in reaching the goal.

3. Buy some stickers with your child—stickers that he or she will really want to earn.

4. Let your child know exactly how and when he or she can earn a sticker.

5. Post the sticker board in a special place.

6. Along the way, praise each small step. Give guidance as necessary. When the goal is reached, have your child place the sticker on the board. Then **smile** together.

Sincerely,

My Sticker Board

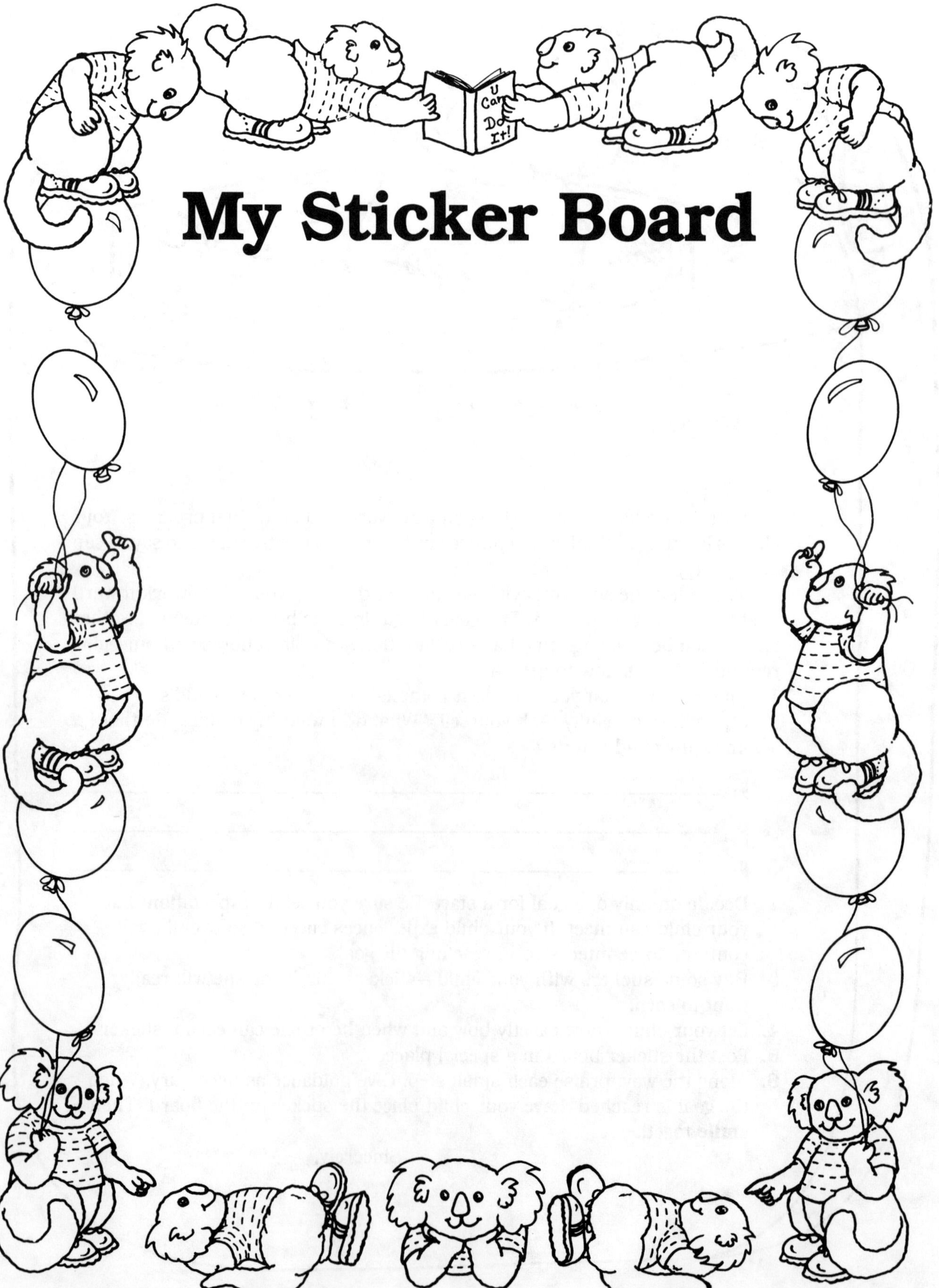

CAN~DO CURRICULUM REVIEW

Teacher: Date:

LANGUAGE ARTS	SOCIAL STUDIES / SCIENCE	MATH

How to Draw Koala-Roo Can-Do

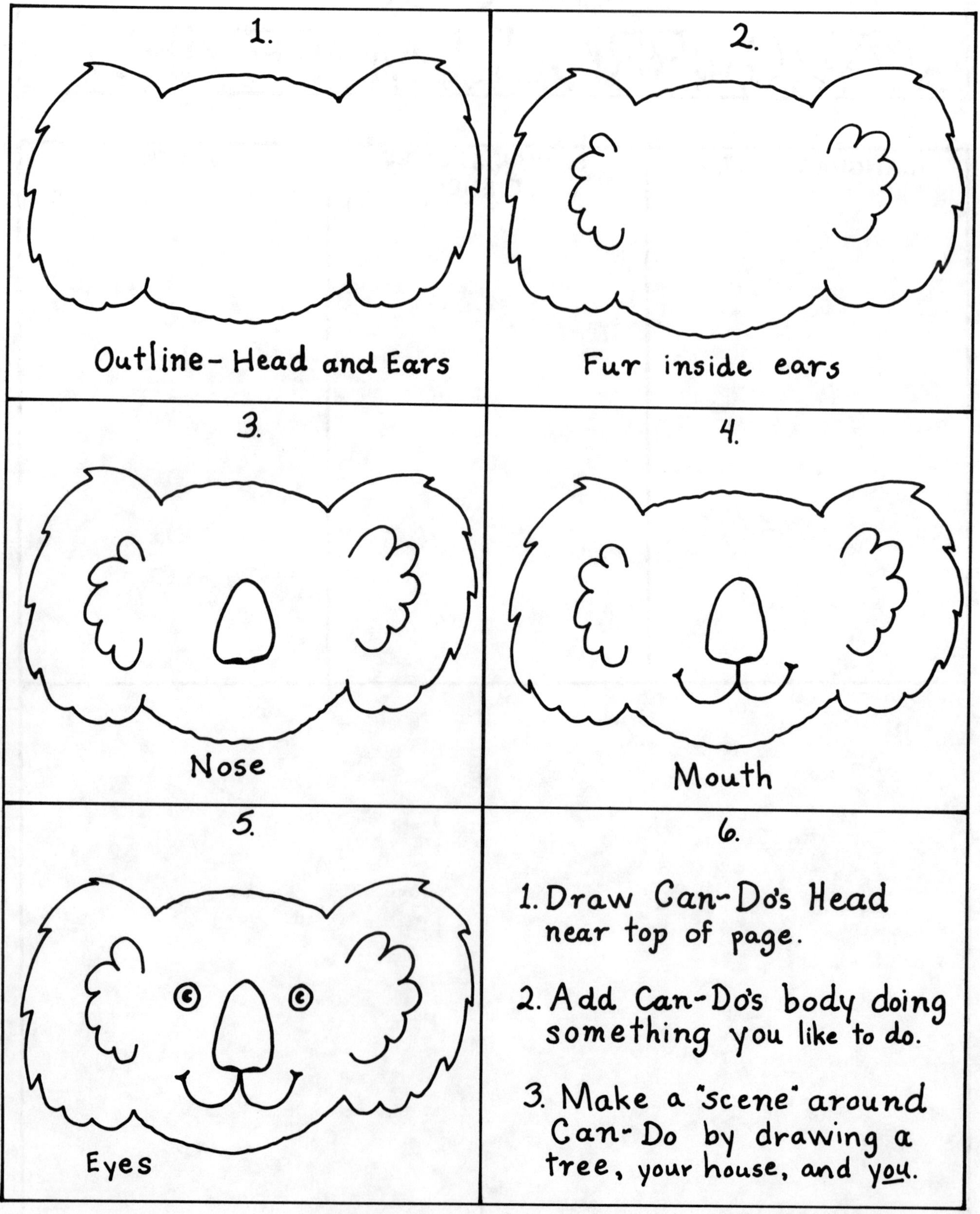

1.
Outline- Head and Ears
2.
Fur inside ears
3.
Nose
4.
Mouth
5.
Eyes
6.
1. Draw Can-Do's Head near top of page.
2. Add Can-Do's body doing something you like to do.
3. Make a "scene" around Can-Do by drawing a tree, your house, and you.

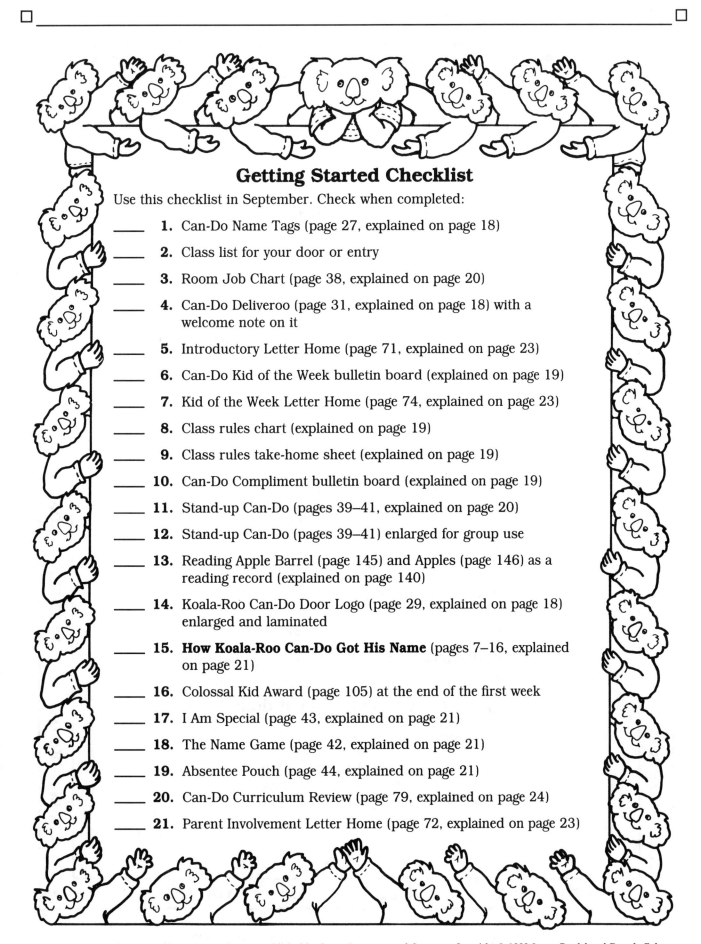

Getting Started Checklist

Use this checklist in September. Check when completed:

____ **1.** Can-Do Name Tags (page 27, explained on page 18)

____ **2.** Class list for your door or entry

____ **3.** Room Job Chart (page 38, explained on page 20)

____ **4.** Can-Do Deliveroo (page 31, explained on page 18) with a welcome note on it

____ **5.** Introductory Letter Home (page 71, explained on page 23)

____ **6.** Can-Do Kid of the Week bulletin board (explained on page 19)

____ **7.** Kid of the Week Letter Home (page 74, explained on page 23)

____ **8.** Class rules chart (explained on page 19)

____ **9.** Class rules take-home sheet (explained on page 19)

____ **10.** Can-Do Compliment bulletin board (explained on page 19)

____ **11.** Stand-up Can-Do (pages 39–41, explained on page 20)

____ **12.** Stand-up Can-Do (pages 39–41) enlarged for group use

____ **13.** Reading Apple Barrel (page 145) and Apples (page 146) as a reading record (explained on page 140)

____ **14.** Koala-Roo Can-Do Door Logo (page 29, explained on page 18) enlarged and laminated

____ **15.** **How Koala-Roo Can-Do Got His Name** (pages 7–16, explained on page 21)

____ **16.** Colossal Kid Award (page 105) at the end of the first week

____ **17.** I Am Special (page 43, explained on page 21)

____ **18.** The Name Game (page 42, explained on page 21)

____ **19.** Absentee Pouch (page 44, explained on page 21)

____ **20.** Can-Do Curriculum Review (page 79, explained on page 24)

____ **21.** Parent Involvement Letter Home (page 72, explained on page 23)

• YOU ARE SPECIAL! • YOU ARE SPECIAL! • YOU ARE SPECIAL! •

YOU ARE SPECIAL! • YOU ARE SPECIAL! • YOU ARE SPECIAL! •
YOU ARE SPECIAL! • YOU ARE SPECIAL! • YOU ARE SPECIAL! •

You Are Special

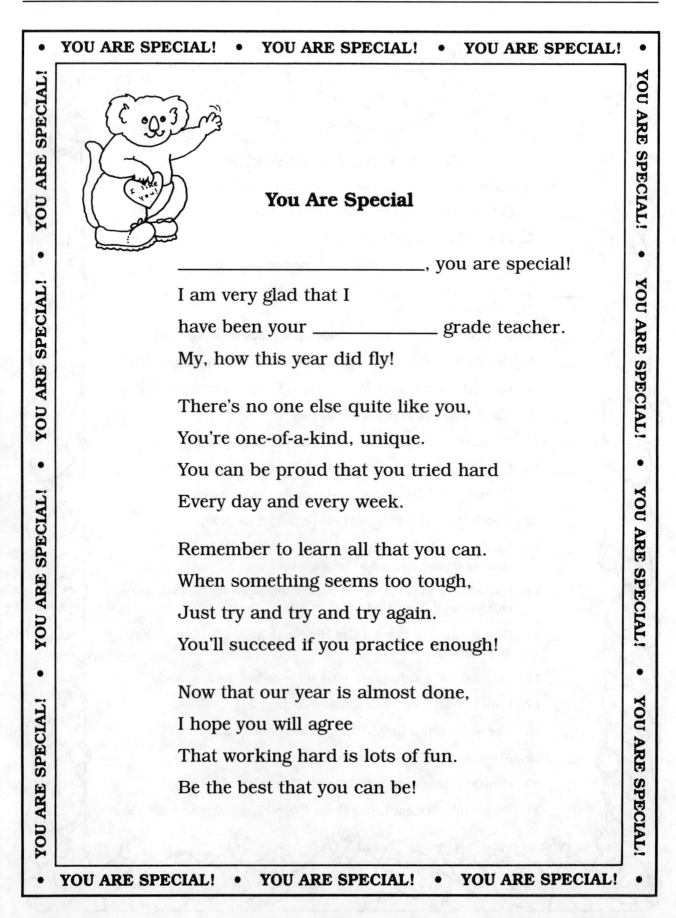

________________________, you are special!
I am very glad that I
have been your ____________ grade teacher.
My, how this year did fly!

There's no one else quite like you,
You're one-of-a-kind, unique.
You can be proud that you tried hard
Every day and every week.

Remember to learn all that you can.
When something seems too tough,
Just try and try and try again.
You'll succeed if you practice enough!

Now that our year is almost done,
I hope you will agree
That working hard is lots of fun.
Be the best that you can be!

• YOU ARE SPECIAL! • YOU ARE SPECIAL! • YOU ARE SPECIAL! •

2

Success Management for Individual Children

Introduction

As you teach, you are constantly observing, evaluating, and guiding your students. From time to time you may work with individuals to help them improve specific behavior or skills so that they can become better learners. After all, our main goal as teachers is to help every student learn.

The following plan for success will help you organize your ideas and strategies in teaching your students to be more effective learners. This success plan is most beneficial for students with prominent problems who require an unusual amount of your attention, but this plan will help you work more positively with everyone in your class. You will find that the tally sheets remove the emotional aspect of problems and help you and your students look at their behavior objectively.

How to Use the Materials

Can-Do Tallies

- **Can-Do Assignments Tally**
- **Can-Do 1-2-3 Tally**
- **Can-Do Hand Raiser Tally**
- **Can-Do Habit Changer Tally**
- **Can-Do Hop-a-roo Tally**

The Can-Do Tally sheets (pages 87–90) are the key materials in your plan for success in changing an individual child's behavior or habit. Their use is discussed in detail as other materials are explained below.

The individual tally sheets can help a child focus on practicing positive behaviors, study habits, study skills, interpersonal relationships, or whatever needs attention. Use the tally sheets when a problem persists and you judge that a positive reward system will be of benefit.

Parents and teachers often apologize for giving children rewards for prescribed behavior, as if such reinforcement were a dishonest form of bribery. There is nothing dishonest in your making a straightforward arrangement with a child, and there is nothing dishonest in what you want the child to do. A positive reward system is essentially contractual. Contracting with children helps them prepare for the adult world, where contracts are commonplace. It also teaches children that their actions have consequences that they themselves can often control.

Think out any individual plan carefully so that the child is always successful in meeting the expectations. Keep in mind, too, that if the reward is not sufficiently meaningful or desired, the child won't work for it. Remember also that the time frame needs to be reasonable, or the goal will seem unreachable. Involving the parents is helpful: the child can receive additional praise at home. You can keep up a form of daily communication with the parents by having the child take the tally sheet home each day.

After you see progress over a period of two or three weeks, you may decide to change the daily tally sheet to a two-day sheet or weekly sheet. You may alter the reward and continue to taper off, observing if the new behavior or skill has been learned. Be sure to continue reinforcing the new behavior with verbal compliments. Continuing your praise and compliments will continually reinforce the learned behavior. The parents will appreciate a periodic follow-up phone call. Parents love to receive praise concerning their child.

Observe the child carefully in the process of growth and change throughout the tally sheet program. As you see change in the child, you may need to change your view or opinion of your student. Consider changing your mental image of the child as he or she shows effort. Visualize the child as a positive learner rather than as disruptive or difficult. See your student as a Can-Do kid. If you feel positive about the child, your nonverbal and verbal communication will convey a flow of positive messages, and the child's self-esteem will grow.

The young child who is having difficulty with behavior and who lacks a sense of self-worth may need extrinsic motivators in the form of tangible rewards, in order to grow and improve. Stickers are an example of tangible rewards. Offering such rewards is sometimes a good beginning. The long-range goal is intrinsic motivation, the child's inner desire to act in certain ways no matter what the external rewards. As the child matures, the hope is that the child will move toward more intrinsic, internal motivation. In other words, the child's personal satisfaction in reaching success will be the reward itself.

The process of working with an individual child and developing a program for success involves many steps and lots of time. Relax! Develop your plan in stages to suit your teaching style and the child's growth. Read the following, and begin discovering what works for you.

Observable Problem Behaviors

Step 1 in the plan for individual success is to observe the behavior of the student. Use the Observable Problem Behaviors checklist (page 91) to track the frequency with which a problem occurs. Each time you see the behavior, record a mark on your checklist. Make a mental note of the time frame. Are you observing the behavior several times in five minutes, or three times an hour?

Focus Sheet

Step 2 in the plan for individual success is to use the Focus Sheet (page 92) to list the positive attributes of the child. Set priorities among the behaviors that need improvement. Determine exactly what you want the child to accomplish. List how you will praise the child when he or she is doing the task correctly. Will you praise verbally, give tangible rewards like special stickers, or what? Be exact.

Things I Like and Ideas for Individual Reinforcers

Step 3 in the plan for individual success is to interview the child. Discuss the need for change. Say that you will work together on a special program so that the child will become more successful at ———. Explain that you will set up a contract together as adults do and that you each will agree to something: the child will reach a goal, and you will give a reward. Talk about things that the child likes by filling out Things I Like (page 93), a questionnaire that may suggest reinforcers. Use Ideas for Individual Reinforcers (page 94) to suggest other rewards your student may want to earn.

Planning Sheet

Step 4 in the plan for individual success is to design a program for your student. Use the Planning Sheet (page 95) to map out in small steps what you need to teach the child in order for him or her to become successful. Sometimes we need to go back and reteach simple tasks that we assumed were already mastered. Choose or adapt an appropriate Can-Do Tally sheet (pages 87–90) to record the number of times the child is on-task, or use Can-Do Clip Art (pages 60–62) to create your own tally sheet.

When designing a tally sheet to fit your particular need, include the following:

1. A statement of the goal: what you want the student to be able to do
2. A statement of the reward: what the student will earn
3. A place to record tally marks
4. Indication of the time frame: one hour, a.m. or p.m., one week, or whatever

5. A place to indicate if the child reached the goal
6. The child's name and the date
7. A picture for interest (see Can-Do Clip Art, pages 60–62)

You can tally just appropriate behavior, praising it when it occurs, or you can tally just negative behavior. Tallying negative behavior helps the child become aware of the problem. Remember, though, that the goal is to reduce the number of negative incidents. If you tally negative behavior, praise the fact that the child is working hard to eliminate it. Quickly switch to tallying both the positive and negative, praising the fine progress. Then tally only positive behavior.

Setting Expectations and Can-Do Contract

Step 5 in the plan for individual success is to set expectations and contract an agreement. Look over Setting Expectations (page 96) for tips on how to approach this crucial task. Then discuss the Can-Do Contract (page 97) with the child. Fill out the contract together. Show the student how the Can-Do Tally works, saying something like: "Each time you raise your hand to share an idea, I will come over to your desk and put a mark on your tally sheet. I will be proud of you. I will also mark each time that you talk out of turn. If you raise your hand more times than you talk out of turn today, you will earn ———. Would you like to work for that reward? At the end of the day, you will take the tally sheet home to share with your parents. They will be proud of you. It will take work to change this habit, but I know you can do it." When the child is ready, teach what you want the child to do. Model the behavior.

Step 6 in the plan for individual success is to begin using the Can-Do Tally sheet, giving compliments for on-task behavior and making tally marks on the sheet. The child at first should earn the reward at the end of each morning, each school day, or some other short period of time. After you have used the tally sheet on a daily basis for several weeks, you can change the reward period to several days or a week.

Step 7 in the plan for individual success is to reward the child at the appropriate time: when the goal has been achieved or shortly thereafter. Delay would dissipate the child's high motivation.

Step 8 is to confer briefly with the child. The most effective time is close to the end of the school day. Look over the tally sheet together. Review how the child reached the goal. Ask, "How does it feel to succeed? What did you do to succeed? What will you do next time?" Say, "I'm so proud of you. I knew you could do it!" When the child doesn't earn the reinforcing reward, continue expressing your confidence in the child: "You didn't make it today, but I know you can do it. Try again tomorrow." The next day, alter the time, the expectation, or the reward so that the child will succeed (see Steps 10 and 11 below). Remember that success breeds success! Studies have shown that it takes about three weeks of daily practice to form a new habit.

Step 9 in the plan for individual success is to send the Can-Do Tally sheet home each day as a communication to the parents.

Child's Success Record

Step 10 in the plan for individual success is to make a plus or minus mark each day on the Child's Success Record (page 98). Post this record sheet on the inside of a closet door, or keep it in a file folder. If the child fails two or three times in close succession and does not earn the reward, you need to readjust the time frame, the expectation, or the reward so that your student can be successful. Adjusting is necessary! The child must succeed if a new behavior pattern is to take hold.

Overview Assessment

Step 11 is to reevaluate the plan for individual success and make changes as necessary so that the child can succeed. Adjust the tally sheet for the next day as appropriate. Always continue verbal compliments as you change or phase out a tally sheet. The Overview Assessment (page 99) can help you keep track of the changes you make, as well as the goals of the program, the child's behavior, the results you achieve, the adjustments you make, and the contacts you have with the child's parents.

Teacher Effectiveness Sheet

Step 12 in the plan for individual success is to use the Teacher Effectiveness Sheet (page 100) to measure how much positive reinforcement you are giving out. This sheet can help you grow professionally. Moreover, if your students see you evaluate yourself, change, and grow, they will be encouraged to imitate your example.

Teacher Effectiveness Checklist

Step 13 in the plan for individual success is to answer the questions on the Teacher Effectiveness Checklist (page 101) from time to time. Make adjustments so that you can be more effective. Praise yourself for the changes that you have made.

Child's Self-Evaluation 1–4

Step 14 in the plan for individual success is to give your student an occasion for self-congratulation by having him or her fill out one of the Child's Self-Evaluations (pages 102–104 and top of page 105). These sheets are self-awards that help students measure their own progress. Use them at report card time, or even at the end of the day or week.

Colossal Kid Award and Can-Do Awards 1–7

Use the Colossal Kid Award (bottom of page 105) and Can-Do Awards (pages 106–112) not only as part of an individual plan for success but also as part of your entire class plan. You can set aside a particular time during the week for giving out awards. Keep track of the recipients, and make sure everyone in the class receives about the same number of awards.

You can attach the spelling award (top of page 112) to the paper of any student who shows spectacular progress in spelling.

You'll even find an award that a child might enjoy giving you (see page 110).

Can-Do Blue Ribbons

Students can wear Can-Do Blue Ribbons (page 113) during Celebrations of Success (see chapter 5). You can post them on special assignments, have students wear them home as reinforcers, or post them on the Can-Do Compliment bulletin board (see page 19).

Can-Do Gram and Good News Note

Use Can-Do Grams and Good News Notes (page 114) as stationery on which to communicate compliments. Children enjoy coloring these cards and sending them to each other, too.

Can-Do Assignments Tally

Name ______________________ Date ______________________

Can-Do says, "You can do it!"

	completed	need to complete
Math		
Reading		
Other		

Goal: Today if I can ______________________

I'll receive ________________

Can-Do 1-2-3 Tally

Name ____________________ Date ____________________

	A.M.	P.M.
1. On task 2. Behavior 3. Completed work		

Total # _____ of "I Did Its"

Can-Do Hand Raiser Tally

Name ____________________ Date ____________________

Be a hand raiser like Can-Do!

A.M. goal: to get less than ___ talk outs.

P.M. goal: to get less than ___ talk outs.

	hand raised	talk outs	Totals
Morning			/
Afternoon			/

Can-Do Habit Changer Tally

Name ______________________ Date ______________________

TRY TO CHANGE A HABIT

I will:

____

A.M.	P.M.

Reward:

____

Can-Do Hop-a-roo Tally

Name ____________________ Week ____________________

Hop-a-roo
With Can-Do

Be on
time!

	Monday	Tuesday	Wednesday	Thursday	Friday	Totals
A.M.						
Lunch						
Home						

Observable Problem Behaviors

Inattention
- Off-task
- Daydreaming, in a fog
- Excessive talking
- Out of seat
- Playing with things
- Not completing work

Immature Behavior
- Thumb sucking
- Baby talking
- Excessive crying
- Temper tantrums
- Talking back (poor turn taking)
- Needing to be the focus
- Interrupting conversation
- Preoccupation with personal interests

Learning and Reasoning Skills
- Not following verbal directions
- Not following written directions
- Illogical answers
- Rarely indicates he or she doesn't understand
- Poor handwriting coordination, direction of letter formation
- Difficulty in remembering, long-term
- Difficulty in remembering, short-term

Organization Skills
(Includes personal habits, time management, work habits)
- Messy desk, desk top, or work space
- Forgetting objects, papers, or homework
- Lack of sequencing (forgetting steps in an activity)
- Forgetting coat, lunch, tickets, etc.
- Needing a lot of reminding
- Not completing work because of poor time planning
- Hyperactivity
- Lack of time deadlines, always tardy

Low Self-Concept
- Underachieving
- Negative self-talk
- Poor eye contact
- Lying
- Fighting or arguing
- Poor attitude, lack of motivation
- Talking back
- Talking out of turn
- Lack of risk taking
- Poor-quality work
- Excessive excuses to get out of classroom or avoid completing work

Focus Sheet

Child ______________________ Date ______________________

List the child's strengths: positive attributes that you can praise.

1. ______________________

2. ______________________

3. ______________________

4. ______________________

List the skills or areas in which the child needs to improve.

____ **1.** ______________________

____ **2.** ______________________

____ **3.** ______________________

In the left margin, renumber the above in order of priority. Decide which **one** you will focus on first.

What is the task you want the child to accomplish (chosen from above)?

____

____

____

____

____

List ways in which you will praise the child.

1. ______________________

2. ______________________

3. ______________________

4. ______________________

Things I Like

1. What are your favorite TV shows? ____________________

____

2. What are your favorite toys? ____________________

____

3. What do you collect? ____________________

4. Name things you like to eat. ____________________

5. What snacks do you like? ____________________

6. Name a favorite person you'd like to do something with.

____

7. Name someone in school you'd like to do something with.

____

8. Name three favorite friends. ____________________

____

9. Name three things you like to do with your mom. __________

____

10. Name three things you like to do with your dad. __________

____

11. Where are the fun places you like to go? ____________________

____

12. Name three things you'd like to have. ____________________

____

13. What would you like to do in school that you haven't been able to do? ____________________

____

Ideas for Individual Reinforcers

- Sit at teacher's desk (work at teacher's desk for ______ minutes)
- Eat lunch with teacher
- Eat with friend and teacher in the classroom
- Wear a button from teacher's button collection
- Earn the privilege to leave five minutes early
- Wear a Can-Do Button home
- Draw a picture in a special art corner of the chalkboard
- Paint with water on the chalkboard
- Earn an award for the entire class (perhaps a ten-minute recess)
- Get small handful of peanuts, pretzels, raisins, chips, crackers, "bagel babies" (Cheerios), marshmallows, pickles
- Get stamp on hand (like a tattoo)
- Get tattoo transfer
- Draw on a ditto and each student gets a copy
- Design an award and the teacher will use it (or the child may give out compliment awards to children who are on-task)
- Run the film projector
- Run an errand
- Turn on flashlight in darkened classroom
- Make shadow creatures at the end of a film when the screen has only light shining on it
- Take a magnet out to recess
- Make a design and it will be made into a button (must have button machine)
- Hammer nails into a board
- Wibble-wobble handshake (teacher keeps hand loose while child controls handshake)
- Have ice cream with teacher
- Earn right for entire class to have paper-airplane-throwing contest

- Choose a friend with whom to do ______________________________
- Give compliments out loud to other individuals while class is doing an activity
- Tape a song or read a story
- Get ten minutes of computer time

- Help another teacher for ______ minutes
- Help the secretary, custodian, cook
- Sit in front or back of the bus
- Be first out at recess time

- Model clay for ______ minutes
- Dismiss the class at day's end

Planning Sheet

Goal

Describe the task you want the child to improve in performing.

____

____

____

____

____

Skills

List the readiness skills. List the smaller parts within the larger task.

1. ______________________________

2. ______________________________

3. ______________________________

4. ______________________________

5. ______________________________

Steps

List the steps you must teach.

1. ______________________________

2. ______________________________

3. ______________________________

4. ______________________________

5. ______________________________

Strategies

List the ways you will alter your teaching strategies to help the child achieve the goal and be successful.

1. ______________________________

2. ______________________________

3. ______________________________

4. ______________________________

5. ______________________________

Setting Expectations

When you set up a positive program for an individual child or the whole class, keep in mind that success depends on many factors working in harmony.

1. Have the child take part in determining the expectations, when appropriate, or you may determine the expectations and rules.
2. Discuss the rules of the program and how the child can earn the reward.
3. Model the behavior that is desired. Have the child practice the new behavior.
4. Limit the number of expectations to no more than three (one at a time is best).
5. Tell the child what you want him or her to **do** rather than what you **don't** want him or her to do. Say, "Raise your hand to share an idea" rather than "Don't call out without raising your hand."
6. Have the child repeat to you what he or she is to do and what happens if he or she succeeds.
7. Write the goals on one of the Can-Do Tallies (pages 87–90) or on the Can-Do Contract (page 97).
8. Tape the tally sheet on the child's desk. The child may sign the contract and put it in a folder.
9. Make the goal realistic, and make the time frame realistic; then the child will be successful. As success is gained, change or extend the goal to achieve further growth.
10. You must give compliments or feedback to the child consistently. Make tally marks on the sheet each time the child is on-task. The sheet forms a record of success for the child.
11. You can send the tally sheet home daily, if you like, as a communication to the parents. The parents can use it to give additional praise.
12. Make sure you give the reward or reinforcer at the time agreed upon.

CAN~DO WANTS YOU TO BE YOUR BEST!

Expectations: I can do this

Reward: I can earn

I will try my best.

Signature

Date

Child's Success Record

Child ____

Date ________________________________

Goal ____________________	Mon.	Tues.	Wed.	Thurs.	Fri.
____________________	☐	☐	☐	☐	☐
____________________					

Date ________________________________

Goal ____________________	Mon.	Tues.	Wed.	Thurs.	Fri.
____________________	☐	☐	☐	☐	☐
____________________					

Date ________________________________

Goal ____________________	Mon.	Tues.	Wed.	Thurs.	Fri.
____________________	☐	☐	☐	☐	☐
____________________					

Date ________________________________

Goal ____________________	Mon.	Tues.	Wed.	Thurs.	Fri.
____________________	☐	☐	☐	☐	☐
____________________					

As a quick daily check, record the child's progress: enter + (a plus sign) if the child achieved the goal or − (a minus sign) if the child did not achieve the goal.

If the child fails two or three times, readjust the time frame, the reinforcer, or the expectation so that the child can succeed. Adjusting is necessary! You're not failing if change is slow. Things sometimes get worse before they get better when you try to help a child change his or her behavior. Keep trying.

Overview Assessment

Child ____________________ Date ____________________

Observed Behavior to Be Changed

____

____

Date ____________________________________

Date ____________________________________

Date ____________________________________

Program (Positive Approach)

Goal (behavior to achieve) ____________________

Reward __________________________________

Results:

Date ____________________________________

Date ____________________________________

Date ____________________________________

Date ____________________________________

Program Changes and Adjustments

Goal (behavior to achieve) ____________________

Reward __________________________________

Results:

Date ____________________________________

Date ____________________________________

Date ____________________________________

Date ____________________________________

Parent Conferences and Contacts Written, phone, in person

Date ____________________________________

Date ____________________________________

Date ____________________________________

Teacher Effectiveness Sheet

Evaluate your effectiveness. Tally all the positive reinforcement, praise, and compliments you give individuals or the class. If you feel comfortable sharing your task with the class, point out to them that teachers are learning new things, too.

Tally before a child or class is on a program:

Date ______________________ Date ______________________

a.m.	p.m.

a.m.	p.m.

Tally while the child or class is on a program:

Date ______________________ Date ______________________

a.m.	p.m.

a.m.	p.m.

Observations:

Teacher Effectiveness Checklist

1. Have I isolated one task at a time for the child to improve?
2. Have I broken the task into small parts?
3. Have I taught the necessary readiness skills?
4. Have I modeled the expectation?
5. Have I explained the program clearly?
6. Have I set up a program for success?
7. Have I praised more than I've criticized?
8. Has the reward been immediate?
9. Have I communicated with the parent?
10. Have I altered the program for success when needed?
11. What have I learned that I can use to be more effective in the future?

    ____

    ____

    ____

    ____

12. What changes have I made already that give me a feeling of accomplishment and growth?

    ____

    ____

    ____

    ____

Name ______________________________

I can think about how I'm doing in my schoolwork.

I am proud of:

1. ______________________________

2. ______________________________

3. ______________________________

I can work on becoming better at:

1. ______________________________

2. ______________________________

3. ______________________________

I'm having an upbeat day!

✓ List

- ◯ I'm trying my best.
- ◯ I'm working hard.
- ◯ I'm concentrating.
- ◯ I can do my ________ very well.
  subject
- ◯ ________ can do it!
  Your name

Dear ________________,

Today in school I liked

______________________.

I learned ______________,

and I tried hard at

______________________.

Tomorrow I want to

______________________.

Love,

____

I DID IT!

Name: ____________________

Date: ____________________

I can organize my work period.

____
subject

Check

☐ 1. ____________________

☐ 2. ____________________

☐ 3. ____________________

☐ I did it!

Can-Do's Colossal Kid Award

☐ 1. Hard worker

☐ 2. Friendly

☐ 3. Helpful

☐ 4. Great listener

☐ 5. Follows directions

Awarded to: ____________________ Date: ____________

Name

is on course today!

	Check
Good listener	
Follows directions	
Working hard	
Gets along with others	
Turns in work	

Date

Teacher

Can-Do Clean Desk Award

for

Name

You worked hard...

You earned it!

CAN~DO
MATH AWARD
to

____

YOU ARE A
HARD WORKER!

______________________ IS A

FABULOUS
READER!
I'M
PROUD
OF YOU!

HURRAY FOR ME!

I DID MY BEST TODAY

I AM TRYING HARD IN

____

Reading today was great!

- △ completed work
- △ caught up
- △ read smoothly
- △ understood what I read

I AM SO PROUD

I ____________________

____

____

____

____
Name

has completed ______*

____________ homework
subject (s)

assignments.

__________ Date:

______________ Teacher:

Can-Do Congratulates:

____
Name

who used gorgeous handwriting.

I'm proud of you!

Love,
Koala-Roo Can-Do

"HATS OFF"
TO
MY TEACHER!

I LIKE YOU BECAUSE

____

____

____
Name

A CAN-DO CLAP-A-ROO
FOR MY

____

I'M GLAD
YOU'RE YOU!

FROM, ______________

CAN-DO
FABULOUS FRIEND

AWARDED TO

____

FOR

____

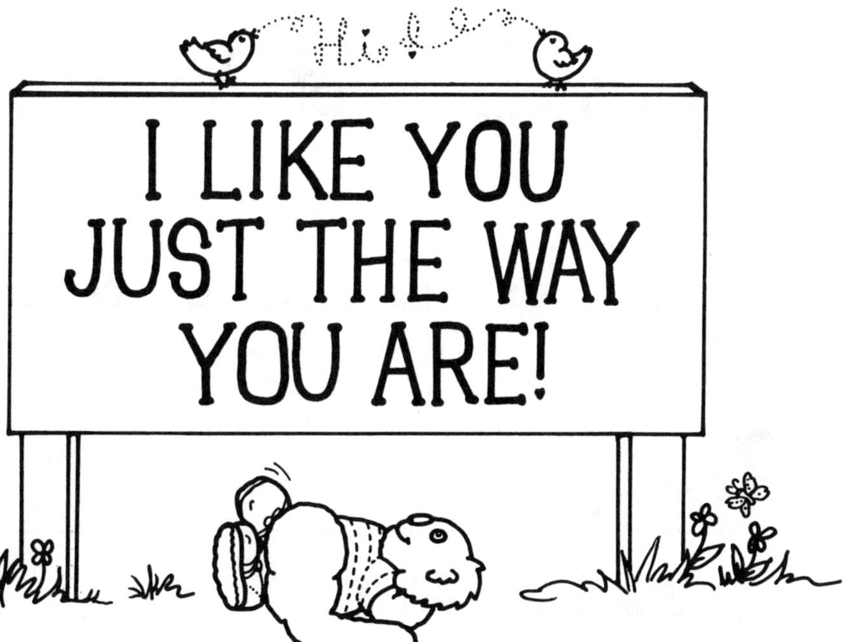
Hi!
I LIKE YOU
JUST THE WAY
YOU ARE!

To: ____________________ From: ____________________

SPECTACULAR SPELLER

____
Name

Place sticker here.

Can-Do's End of Year Award

☆ ☆ ☆ ☆ ☆ ☆ ☆ ☆

I'm proud of ______________________

Who has excelled in ______________________

______________ Date

______________________ Teacher

Can-Do Blue Ribbons

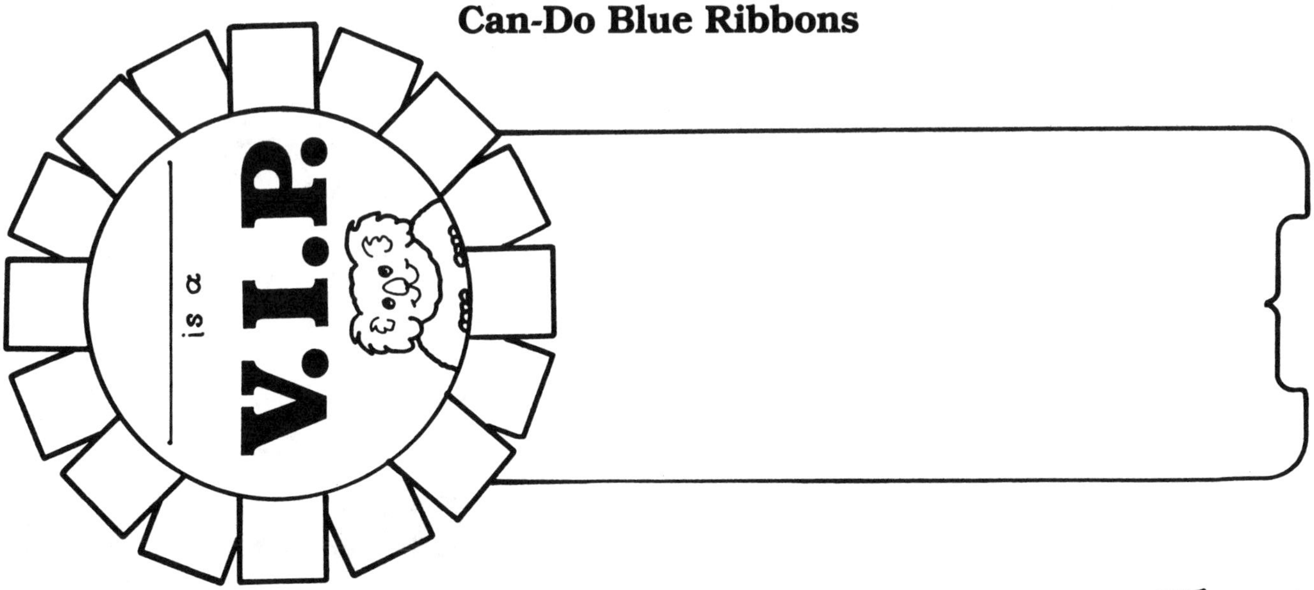

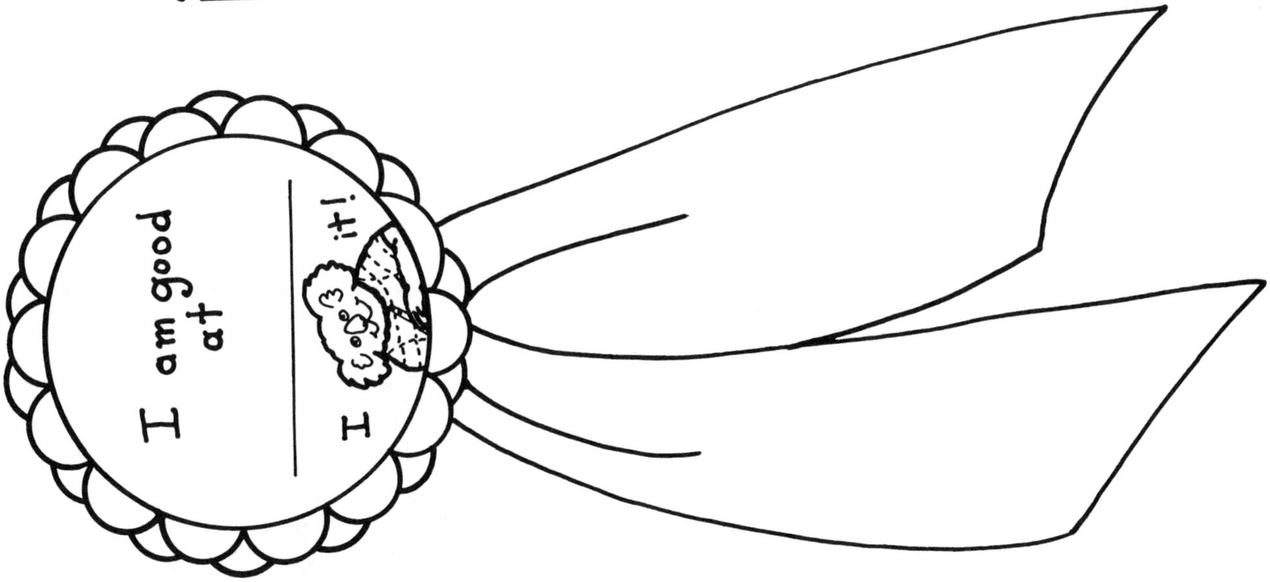

Can-Do
Gram

Good
News
Note

3

Success Management for Small Groups

Introduction

The principles underpinning a program for group success are the same as those on which programs for individual success are based (see chapter 2). Be accurate about the situation as it exists, be clear about your goals, analyze the steps that will get you to your goals, and then consistently reinforce positive behavior. Again, don't be afraid to revise along the way!

Many of the materials in chapter 2 are useful with small groups as well as individuals. You will find materials designed especially for use with groups here in chapter 3.

How to Use the Materials

Compliment Grids

- **Apple Compliment Grid**
- **Backpack Compliment Grid**
- **Balloon Compliment Grid**
- **Bucket Compliment Grid**
- **Gingerbread House Compliment Grid**
- **Heart-Flower Compliment Grid**
- **Ice Cream Compliment Grid**
- **Igloo Compliment Grid**
- **Kite Compliment Grid**
- **Knapsack Compliment Grid**
- **Leaf Compliment Grid**
- **Pumpkin Compliment Grid**
- **Spaceship Compliment Grid**
- **Turkey Compliment Grid**
- **Umbrella Compliment Grid**
- **Balloon Detailed Compliment Grid 1**
- **Balloon Detailed Compliment Grid 2**
- **Bouquet Detailed Compliment Grid**
- **Can-Do-Fly Detailed Compliment Grid**

The Compliment Grids (pages 120–138) are the key materials in your plan for success with small groups or the whole class. Their use is discussed fully as other materials are explained below. The last four grids—the Detailed Compliment Grids (pages 135–138)—provide you with more spaces for compliments and are described on page 117.

Use the Compliment Grids to reinforce on-task behavior throughout the day or while you are teaching certain subjects. A Compliment Grid is a picture divided into sections, or spaces. Each section can represent a compliment. As you see a group demonstrating the on-task behavior that you are working to achieve, you compliment the group orally. Then call on someone in the group to color in a space on the group's Compliment Grid.

Ideas for Group Reinforcers

When all the spaces on the Compliment Grid are colored in, the group earns the reinforcer or reward (see Ideas for Group Reinforcers, page 118). Each group earns the reward when all the spaces have been filled in on the grid: each group earns the reward, but at its own pace. Everyone is a winner.

Organize your class into groups (perhaps according to the placement of desks: one row of desks could be a group, for instance). Give each group a name (for example, if you have organized groups by tables, you can name the groups Table 1, Table 2, and so on). Each group will have its own Compliment Grid. Reproduce the same grid for each group. Label each copy with its group name, and mount the grids on your Can-Do Compliment bulletin board (see page 19). Try to balance the groups so that each contains children with various learning styles and behavior patterns: you want each group to contain some children who will model appropriate behavior.

Your plan for success with small groups is much like your plan for success with individual children:

1. Observe the class's behavior or study skills.
2. Make a list of behavior patterns or skills you would like the children to improve or change.
3. Number the list in order of priority.
4. Determine the goal and reward (see the discussion of the Goal and Reward Sheet below and Ideas for Group Reinforcers, page 118).
5. Set a time frame within which to reach the goal. One or two weeks seems to work well with young children. You may choose to keep the schedule to yourself. Doing so may encourage you to give compliments on a consistent basis. The more immediate positive feedback you give, the quicker the behavior will be mastered. Remember that your students will lose interest if there is delay: the goal will seem unreachable.

Goal and Reward Sheet

After you have posted the Compliment Grid for each group, fill out a Goal and Reward Sheet (page 119) with the whole class.

Guide the students to set a worthwhile goal when you fill out this sheet with them. The goal must be one that is measurable and that can be reached in a reasonable length of time. Make sure the wording is specific. Work on one goal at a time.

Decide together on a desirable reward, one that the students will work eagerly to receive (see Ideas for Group Reinforcers, page 118). Note the reward in the right-hand column of the Goal and Reward Sheet.

Mount the completed Goal and Reward Sheet near the Compliment Grids on your Can-Do Compliment bulletin board (see page 19).

Implementing the Compliment Program Model and teach what you expect the class to do in order to reach the goal. Have the children model the expected behavior.

Every time a group shows you that it is meeting the expectation, give lots of praise. After you give the compliment, ask someone in the group to go up to the Can-Do Compliment bulletin board and fill in a space on that group's Compliment Grid. The object is to color in the entire set of spaces on the grid and earn the reward.

Reinforcing Your Expectations Each day or before specific lessons, remind the class of the goal. Be specific and positive in tone, saying something like: "You are going to learn to write letters that go below the baseline. I'm going to see if the class can listen carefully and follow directions. You can earn compliments for the Compliment Grid. I like the way Danny and Jessica are listening to me right now. You are super listeners. How can you earn compliments when you're doing handwriting today? You can earn compliments by listening and following directions. That's right, Jason."

Young children must receive feedback immediately if it is to have impact. Give compliments quickly, therefore, and freely. Use a variety of compliments (see Positive Teacher Talk, page 4, for dozens of ideas for wording). Say things like "I'm so proud of Table 2. They were all watching me as I wrote that letter. Sara, give your group a compliment" and "Max, give your table a compliment. Everyone at your table formed the letter **g** correctly."

- **Be specific.** Let the children know exactly what they did correctly.
- **Praise improvement, not just mastery.** If your class is showing effort, encourage them with praise and compliments.
- **Be sincere.** Share warmth, love, genuine caring, and confidence in each child that he or she **can** do it, whatever it is. Children detect hypocrisy instantly. Hold an image of each child at his or her best so that the children sense your affection and respect (see Fostering an I-Can-Do-It Attitude, page 2). Let your students know that you expect not perfection, but effort and the best they can do at the time.

Reinforcing Your Purpose If Your Students Become Competitive The goal is compliments rather than competition. Stress that **each** group will earn the reward when its compliment grid is completed. There can be no losers.

You can use competition positively, too. If one group, say Table A, is not performing to expectation, then compliment another table, say Table B, by praising its behavior. Choose someone to fill in a compliment on the Table B Compliment Grid, and you will probably observe immediately that Table A corrects its behavior. Be sure to compliment Table A as soon as it is appropriate. This approach is more effective than saying negative things like "Table A, you're talking too loudly."

Here is another illustration of this approach. You notice Group 1 visiting and not working independently. Praise Group 3. "Oh, Group 3, you are working so well and concentrating without visiting. I'm impressed. Ian, will you color a compliment on the Group 3 Compliment Grid?" You notice that Group 1 quickly changes its behavior. "I see Group 1 is trying harder to concentrate. Oh, I see Group 2 doing a fine job: Renee, give your group a compliment. Group 1, you are working quietly: Josh, give your group a compliment."

Reaching the Goal When all the spaces on the grid have been colored in by a group, then that group has earned the reward. If the reward is a lunch date with the teacher, for instance, then plan the very next day, at the latest, to have lunch with that group. Make the reward fun and exciting, to celebrate the success of the group. Perhaps you could have the lunch in the classroom instead of the lunchroom. Use a tablecloth. Turn on the radio, and let the children choose the station. Remind the first group that completed the grid not to gloat but to encourage the others to continue trying. Even though the first group has completed the grid, be sure to continue the verbal praise—the compliments. Be assured that they will still enjoy the praise.

Remember, it is important to give the reward immediately or as soon as possible.

Using a Compliment Grid with the Whole Class You can use one Compliment Grid for the entire class. Determine your goal. There might be something specific on which your entire class needs to work: for example, lining up without pushing and shoving. Now choose a Compliment Grid. Each grid has a different number of spaces, and you may choose the number for a shorter or longer time period. Choose a grid with few enough spaces to allow your students to reach the goal fairly quickly. Then determine an appropriate reward, say a five-minute extra recess.

Detailed Compliment Grids Another way to use a Compliment Grid with the entire class is purposely to choose a grid with many spaces. The Detailed Compliment Grids (pages 135–138) have many segments to be colored in by students. You don't even need to offer a reward as a reinforcer. The finished grid will be a colorful mosaic, a work of art that can itself be a reward of success.

You might enlarge a Detailed Compliment Grid before you mount it on your Can-Do Compliment bulletin board. After you post the grid, tell the class you'll give compliments throughout the days ahead to individual children and the class. Say, "We'll earn compliments for all kinds of things we do. Let's watch the design fill with color."

Since a Detailed Compliment Grid has so many spaces to fill in, you might add a twist of excitement by occasionally asking a child to color in two or three spaces for a job well done.

Holding a Drawing for the Finished Grid When a Detailed Compliment Grid or any of the other grids is completed, you may distribute Can-Do Chances (page 57) to compliment on-task behaviors. Distribute them freely throughout the day. Let the class know that at the end of the day there will be a Can-Do Chance drawing. As a child receives a Can-Do Chance, the child writes his or her name on the back. Put all the Can-Do Chances in a container. At the end of the day, have someone draw a Can-Do Chance. The person whose name is drawn may keep the completed grid.

Ideas for Group Reinforcers

- See a funny film
- Have an indoor picnic (spread tablecloths on the floor and eat in the classroom)
- Be dismissed from class five minutes early
- Have a Games Party (everyone brings board games and plays for thirty minutes)
- Have a Record Party
- Have Crazy Hat Day
- Have teacher dress up in costume
- Have a talent show
- Have a treasure hunt (hide clues leading to a basket of fresh flowers, one for each child, or a "pot of gold," one chocolate coin for each child)
- Have a White Elephant Swap (everyone bring unwanted games, toys, books)
- Wear slippers for the afternoon
- Be in the movies (videotape the class)
- Weave a tent (make a wooden A-frame, line the top piece and bottom pieces with nails, string heavy cord vertically, cover nail heads with duct tape for safety, have children weave rag or fabric strips to make a tent, call it the Reading Hut, and let children sit in it to read books)

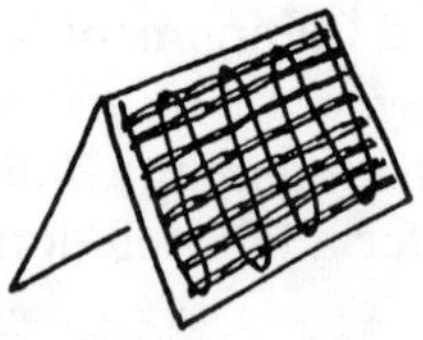

- Have T-Shirt Day
- Make a class rainbow (draw rainbow on large piece of butcher paper, have children cut solid-color blotches from magazines, let children fill in each band bit by bit with the proper color so that each band shows all shades of its color, and have a magnificent final product!)
- Have a Share-Your-Furry-Friend Pet Party
- Bring favorite stuffed toys for a Stuffed Toy Parade
- Have a hobby display
- Have a display of collections
- Have a Reading Safari (class travels to a different part of the school and listens to or reads books)
- Have an extra recess
- Trade teachers with another class for one activity
- Have a mystery guest (invite older child to do magic tricks or tell jokes)
- Send off a helium-filled balloon with message on it
- Have the principal visit and share hobbies
- Take out ad in local newspaper to announce class's success
- Have a Popcorn Party
- Have a Yogurt Sundae Party (everyone bring toppings to sprinkle on top)
- Make ice cream floats (need paper cups, plastic spoons, bottle of root beer, and carton or two of vanilla ice cream)
- Get to squirt your initials on graham crackers with whipped cream

A Weekful of Success Celebrations

See chapter 5.

- Magnificent Monday: Popcorn Picnic
- Tea Party Tuesday: Friendship Tea and Colossal Cookie
- Wonderful Wednesday: Chips and Dips
- Thoughtful Thursday: Koala-Roo Malted Milk
- Fabulous Friday: Dessert Pizza

Special Occasions

See chapter 5.

- Koala-Roo Can-Do's Birthday: Koala Cake
- Grandparents' Day
- Fall Festival: Koala Apple Crispy
- Book Bash: Koala Frozen Yogurt
- Success in All Seasons: Chocolate Soup à la Can-Do
- Games Galore: Peanut Butter Hors d'Oeuvres
- Spring Fling: Koala Cooler
- Summer Circus Celebration

TRY HARD  and SUCCEED

GOAL

We can ____________________

____

____

____

____

REWARD

We can earn ____________________

____

____

____

____

TRY HARD  and SUCCEED

GOAL

We can ____________________

____

____

____

____

REWARD

We can earn ____________________

____

____

____

____

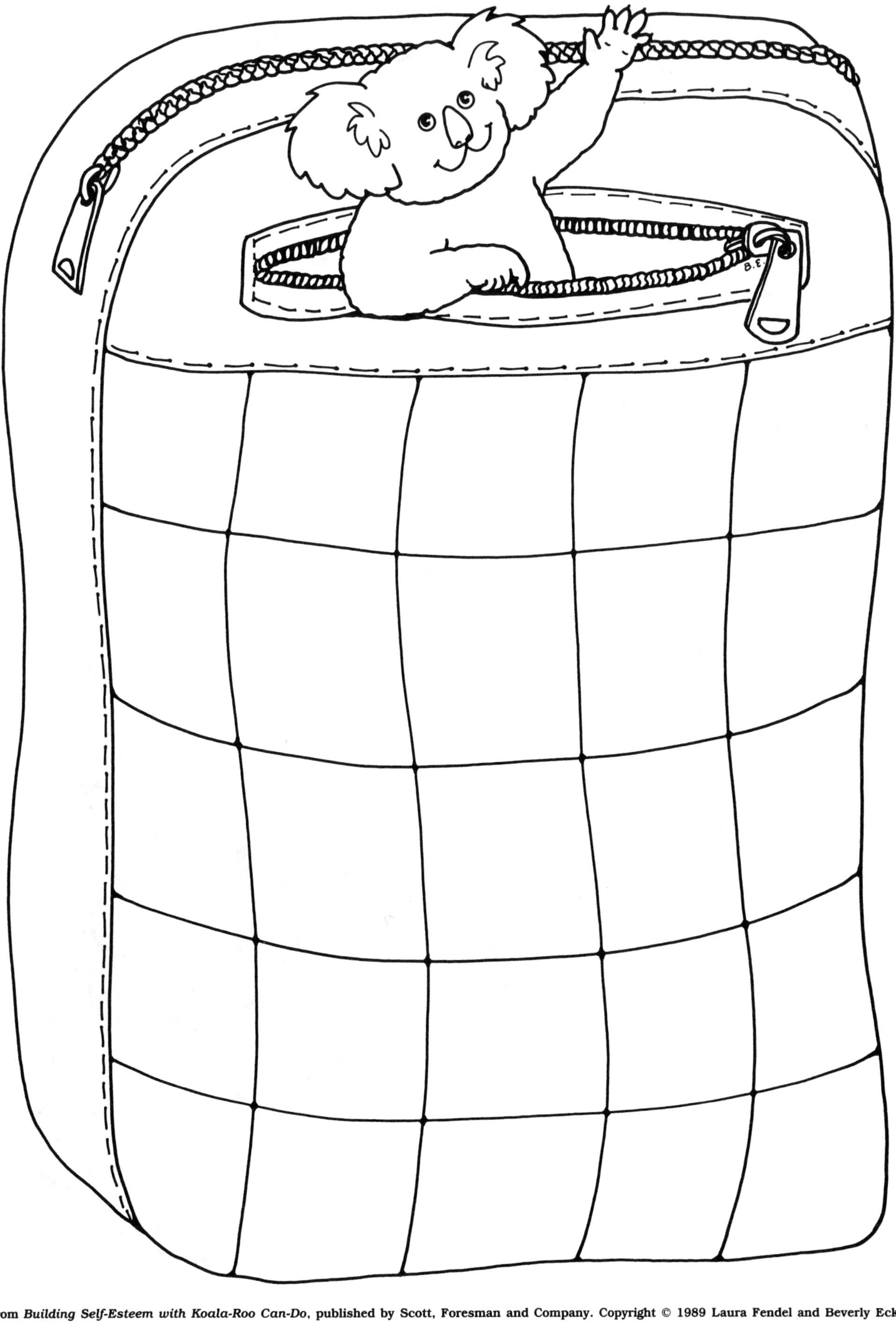
B.E.

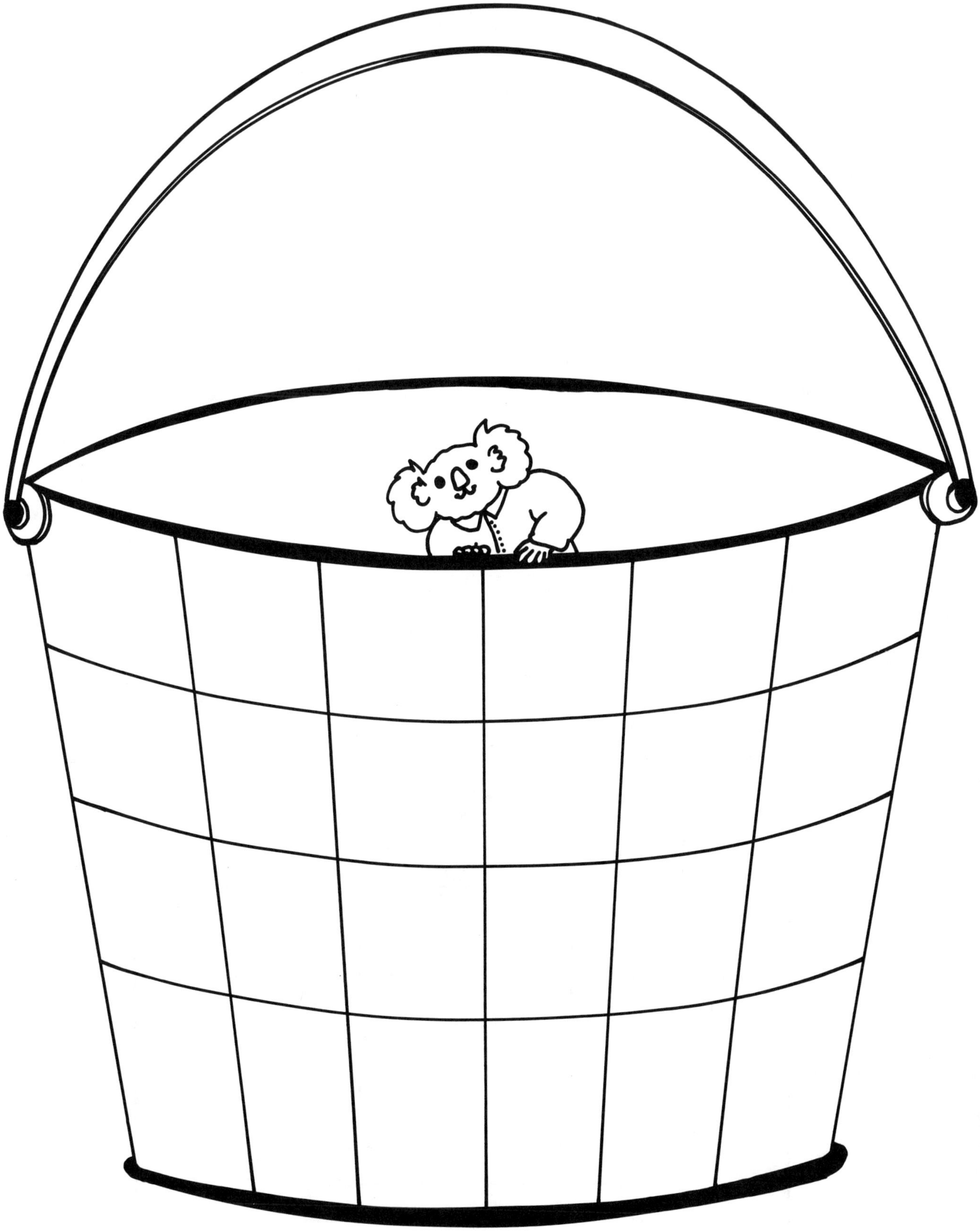

Welcome

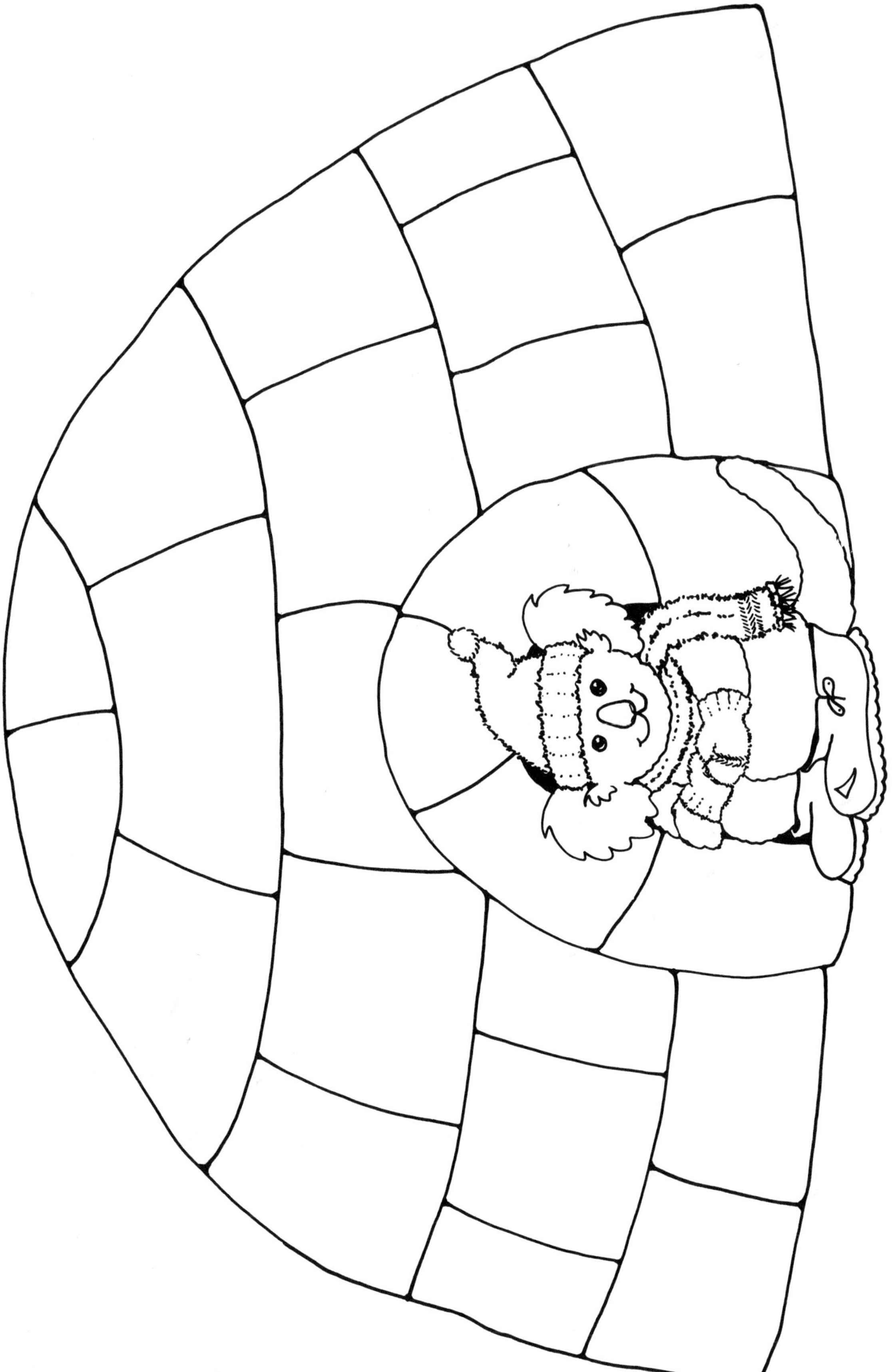

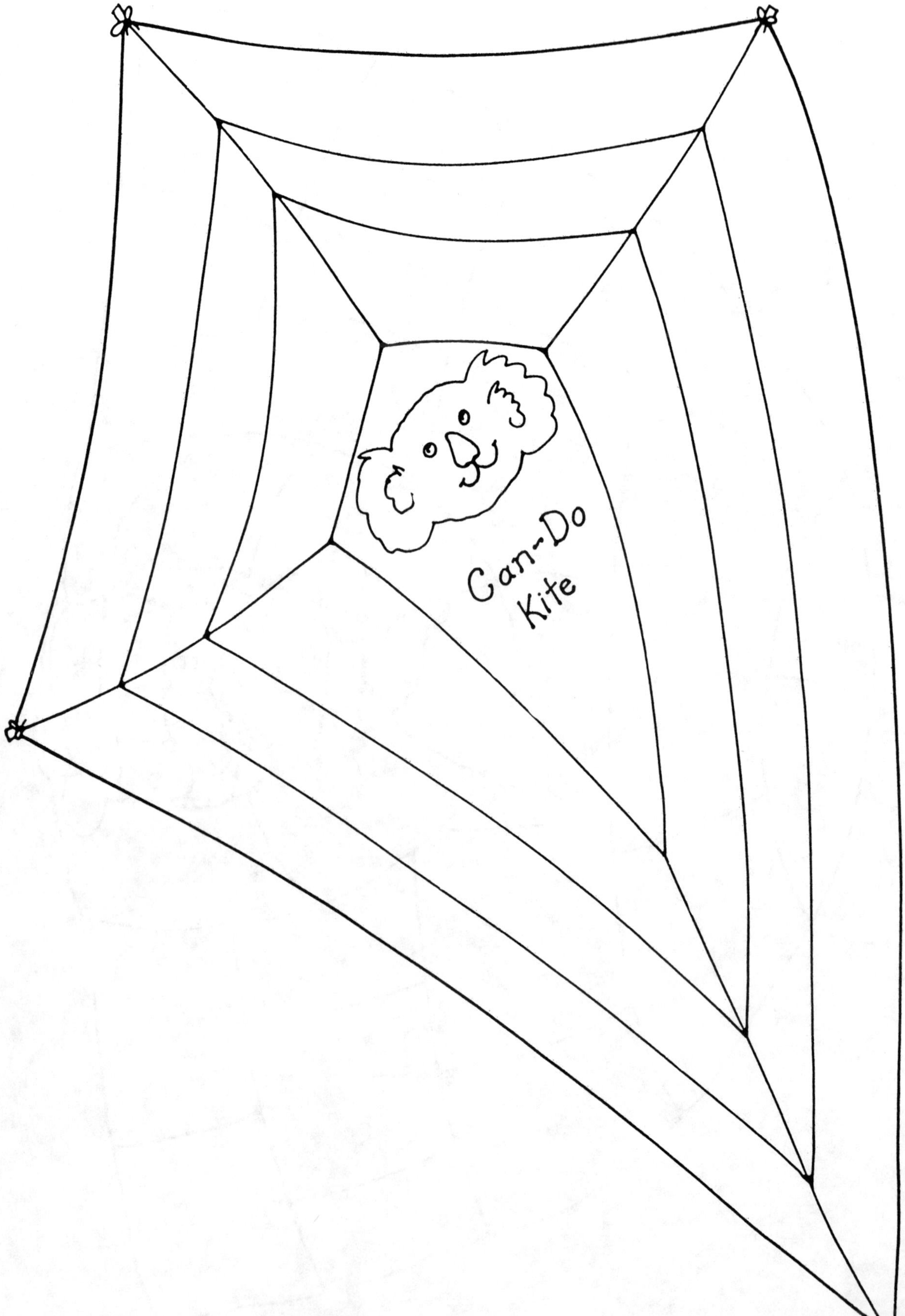
Can-Do
Kite

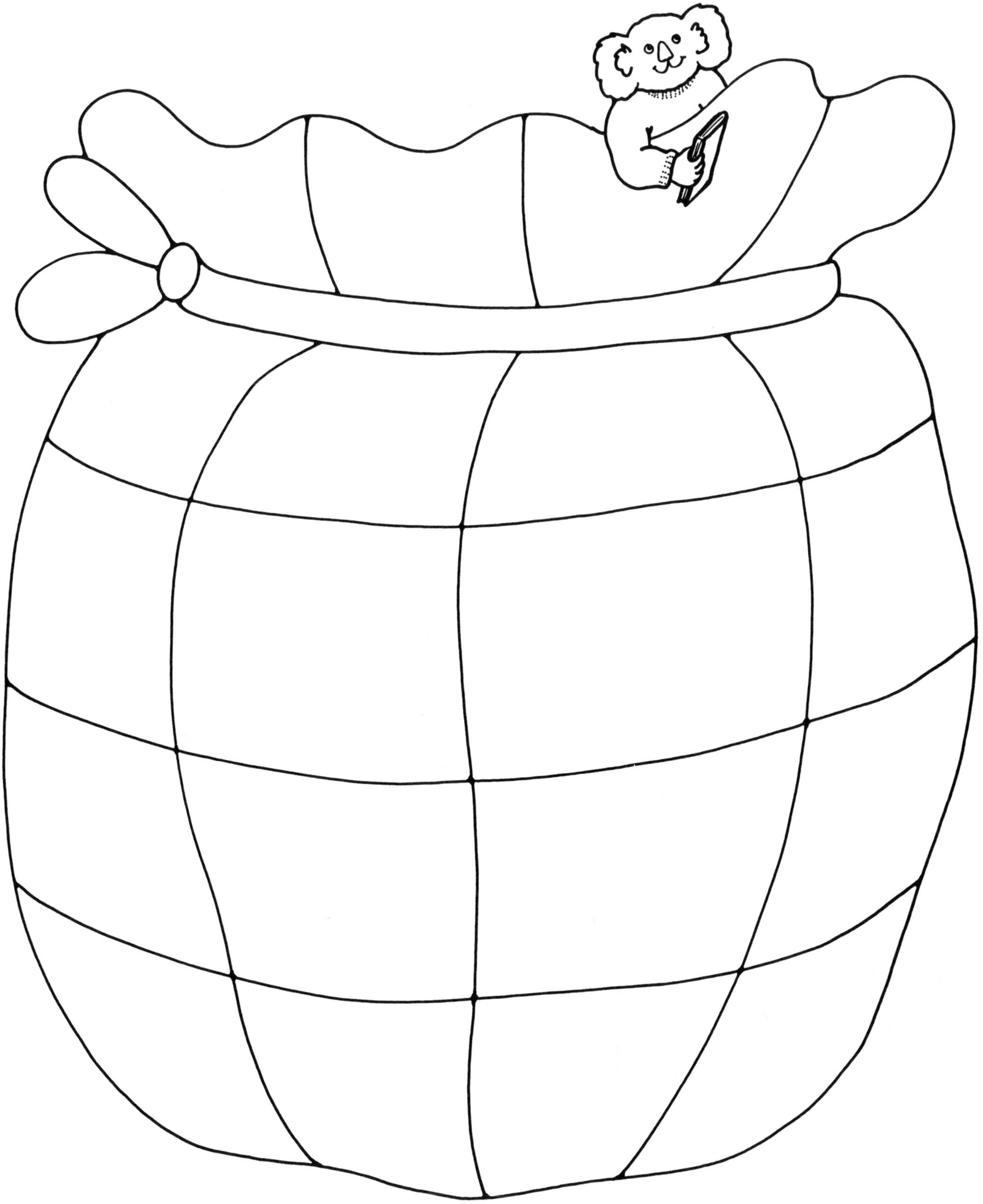

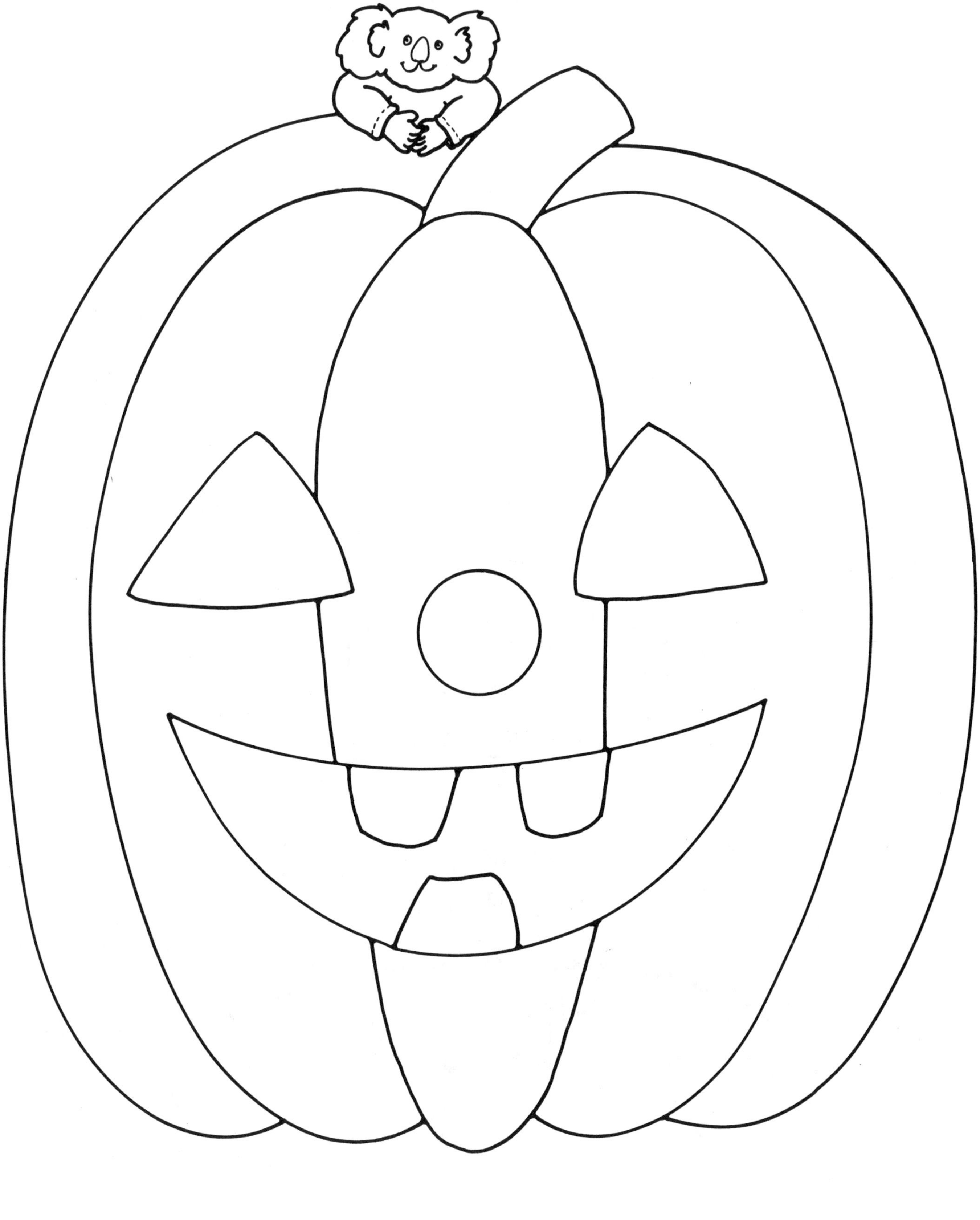

CAN-DO
USA

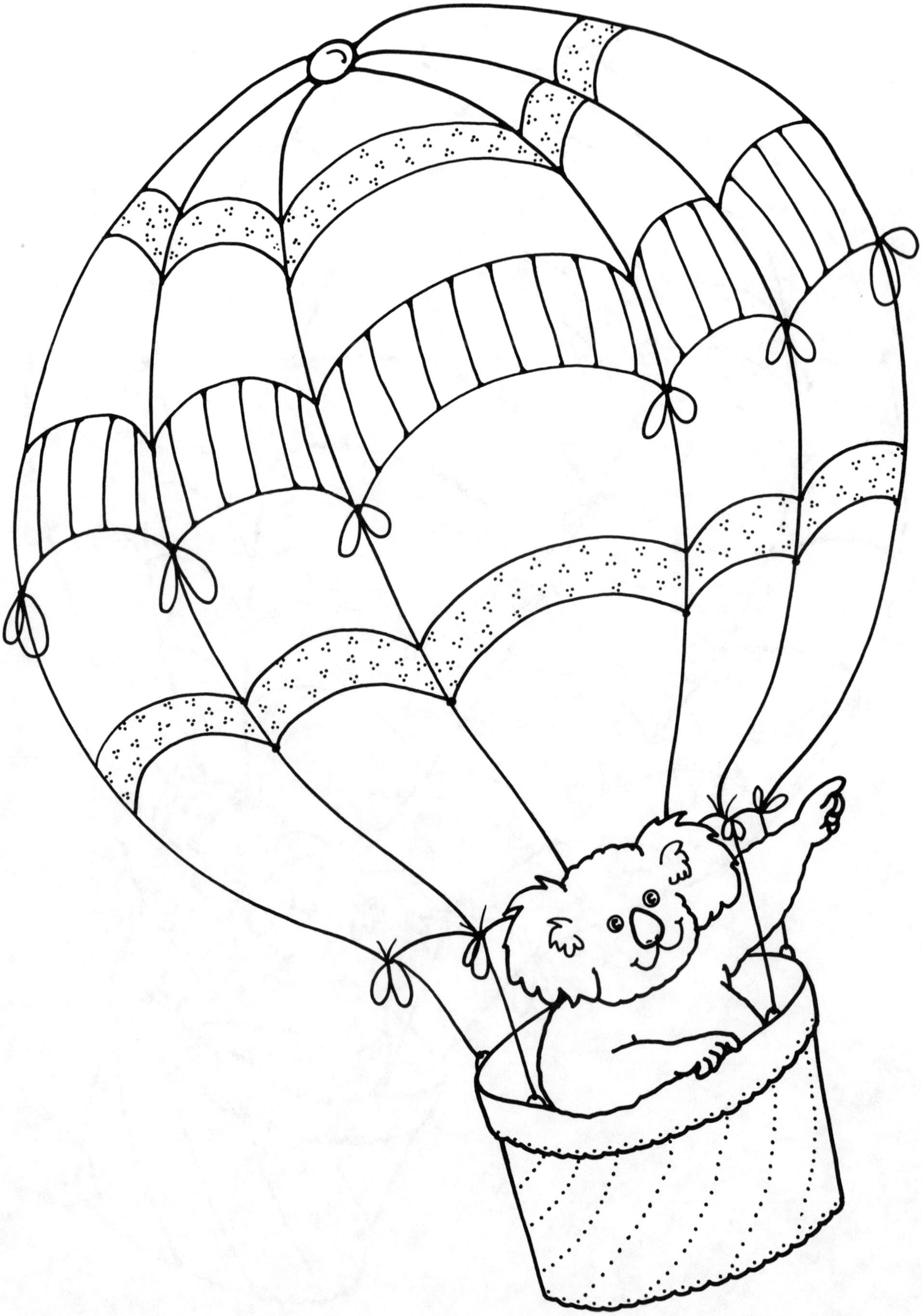

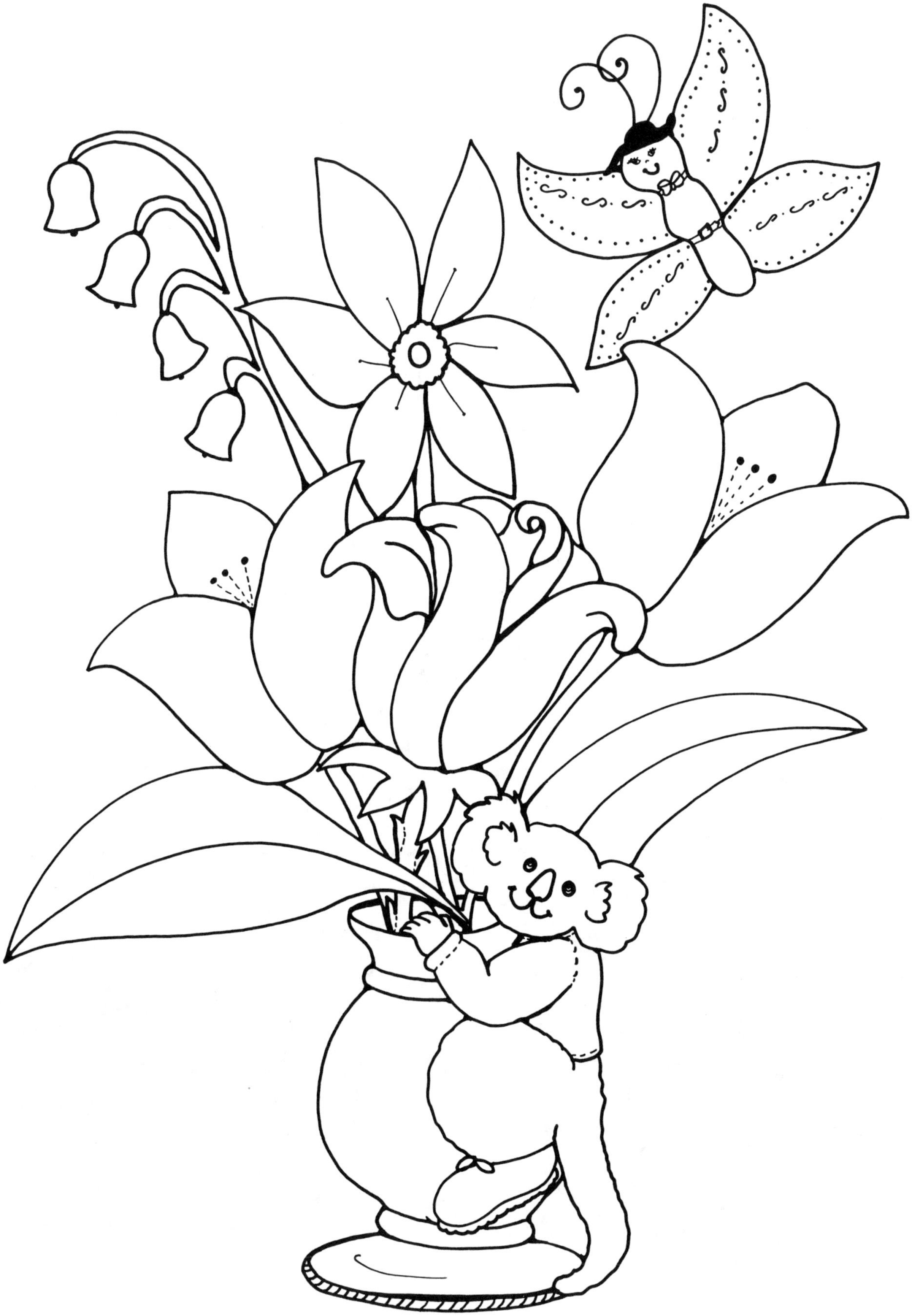

HOW HIGH
CAN~DO~FLY

4

Can-Do in the Curriculum

Reading

Introduction

Koala-Roo Can-Do will hop his way onto your reading bookshelf and encourage your students to become confident readers by keeping records of the many books they have read. The more they read, the more success they will experience.

Discourage your students from waging contests to see who can read the most books. If amassing lengthy lists of titles becomes the object, your students will want to read only the briefest and simplest books. The goal is to enjoy and learn from reading.

Have your students look back at their growing lists of book titles so as to be able to discuss such interesting topics as:

- Who is your favorite author? Why?
- Describe the funniest story you have read.
- Tell about a book character who had a problem and solved it. How would you have solved the problem? What are other solutions?

Brainstorm other discussion ideas with your class.

The activities and materials discussed below encourage children to read, keep records of their reading, and take pride in their reading accomplishment.

Can-Do Reading Pockets

Before you embark on the special activities associated with the reading materials described below, make a Can-Do reading pocket for each student. A Can-Do reading pocket is a holder for book reports and a place to write or store titles of books each student has read.

To make a Can-Do reading pocket, fold an 8½-by-11-inch piece of construction paper, and fasten the sides together with a thin line of glue. Leave the top open. Color and then fasten to the front of the pocket any of the following:

- Stand-up Can-Do Body (page 40)
- Apple Compliment Grid (page 120)
- Backpack Compliment Grid (page 121)
- Igloo Compliment Grid (page 127)
- Knapsack Compliment Grid (page 129)
- Spaceship Compliment Grid (page 132)
- A Can-Do Reading Shoe (page 144; see page 140 for a discussion of the Can-Do Reading Shoes' primary use)

Tape the Can-Do reading pockets to a wall in the classroom or hallway, or glue each pocket to the inside of a folder.

Cut slips of paper about 3 by 8 inches. When a student reads a book, then you or the student write the book title, the author's name, and the student's name on one of the slips. Have the student put the slip into his or her own Can-Do reading pocket.

If you use Compliment Grids on the pockets, older students can note authors and titles in the grid spaces (instead of on slips of paper) and put book reports inside the pockets.

Be sure to discourage contests for most titles listed. Again, the goal is enjoyment and learning.

How to Use the Materials

Book Record Sheet and Favorite Book Awards with Pouch

Use the Book Record Sheet (page 142) and the Favorite Book Awards with Pouch (page 143) to build your class's interest in evaluating the qualities that they think make a book good.

Get standard manila folders, or fold pieces of construction paper, one for each child. Glue a Stand-up Can-Do Body (page 40) to the inside of each folder. Glue a Favorite Book Award Pouch (page 143) to the Stand-up Can-Do Body so that the Pouch forms a storage pocket within each folder. Duplicate the Book Record Sheet (page 142), and place one copy inside each folder. Have extra copies of the Book Record Sheet available for students to pick up as they need new sheets. Duplicate Favorite Book Awards (page 143), and set them aside for future use.

Have each student, after reading a book, write the title and author on the Book Record Sheet. After several weeks, have a discussion about favorite books. Begin by talking about favorite foods, toys, television shows, and friends. What makes them favorites? Proceed to the topic of favorite books the students have read in the last several weeks.

Then have each of your students fill out Favorite Book Award slips and put them in the Favorite Book Award Pouches on the Stand-up Can-Do Bodies inside the folders.

Can-Do Reading Shoes

Have a read-a-thon involving all the members of the class. Treat the read-a-thon not as a contest but as a group effort to reach a long-distance goal. Use Can-Do Reading Shoes (page 144) to mark progress. Choose a shoe (there is one pointing in each direction). Duplicate many copies of it. As a child finishes a book (or some specified number of books), write the book title (or titles) and the child's name on a copy of the shoe. Once a week, tape the collected filled-out Can-Do Reading Shoes around the walls of your room to form an ever-lengthening path. When the shoes go all the way around the room, have a Celebration of Success (see chapter 5).

A Can-Do Reading Shoe also makes a nice cover for a Can-Do reading pocket (see page 139).

Reading Apple Barrel and Apples

The Reading Apple Barrel (page 145) and Apples (page 146) give your students another means of recording books read. Have each child color a barrel, cut it out, and glue it to an 8½-by-14-inch piece of construction paper or a large piece of butcher paper. Mount each poster on a wall or bulletin board. Duplicate the apples. As a child completes a book, have the child write the title on an apple and glue the apple above his or her barrel. Continue adding apples to the posters as children read more books.

Koala-Roo Reading Tree

Post the Koala-Roo Reading Tree (page 147) or A Tree for All Seasons (page 45). You might want to enlarge the tree first. Hang book jackets on the tree, and have children write book titles on apples to scatter under the tree. An alternative is to eliminate the jackets and hang the apples themselves on the tree. If you hang book jackets, try to see that they represent books that are available in your school library so that your students will be motivated to use it.

Pouch Book Report and Dear Can-Do Book Report

The Pouch Book Report (page 148) and Dear Can-Do Book Report (page 149) help older primary students master the rudiments of the book report form. Students can place finished Pouch Book Reports and Dear Can-Do Book Reports in their Can-Do reading pockets.

Color Code for Can-Do Reading and Can-Do Reading Tickets

Use a color code to encourage your students to read a variety of books. Gather five kinds of books, all appropriate to your class's reading level:

1. Stories with human characters
2. Stories with animal characters
3. Books about science and nature
4. Books about places of interest
5. Literature: poetry, fairy tales, and folktales

Assign each category its own color. You may want to prepare five color-coded boxes or tubs to hold the books. Cut colored paper into long bookmarks, and place a bookmark in each book according to its category so that each book can be returned to the appropriate container.

Give each student a copy of the Color Code for Can-Do Reading (page 150), and have the class color in the circles with the five chosen colors. Make copies of the Can-Do Reading Tickets (page 151) on white paper or, if possible, on paper of the five chosen colors. You as the teacher decide how many books in each category a student should read. After a child has read a book, he or she colors a reading ticket appropriately or chooses a reading ticket of the appropriate color. The child glues this reading ticket on the back of the Color Code for Can-Do Reading.

When all the students have reached the goal, you can have a Success Celebration (see chapter 5).

Koala-Roo Can-Do Bookmarks

Each student earns a Koala-Roo Can-Do Bookmark (page 152) for every book he or she reads.

Koala-Roo Can-Do Bookmark Mobile A student who has collected five Koala-Roo Can-Do Bookmarks can use them in a mobile. Set up an independent center where children can make their mobiles. Equip it with scissors, a hole punch, yarn, and copies of the Can-Do Door Decor Head (page 51). Assemble a sample mobile yourself, and have it on display.

Write out the directions, and post them:

1. Color Can-Do's head, and cut it out.
2. Punch a hole in the top of each of your five bookmarks. Punch five holes along the bottom edge of Can-Do's head.
3. Cut five pieces of yarn, all different lengths.
4. Tie the bookmarks to Can-Do's head so that the bookmarks dangle.
5. Display your mobile by hanging it.

Variations Use Can-Do Reading Tickets (page 151) to add incentive if your students are avid and capable readers. Give each child a Koala-Roo Can-Do Bookmark in advance. Give a Can-Do Reading Ticket each time a book is read, and have the child glue it on the back of the bookmark. Set a quota: seven Can-Do Reading Tickets fit easily on the back of a bookmark. You may choose to ask for five or fewer. When the back of the Koala-Roo Can-Do Bookmark is covered with reading tickets, laminate it or protect it with clear contact paper. When a student has five completed bookmarks, the student can make the Koala-Roo Can-Do Bookmark mobile.

You can also use Koala-Roo Can-Do Bookmarks with Can-Do Reading Tickets in an activity that results not in a mobile but in a useful bookmark that is a handsome reinforcer. Again, give each student a bookmark in advance and then a reading ticket each time a book is read. Have each student glue the tickets on the back of the bookmark until the prescribed number of reading tickets is reached. Laminate the bookmark, punch a hole at the top, and add some yarn fringe.

Name ____________________ Date ____________________

Book Record Sheet

Being a Can-Do Reader means reading lots of books!

Here is a record of books I have read.

1. Title ________________________________

Author ________________________________

2. Title ________________________________

Author ________________________________

3. Title ________________________________

Author ________________________________

4. Title ________________________________

Author ________________________________

5. Title ________________________________

Author ________________________________

6. Title ________________________________

Author ________________________________

7. Title ________________________________

Author ________________________________

8. Title ________________________________

Author ________________________________

9. Title ________________________________

Author ________________________________

10. Title ________________________________

Author ________________________________

Favorite Book Award to:

Title ______________________________

Author ______________________________

Favorite Book Award to:

Title ______________________________

Author ______________________________

Favorite Book Award to:

Title ______________________________

Author ______________________________

Favorite
Book
Award

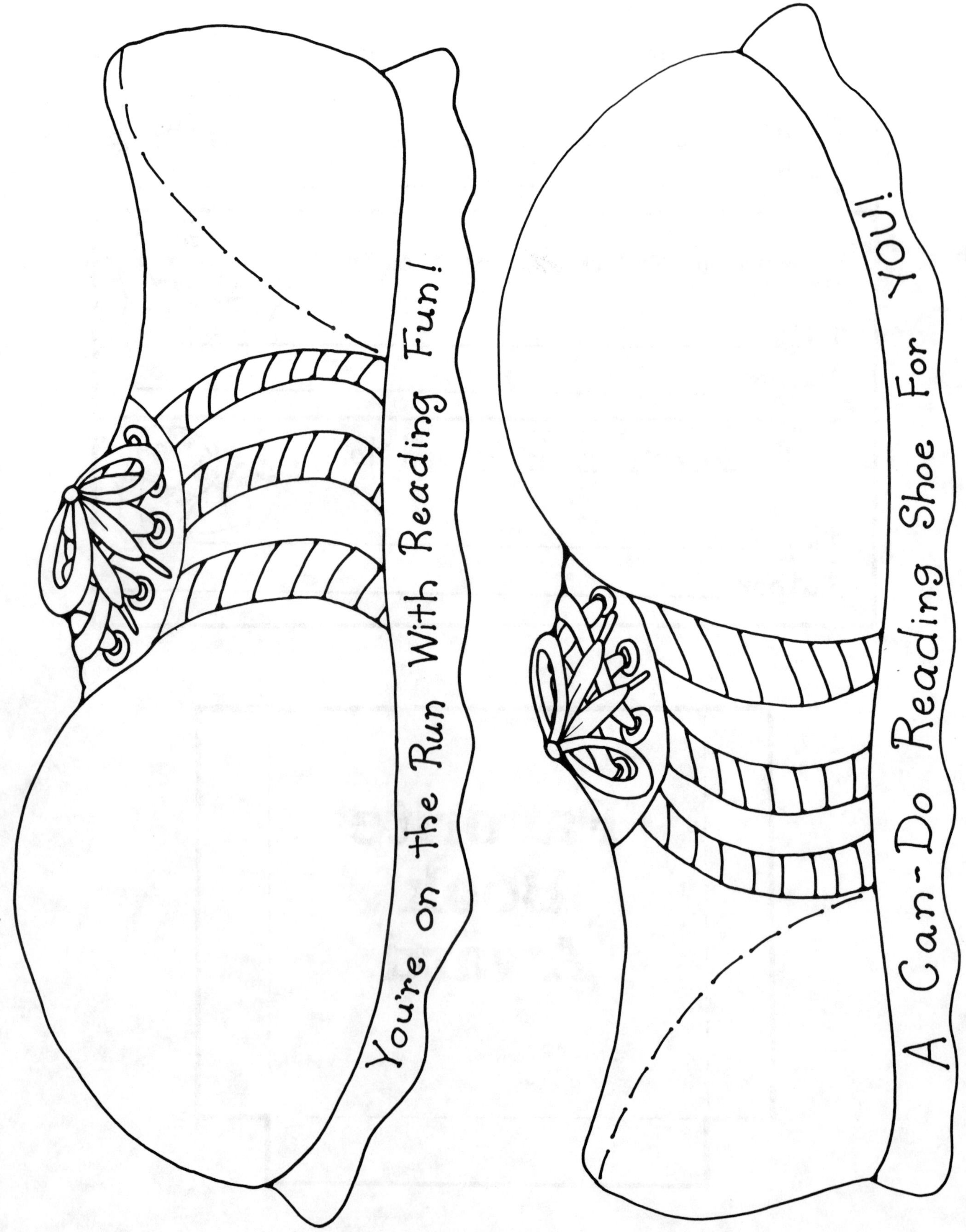
You're on the Run With Reading Fun!
A Can-Do Reading Shoe For YOU!

Reading Apple Barrel

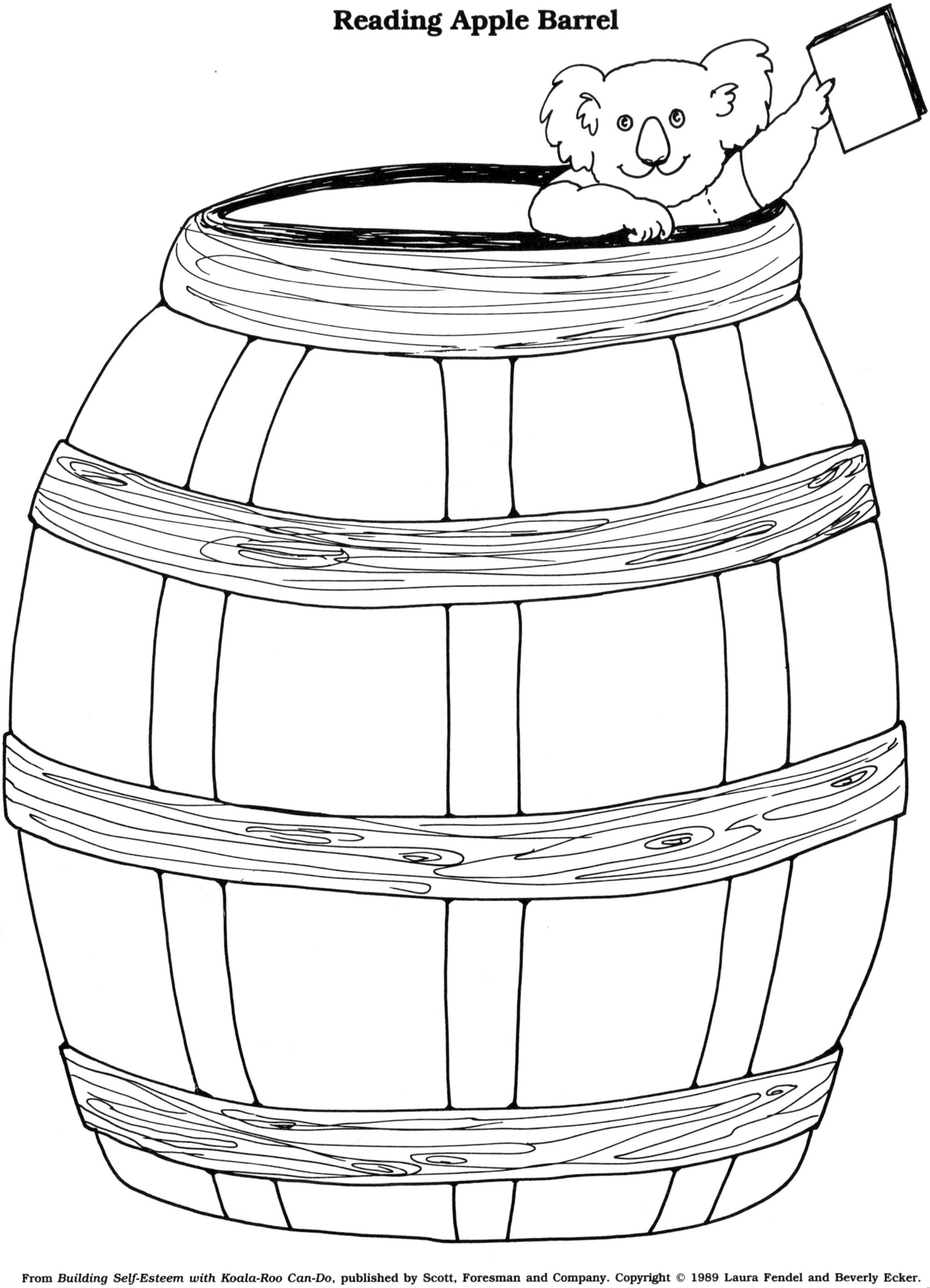

Apples

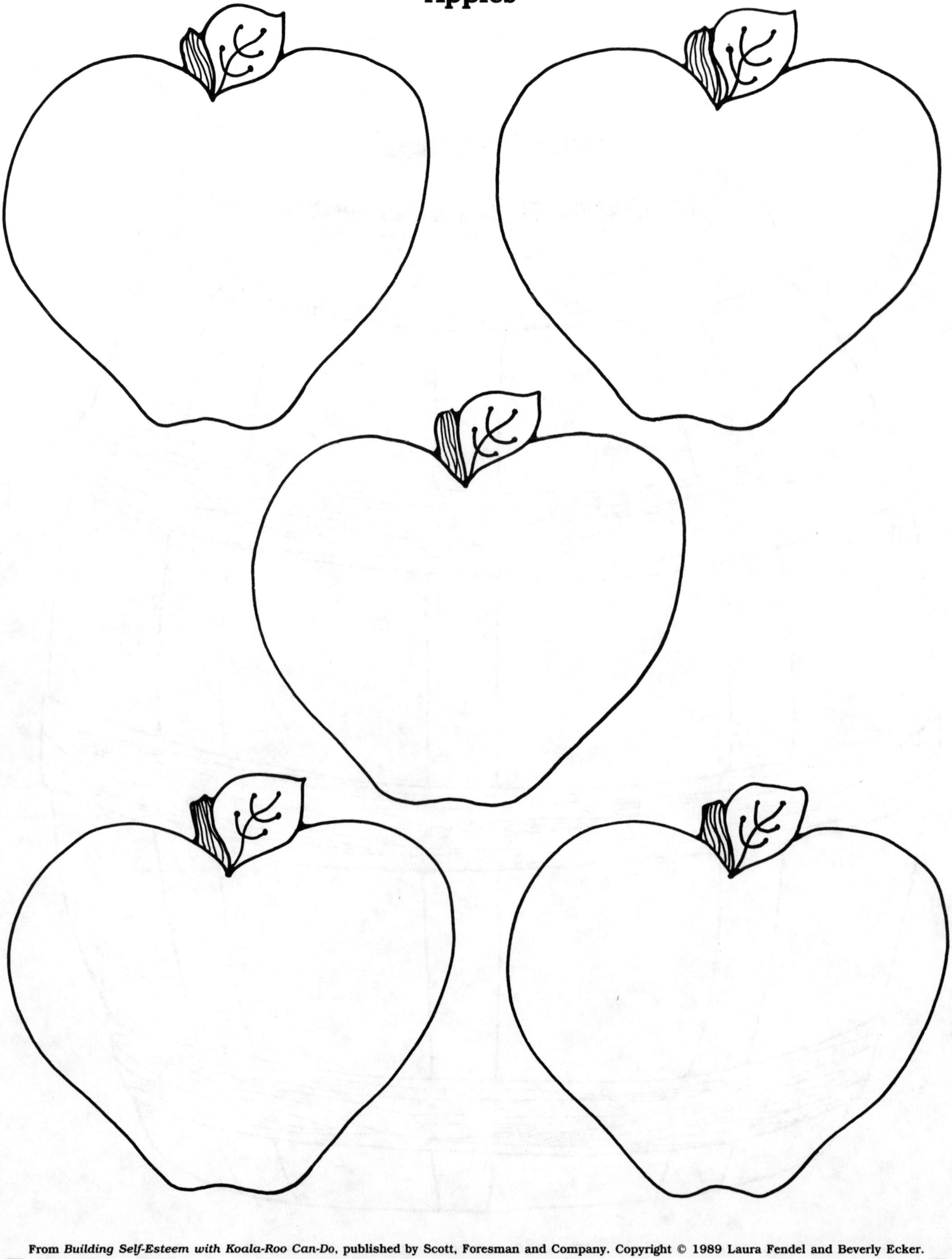

Mini-Portrait of

Name of your favorite character

Book Brief

Title:

Author:

Write three things you liked about your favorite character:

Pouch Report

By:

Thinking It Through...

Name: ______________ Date: __________

Title: ______________________

Author: ______________________

Write about four important events that happened in the story. Tell them in order.

1. ______________________

____

2. ______________________

____

3. ______________________

____

4. ______________________

____

Date: __________

Dear Can-Do,

I read ______________________

It was by ______________________

The story was about ______________

____

____

____

____

____

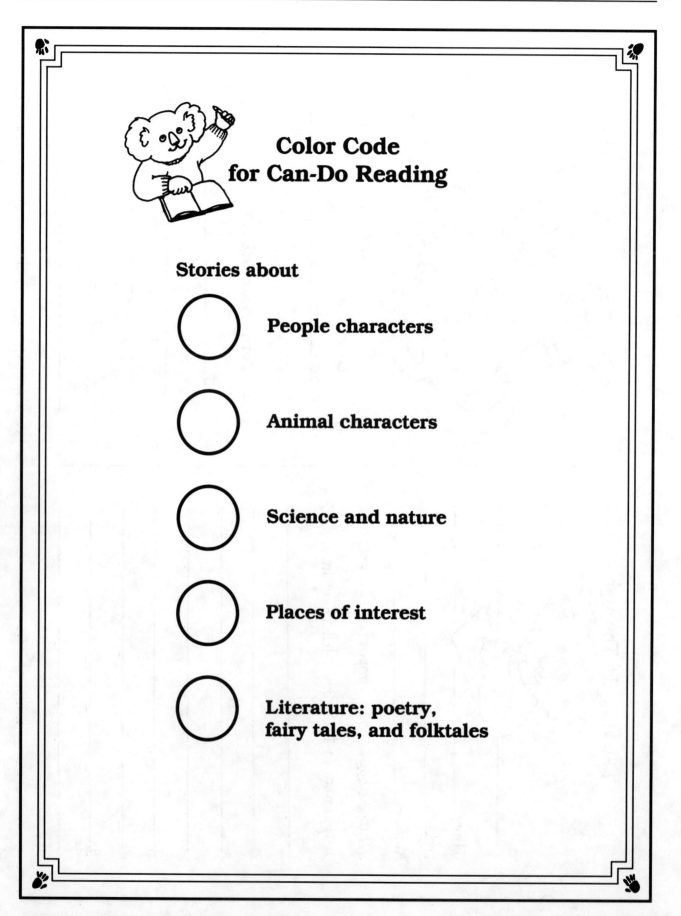

Color Code for Can-Do Reading

Stories about

◯ **People characters**

◯ **Animal characters**

◯ **Science and nature**

◯ **Places of interest**

◯ **Literature: poetry, fairy tales, and folktales**

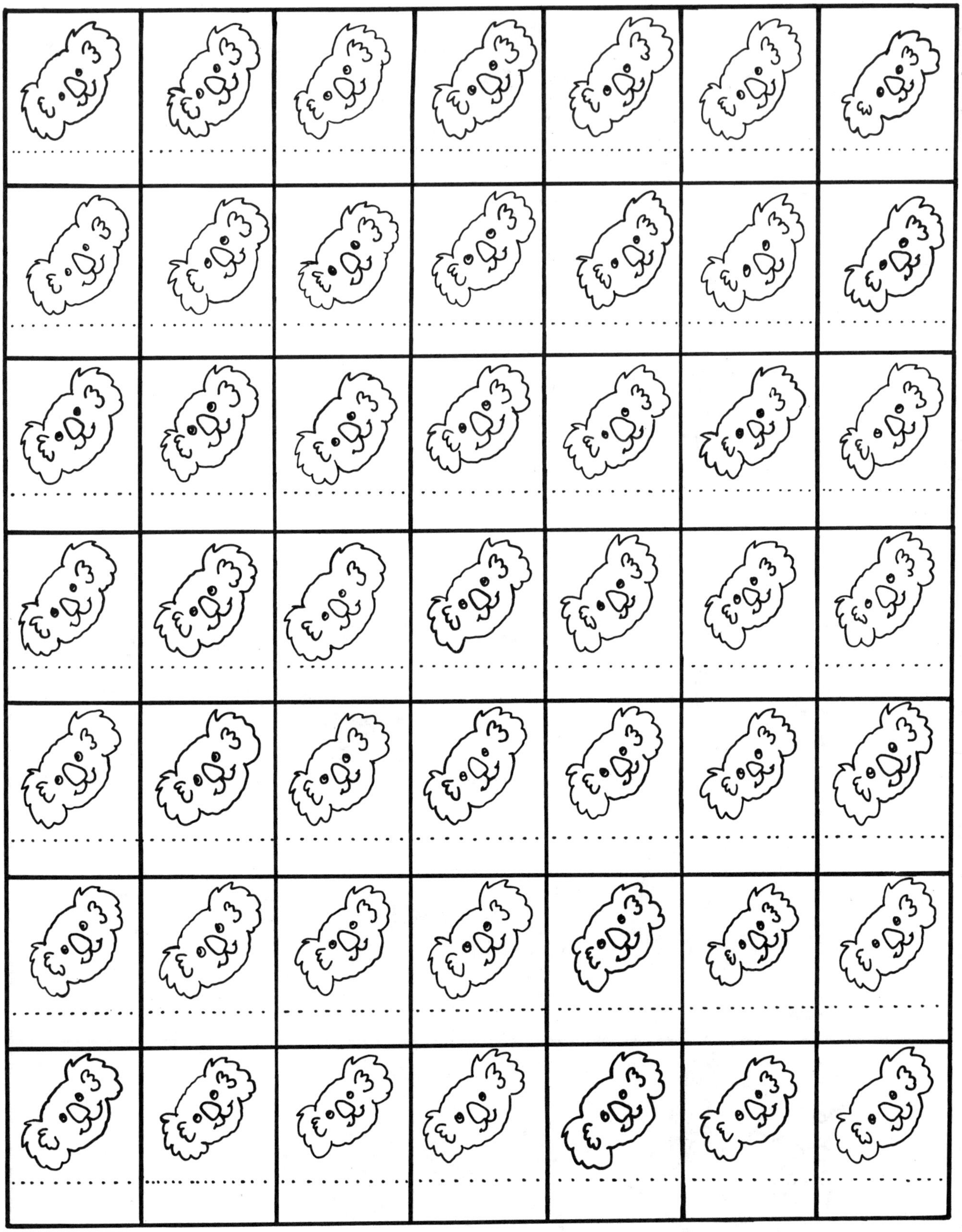

YOU CAN DO IT!
YOU ARE A CAN-DO KID!
HANG IN THERE
DON'T GIVE UP!
BE PROUD OF YOUR WORK!
TRY HARD
AND IMPROVE

Math

Introduction

The Can-Do math success program lets you guide and reinforce positive behavior, study habits, and attitudes in your classroom. It is detailed and time-consuming. Use it in difficult learning situations with students who are discouraged or have behavior problems and need a boost of motivation to get them going.

Children invariably sense when they are not fast learners, but when they experience success on their level of ability, they can achieve because they feel good about themselves. The program can also be successful with a group of bright students who are not motivated or have poor study habits. The reward is a class of children filled with pride at their own success.

All the children in your class will enjoy the math games and projects presented below after the discussion of the plan for math success.

How to Use the Materials

The plan for math success works with groups of students. You can adapt it to other curricular areas if you like; the principles underlying it are widely applicable. By giving lots of praise with compliment slips, you help each child and the entire group achieve expectations, thus motivating them to continue trying to do their best. What gives the plan its math focus is the set of culmination and evaluation activities that provide lessons in adding large numbers and regrouping sums.

Step 1 in the plan for math success is to duplicate many copies of the Can-Do Compliment Slips (page 25).

Step 2 is to determine the expectation for your group and communicate the expectation. You may need to model what you expect your class to do. You may have to back up with your class and have different children share their ideas of what the expectation means. For example, say you feel the need for your children to listen to directions more carefully. You may have to explain that in order to listen to directions carefully, they must stop what they are doing, keep their bodies still, give you eye contact, and look alert. Break down into smaller parts the meaning of your expectation so that your students can really understand it.

Step 3 in the plan for math success is to determine with the group how many compliment slips it will accumulate collectively to reach its goal: perhaps two hundred compliments collectively. Then decide what the class or group will earn as a reward. (See Ideas for Group Reinforcers, page 118, or choose a Celebration Success Party, chapter 5.) Fill out a Goal and Reward Sheet (page 119), and post it.

Step 4 is to start giving compliments. As the group is working or you are teaching directed lessons, distribute Can-Do Compliment Slips to each child who meets the expectations you have set. It is essential that you tell the child in specific terms what he or she is doing that is appropriate. If you are giving ten compliments to different children all for the same reason, state that, too. And be sure that you smile as you do it! If you tell a child, "You're an absolutely super learner," but the expression on your face is blank, you send a mixed message.

It is important not only that you be sincere but also that you distribute the compliment slips freely and to everyone. A child who is trying hard but hasn't quite achieved his or her overall long-range goals can reach smaller goals. When you see that child making efforts, be sure to reinforce the positive behavior. Success is a reinforcing motivation, so make each child feel successful.

Can-Do Group Tally Sheet

Step 5 in the plan for math success is to prepare a pocket pouch for each child. A sealed envelope, cut in half, will provide two pockets. Library pockets (the kind that are glued into books) work well, too. Each child may store his or her compliment slips in the pocket. Have the children write their names on the backs of compliments before storing them if you think ownership might become an issue. At the end of each class time, have each child count his or her Can-Do Compliment Slips.

Record the number on the Can-Do Group Tally Sheet (page 158).

A note on competition: Some competition is healthy. Continue reinforcing the expectation and the collective goal of the group, and emphasize that everyone's effort is important. Each person's compliments add to the total number of compliments.

Individual Can-Do Counting

Step 6 in the plan for math success is, at the end of the week, to have each child fill out an Individual Can-Do Counting sheet (page 159) to evaluate progress. Adding several numbers and discovering how each person's success contributes to the overall effort to reach the goal is exciting to young children. Reinforce their perception of the benefits of individual contribution to a group goal.

Step 7 in the plan for math success is to have the whole group add the totals from each child to determine the group total for the week.

Group Can-Do Counting

Step 8 in the plan for math success is to use the Group Can-Do Counting sheet (page 160) to evaluate further with the group. Continue adding numbers of compliments. Praise the group:

- "Look at all the compliments you have earned."
- "I'm so impressed with how well each person has done."
- "Can you believe we could work so hard?"
- "This is wonderful."
- "We're getting closer to our goal."

If your students have not learned how to regroup and add large numbers, your modeling the addition process will let them see its usefulness. If your students already know how to regroup, you could have them do the adding in order to reinforce that skill.

Yes, this is time-consuming! How well we all know that there are some groups of children and indeed some classes that in fact need special consideration and demand our attention and energy more intensely than others. But there is an excitement and intrigue in working toward a goal of one or two hundred compliments, adding the numbers each day and week, that I'm sure you will find infectious.

Reaching the goal should take two or three weeks, but no longer.

Math Games and Activities All your students, not just those requiring special attention, will enjoy a variety of Koala-Roo Can-Do math games and activities.

Place Value Game Enlarge the Stand-up Can-Do (pages 39 and 40) to about 3 feet in height. Make individual pockets for each of the placeholders (ones, tens, hundreds, and thousands). You will be attaching these pockets to the front of the Stand-up Can-Do's pouch.

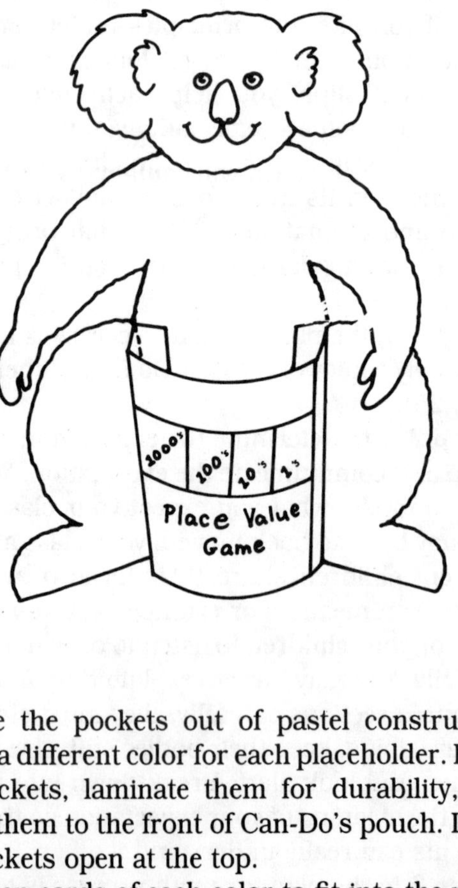

Make the pockets out of pastel construction paper, a different color for each placeholder. Label the pockets, laminate them for durability, and fasten them to the front of Can-Do's pouch. Leave the pockets open at the top.

Cut ten cards of each color to fit into the pockets. On each card write one digit from 0 through 9.

Here's how to play:

1. Hand out all forty cards. Some children may have more than one card.
2. Call out a number like this: "two hundreds, five tens, and seven ones."

3. The children must then associate the color code with their cards to see if they have the correct digits for the correct places. Students with the proper cards run up and put their cards into the correct pockets so that the digits show.
4. When the students can read the four-digit number in the pockets, they raise their hands.
5. When you call out a signal, everyone says the number together.
6. The children run up and take their cards out of the pockets, and the play begins again.

Can-Do Backpack Bingo Board

Can-Do Backpack Bingo gives practice in addition and subtraction facts.

Duplicate one Can-Do Backpack Bingo Board (page 161) for each student. Have the students write numbers from 1 through 20 at random in the spaces on their boards. There are twenty-four spaces, so each board will contain duplicate numbers. Ahead of time prepare addition and subtraction equations to 20. Call out the equations in no particular order, keeping notes of the sums and remainders in the equations you call out. Students cover the numbers on their boards that correspond to each sum or remainder in the equations you call out; they can use standard bingo markers to do the covering.

The first student with a line of covered numbers calls, "Bingo." Check the covered numbers against your notes. Play again.

Can-Do Coins and Can-Dollars

Use Can-Do Coins (page 162) to give practice in counting by fives, tens, twenty-fives, and fifties. Duplicate fifty to one hundred coins. Distribute them like compliments, but tell the class they are like dimes. At the end of the day, have each student add up the value of his or her dimes by counting by tens.

Another day assign a different value to the Can-Do Coins. Another day hand out Can-Dollars (page 162) along with the Can-Do Coins. Assign a value to the coins as before. Have students count their money at the end of the day. Set up a bank where Can-Do Coins can be converted into Can-Dollars.

Valentine Post Office Project All the rest of the reproducibles in this section have to do with a Valentine Post Office project that lets your class simulate a post office system and assembly line. The activities call for math, social studies, and life skills. The students will have responsibilities for several jobs. The class will estimate large numbers and see, for example, what 2,328 looks like.

First, make a Valentine Post Office booth from which to distribute employment forms, schedules, and other materials. Use a cardboard refrigerator box. Cut a square window in the front and a door on the side of the box. Make shingles of railroad board or heavy cardboard. Cover the box with colored paper, and glue valentines made by your class all over it. Leave some decoration to be done by the official Valentine Post Office artists (see the discussion of the Valentine Employment Form, below). On the box hang a sign that says **Valentine Post Office**.

Make mail drop-off boxes. Cover boxes that are 1½ or 2 feet high. Cut slits 2 inches wide through which mail can drop. Cut flaps that open in the back of each box to allow mail collection.

Now invite other classes to mail their valentines through your post office.

Valentine Post Office Flyer

Use the Valentine Post Office Flyer (page 163) to explain the guidelines for addressing envelopes.

Practice addressing valentines. Send home the flyer along with a class list and a list of the room numbers of all the classes participating so that children can send valentines to other teachers and friends.

Valentine Employment Form

Distribute Valentine Employment Forms (page 164), and explain the Valentine Post Office jobs to your class. (The jobs are further described under Valentine Postal Worker Schedule, below.)

1. **Postal pickup workers** pick up mail from the mail drop-off boxes.
2. **Counters** count the letters each day.
3. **Date stampers** stamp the date on each letter.
4. **Cancel letter stampers** cancel each letter with a special stamp.
5. **Sorters** sort the letters by classroom.
6. **Mail carriers** deliver sorted and packaged letters to each classroom.
7. **Publicity people** speak to each class, describing the Valentine Post Office and explaining how to address the valentines.
8. **Postal managers** coordinate all the jobs and check that each person is at work on time.
9. **Booth helpers** stand in the Valentine Post Office booth daily when the valentines are being mailed, hand out free valentines, and answer questions.
10. **Artists** decorate the Valentine Post Office booth and the mail drop-off boxes and organize sorting boxes for the mail room.
11. **Office workers** post the numbers of letters that pass through the Valentine Post Office each day and make out checks at the end of the week. (See the discussion of Valentine Postal Worker Checks, below.)

Have the students fill out their Valentine Employment Forms.

Now estimate with your class the numbers of cards that will pass through the Valentine Post Office. Write down all the estimates. Save them for later comparison with the actual numbers.

Valentine Postal Worker Schedule

Set up each student's work schedule on the Valentine Postal Worker Schedule (page 165). Write down the job titles, the work times, and the workers' names.

Now the artists organize the sorting boxes in the mail room, labeling one box for each class participating.

Each day after the children have mailed their valentines, the postal pickup workers collect the cards from the mail drop-off boxes. Counters then count the total number of cards for the day and record it. In an assembly line, date stampers stamp the date on the cards, and cancel letter stampers stamp the corner of each letter with a rubber stamp that has a picture on it. Down the assembly line, some sorters sort the cards by room number while others then sort according to the first letter of the addressee's last name into two piles for each classroom: A though K and L through Z. Other sorters then bundle the letters and label them with the number of the room to which each bundle should go. Mail carriers deliver the valentines to the classes. Then each class is responsible for the distribution to each child.

Valentine Graph

If several classes are participating, color in the Valentine Graph (page 166) to show the number of cards per day that passed through the Valentine Post Office. At the end of the week, add the daily totals, and determine the total number of cards that passed through the Valentine Post Office. Then figure out with your class how many fifties, hundreds, and five hundreds there are in the total number of cards. Finally, compare the actual number of valentines that went through the Valentine Post Office with the estimates your students made earlier.

Fifty-Valentine Pattern Sheet

Duplicate the Fifty-Valentine Pattern Sheet (page 167), and have each student color a copy with only two or three colors to make a pattern. Post the colored Fifty-Valentine Pattern Sheets as part of a large display. Make a big sign or sentence strip that tells the total number of valentines that went through the Valentine Post Office, and incorporate the sign or sentence strip into the display. Mount the display in the hallway, if possible, so that children from all participating classes can see it.

If the display is posted in your room, use the

Fifty-Valentine Pattern Sheets in an extension lesson. Point to the sheets as you count out loud with the class by fifties, hundreds, and five hundreds. Ask how many Fifty-Valentine Pattern Sheets equal one hundred valentines. Then ask how many sheets equal two hundred valentines. Try to get your students to notice the relationship between the number of sheets and the number of valentines (two, four, six sheets; one hundred, two hundred, three hundred valentines) and other mathematical patterns.

Valentine Postal Worker Checks

Have the Valentine Post Office project's office workers fill out Valentine Postal Worker Checks (page 168) and distribute them to all the students in the class, including themselves.

Valentine Math Report

To each participating class, send a Valentine Math Report (page 169) telling the number of valentines that came through the Valentine Post Office each day. Fill in all the blanks except the total.

Leave the total blank so that each class can do its own addition and discover the grand total number of valentines that came through the Valentine Post Office.

I "Chews" You Valentine

I "Chews" You Valentines (page 170) are for you, the teacher, to give to each of your students. Duplicate the I "Chews" You Valentine, cut out each copy, cut the two slits with an X-Acto knife or scissors point, fold the valentine, sign it, and insert a piece of sugarless gum in the slits.

CAN~DO GROUP TALLY SHEET

Daily each child counts compliment slips and records the number.

NAME	M	T	W	Th	F	Total

_______________ Name

________ Date

CAN~DO COUNTING

Individual Evaluation

~ End of the Week Report

I earned ____ Can-Do Compliment Slips in ________

I did the following:

- [ ] 1. ______________________________
- [ ] 2. ______________________________
- [ ] 3. ______________________________
- [ ] 4. ______________________________

Our ______ (name of group) group earned ____ Can-Do Compliment Slips

Our class earned _____ Can-Do Compliment Slips

Do math addition here:

Name ________ Date ________

CAN~DO COUNTING

Group Evaluation

~End of the Week Report

I earned ______ Can-Do Compliment Slips this week.

My ________ group earned ____________.

Group's weekly totals: ________

____

____

____

____

____

Add group totals:

I am proud: ________

____

____

Class goal: ________

Reward: ________

____

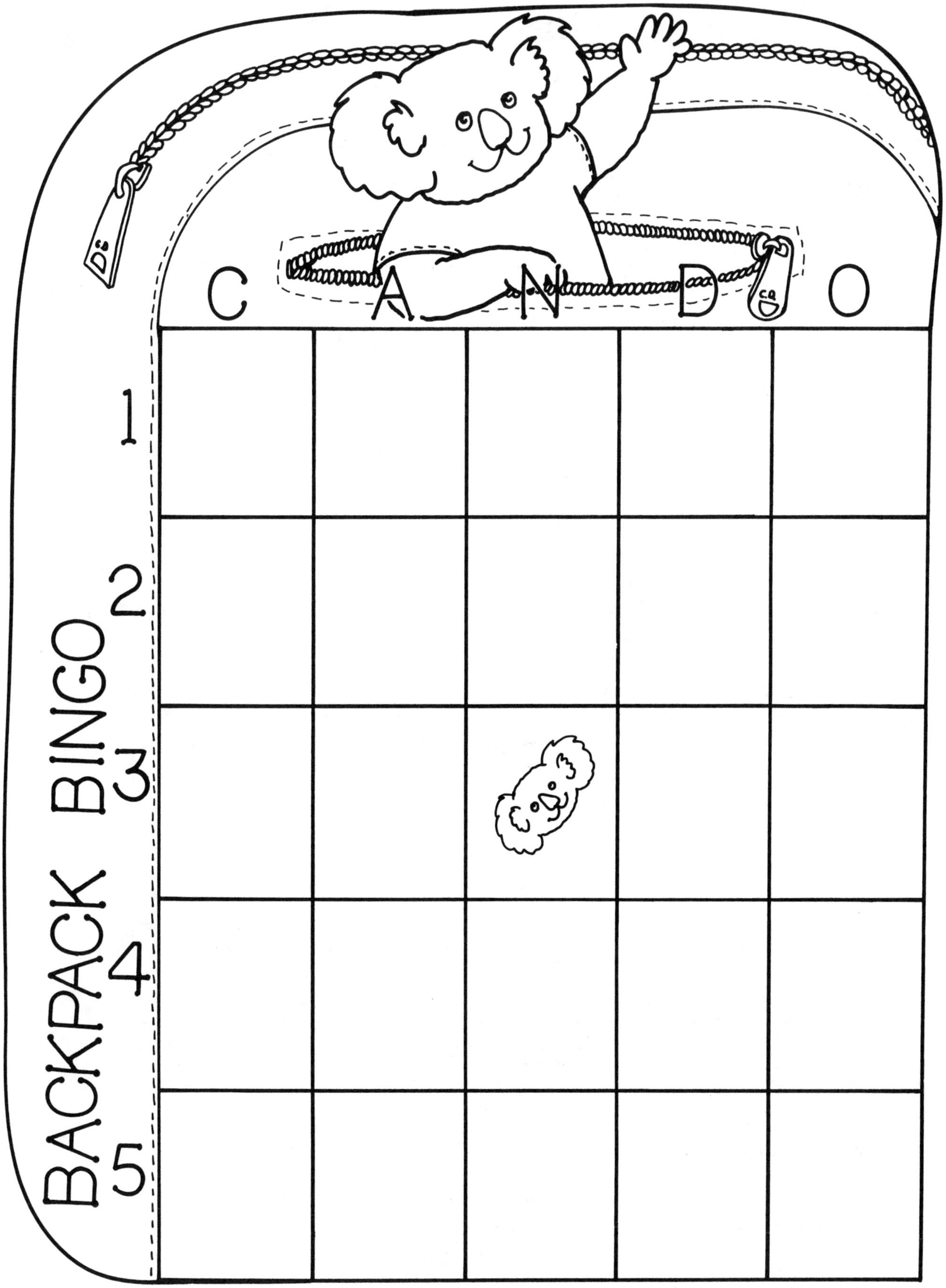
C A N D O
BACKPACK BINGO
1
2
3
4
5

CAN-DO COIN
CAN-DO COIN
CAN-DO COIN
CAN-DO COIN
CAN-DO COIN
CAN-DO COIN
CAN-DO COIN
CAN-DO COIN
CAN-DO COIN
CAN-DO COIN
CAN-DO COIN

CAN-DO CURRENCY NOTE
1
1
I'm a
CAN-DO
Kid!
I
CAN DO
It!
CAN-DO
1
1
IAMOKTOO
ONE CAN-DOLLAR
UROKTOME

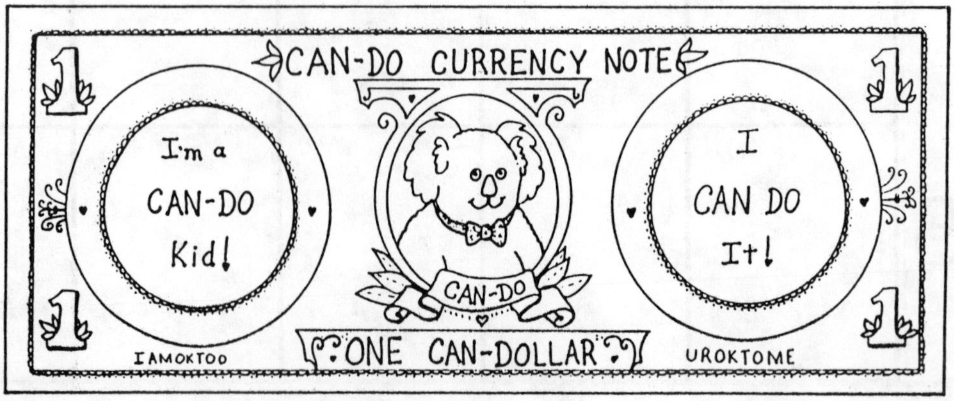
CAN-DO CURRENCY NOTE
1
1
I'm a
CAN-DO
Kid!
I
CAN DO
It!
CAN-DO
1
1
IAMOKTOO
ONE CAN-DOLLAR
UROKTOME

ANNOUNCING:

____

School name

Valentine Post Office

Valentine Collection

- ♡ Time:
- ♡ Drop your cards in the mailbox early!
- ♡ Postal Workers will sort, cancel, date, and deliver. Your class workers will distribute the cards.
- ♡ Address your cards correctly!

♥ FRONT ♥

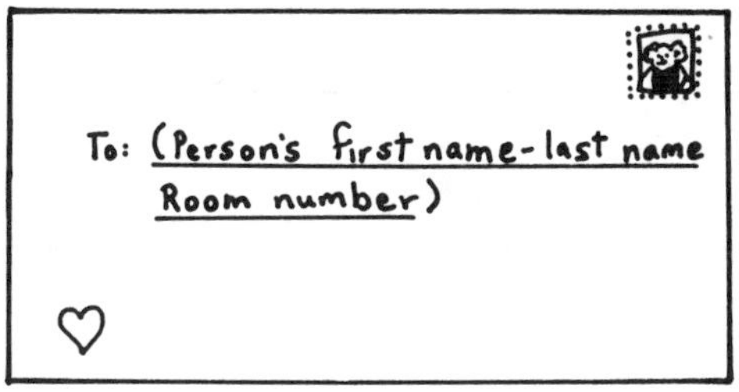

♥ BACK ♥

Employment Form for Valentine Post Office

Date: ____________

Name ______________________________

Age __________

Address ______________________________

Job you would like ______________________

List your second choice __________________

List your third choice ___________________

Why do you think you would do a good job? ______________________________

____

____

Valentine Postal Worker Schedule

JOB TITLE	WORK TIME	WORKER'S NAME

Valentine Graph

Color in the boxes to show how many cards went through the post office each day. Each box stands for 100 valentines.

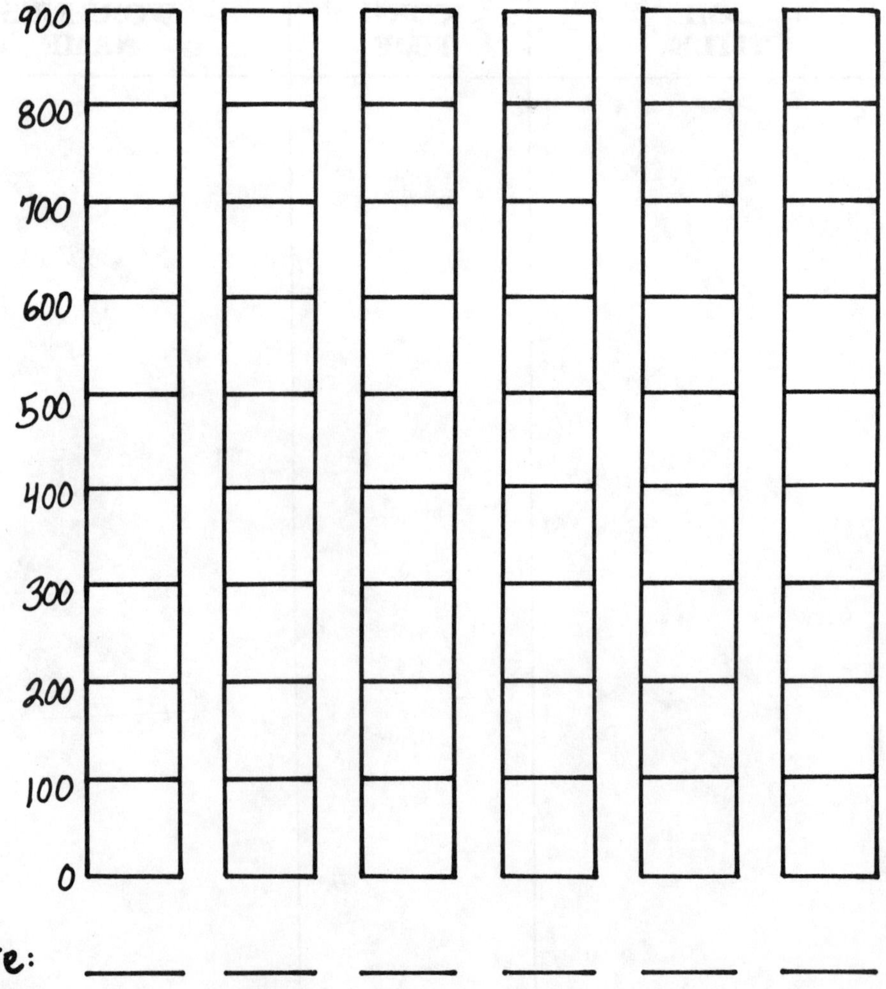

Date: ____ ____ ____ ____ ____ ____

\# ♡'s: ____ ____ ____ ____ ____ ____

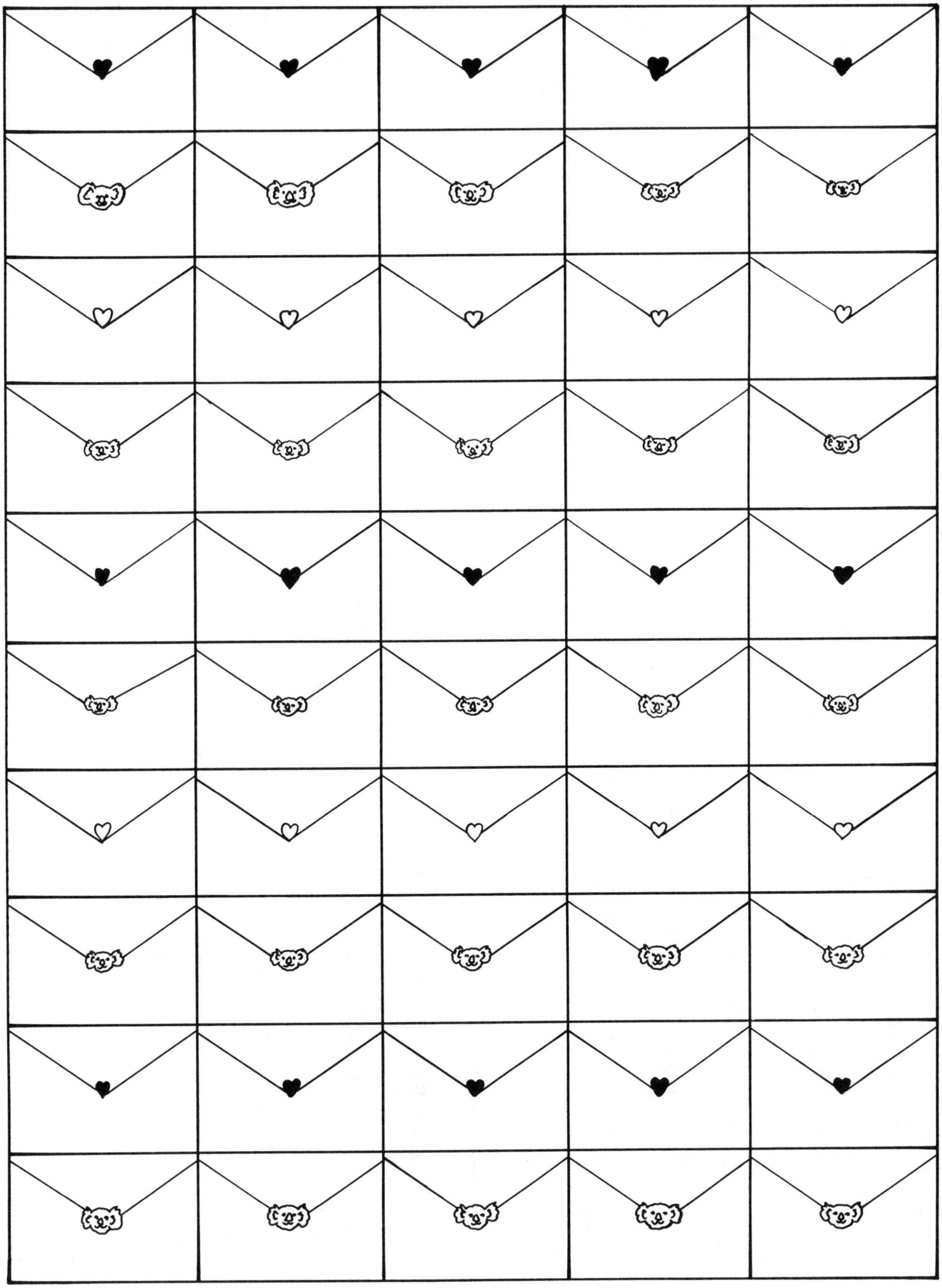

POSTAL WORKER CHECKS

Valentine Post Office

Grade ________ School

________ 19____
Date

Paid to the Order of ________________
Worker's name

For helpful service we pay you ________ ♡♡♡XXX

and lots of thanks for a job well done.

____
Postmaster

Valentine Post Office

Grade ________ School

________ 19____
Date

Paid to the Order of ________________

For helpful service we pay you ________ ♡♡♡XXX

and lots of thanks for a job well done

____
Postmaster

Valentine Math Report

Date	Number of Valentines Posted and Delivered

Total:

Number of letters incorrectly addressed: ________

cut & insert gum
FOR MY
VALENTINE!

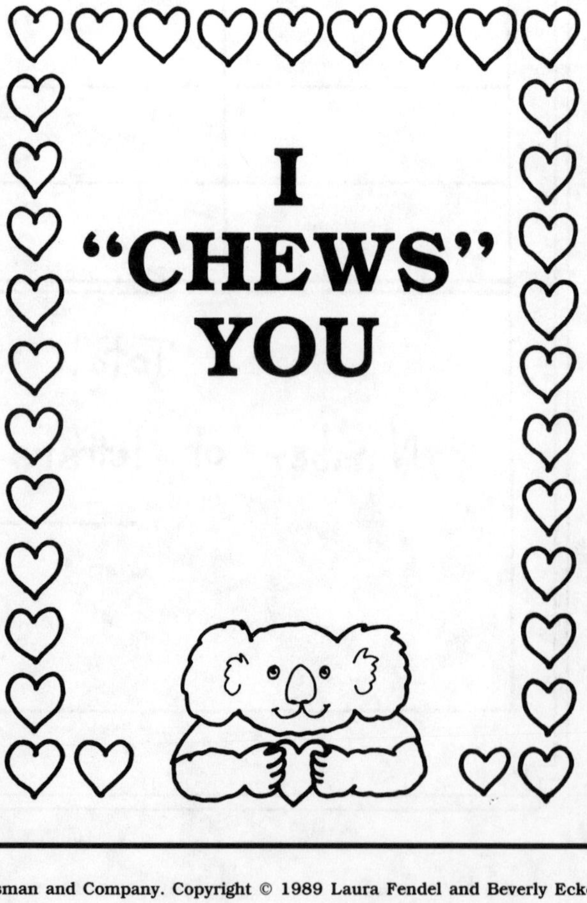
I
"CHEWS"
YOU

Language Arts

Introduction

The activities and materials discussed below incorporate Koala-Roo Can-Do to build self-esteem and promote writing and speaking skills.

In the appendix (Suggested Reading, page 207) under the heading Books about Self-Esteem, you will find suggestions for related activities (as well as dozens of titles of books your students will enjoy reading and discussing).

How to Use the Materials

Can-Do Chronicle

The Can-Do Chronicle (page 173) is a child-written newspaper that reports on your curriculum from the students' point of view. It is most successful if completed each week. Brainstorm ideas for features: things your students are learning in school, the seasons, important events, classroom successes, the Can-Do Kid of the Week, the art corner, a joke, a poem, a short story, a book review. Then choose who will write each article. You decide whether the children will write a draft that you will edit for spelling or if they are to use their own invented phonetic spelling. If you allow invented spelling, be sure to write the parents an introductory note explaining your purpose and rationale (perhaps to let parents see their child's development in writing as compared to that of other children in the class). If the students write firmly with a number two pencil right on a Can-Do Chronicle sheet, many copy machines will print a legible copy.

Ideas for Show-and-Tell

The show-and-tell concept has been around for decades. Show-and-tell gives children in early grades an introduction to speaking in front of a large group. It develops self-confidence and pride.

Some children are shy or afraid to speak in front of the entire class. You can achieve success with these children by forming a small sharing group that meets privately to share ideas, objects, or experiences in a nonthreatening atmosphere. After much time, perhaps these children can be encouraged to share with the entire class.

You can use show-and-tell to extend learning and promote conversation skills by encouraging children to speak in complete sentences and to give clear explanations or presentations. Encourage discussion after a child has shared by having the group ask questions of the speaker.

To get ideas for creative sharing, look over Ideas for Show-and-Tell (page 174). You can read this list to your class, post it, or even distribute copies of it.

Send the Show-and-Tell Letter Home (page 75) to parents so that they can help their children find interesting things to share.

Can-Do Cards

- **Can-Do Birthday Card**
- **Can-Do Giving Card**
- **Can-Do Note Card**
- **Can-Do Thanksgiving Card**
- **Can-Do Triangle Card**

Can-Do Cards (pages 175–179) are note cards suitable for different occasions and various uses. You can use them to teach your students how to write letters or notes. Your students can use the cards to send compliments to one another.

You might add a simple puzzle or maze—one that is appropriate to your class's grade level—to the inside of the Can-Do Birthday Card (page 175). Duplicate many copies, and have them available for birthdays and unbirthdays.

Story Writing Your students can write stories in Can-Do Cards. Children enjoy writing on special paper, particularly paper that carries decoration, as these note cards do. (Keep in mind that you can give your students duplicated Can-Do Borders, pages 63–69, for this purpose, too. Add lines, if you choose, before duplicating.)

Pouch Stories You can write the following ideas on cards or slips of paper, put them in the pouch of a Stand-up Can-Do (pages 39–41), and have students draw them as topics for discussions, impromptu speeches, or invented stories. The story starters call upon the children to draw either mainly on experience or mainly on imagination.

Experience These ideas call mainly upon the children's own experiences:

- I'm terrific because . . .
- Wishes
- My lucky day
- I am proud of . . .
- Gee, was I angry!
- My first day of school
- Moving was a difficult thing; moving was a wonderful thing
- Birthdays can be difficult days
- Someone called me names. I felt . . .
- I like it when my friend comes to visit. We can . . .
- I do not like it when my friend comes to visit . . .
- Everyone makes mistakes sometimes
- I was jealous: my friend had something I wanted
- Something my mom or dad wouldn't buy for me
- A special grown-up whom I admire
- Something I had to give up because I was getting older
- I helped a friend
- I am proud of myself when I . . .
- I am a big help when . . .
- My mother is the most beautiful woman or my dad is the most handsome man because . . . (see *My Mother Is the Most Beautiful Woman in the World*, page 215)
- My favorite quiet-time activity
- Something I'm scared of
- A terrible, horrible day
- A fantastic day
- I had a problem
- I wish something were different
- Something I want to do someday
- Something I want to do that will take a long time to learn
- My favorite place
- Our family likes to . . .
- My favorite meal
- I did something nice for someone without being asked

Imagination These ideas call upon imagination:

- If I were a turtle or a frog (choose one)
- The exciting dream
- My dream to be a . . .
- In the land where everyone gives compliments and no one puts anyone down
- The incredible gift that you can't see but is really there
- The good feeling spread all over the room . . .
- And we lived happily ever after
- The magical mountain
- The magical ———
- The machine that could ———
- The robot who loved me
- A ride on Can-Do's balloon
- A visit to the enchanted forest

Koala-Roo Finger Puppets

Koala-Roo Finger Puppets (page 180) are so small that it's important to share stories in groups made up of only a few children so that everyone can see the characters speaking. Act out the following ideas:

- **How Koala-Roo Can-Do Got His Name** (pages 7–16)
- Trying to succeed at different things
- Different ways to succeed at one thing
- Praising others, and accepting praise by saying thank you
- Something is difficult, and it's hard to keep trying
- Can-Do wants to swim but is afraid to jump in
- Can-Do called a friend to come over to play, and she said she couldn't
- Can-Do wants to have a birthday party in the summer, but his friends are busy
- Can-Do knows someone who keeps calling to play, but Can-Do doesn't like to play with that koala-roo
- Can-Do compliments Auntie Kanga-Lou when she does something special for a friend
- Can-Do tells his koala-roo friend why he's a fantastic friend
- Auntie Kanga-Lou's garage needs cleaning, and she and Can-Do think of a plan to organize it

CAN~DO CHRONICLE

Teacher: Date:

Ideas for Show-and-Tell

Each of the following ideas could be used for a different week. A weekly theme adds purpose to the activity.

- Something old, older than my parents
- Something I found
- Something I made
- Something someone made for me
- A favorite book from home
- A fairy tale book from home (maybe one with a special version of a favorite story)
- Something that's been in our family for a long time
- My favorite baby toy
- My favorite stuffed animal
- Something I received for a birthday
- Something from another country
- Something I can do
- Something I can teach everyone else to do by showing how (for example, origami)
- A collection
- Something that moves
- Something that makes a sound
- Something that smells good
- A pet or an insect
- A food sculpture I can make to share
- An experience I can share

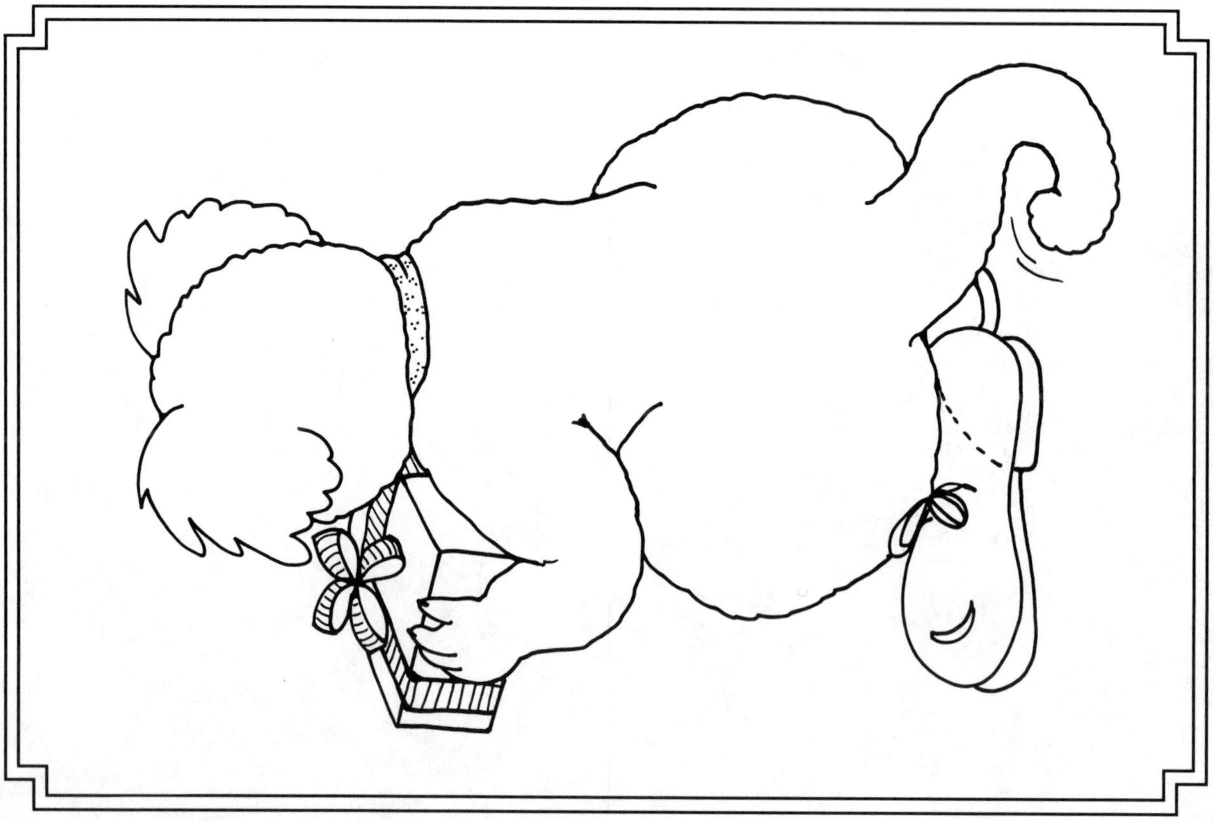

Happy Thanksgiving

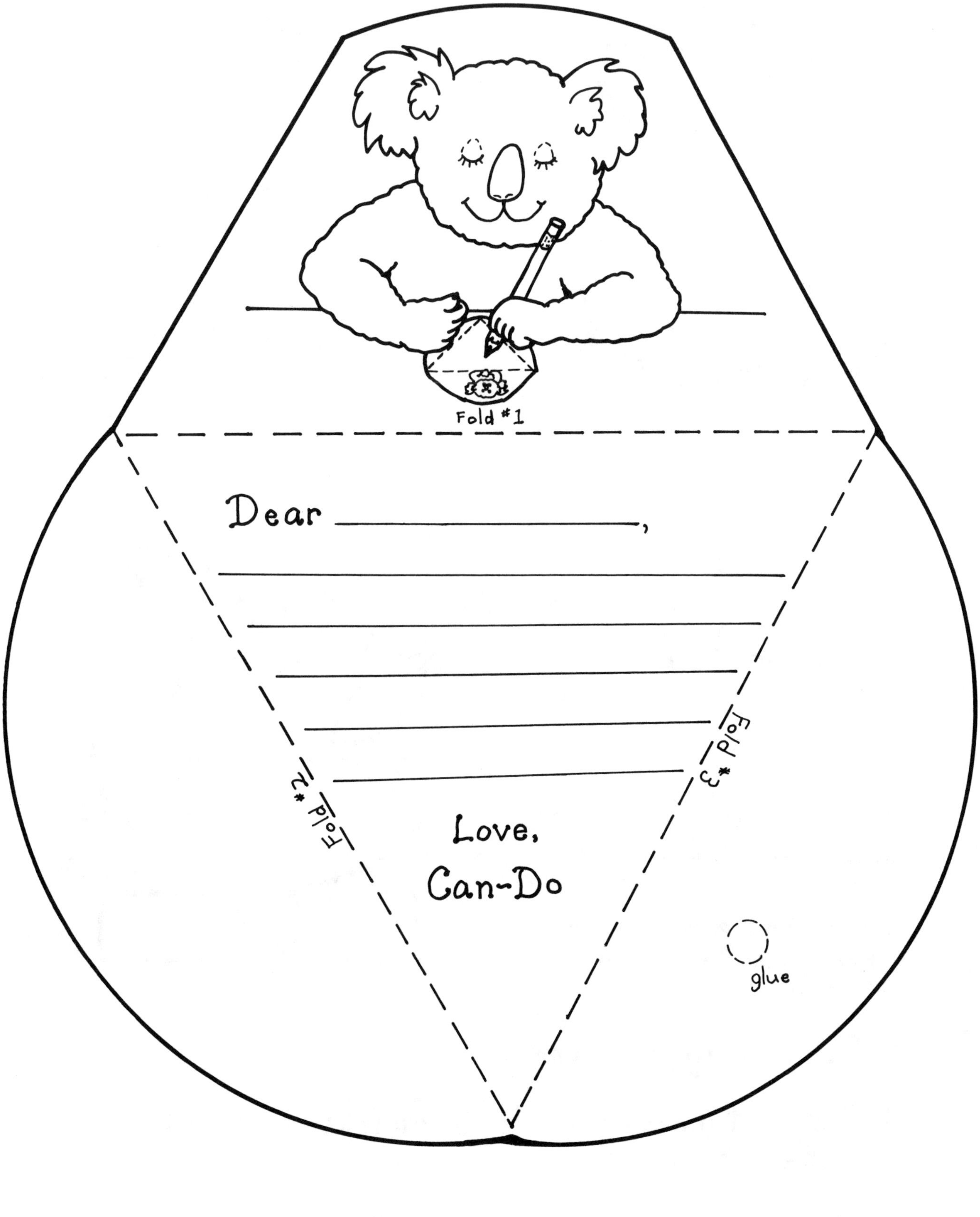
Fold #1
Dear ,
Fold #2
Fold #3
Love,
Can-Do
glue

Koala-Roo Finger Puppets

Can-Do

Auntie Kanga-Lou

Friends

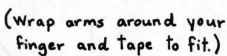

(Wrap arms around your finger and tape to fit.)

1. Color finger puppets.
2. Cut out carefully along outside lines of patterns.
3. Wrap strip around your finger. Tape to fit.

5

Celebrations of Success

Introduction

Celebrations lift the spirits and help to reinforce the progress we've made. Celebrations help us share in being proud of our accomplishments.

Choose special times to celebrate. Completing a textbook, ending a unit, completing a Compliment Grid, reaching one or two hundred compliments, or arriving at the end of a grading period are all excellent occasions for Celebrations of Success.

Several children working on individual goals could collectively earn a celebration for the whole class: each child would have his or her own target, but everyone together would celebrate the attainment of the goals. Keep in mind that each child should be involved in a program oriented toward success so that each child can and will reach his or her own goal.

How to Use the Materials

The reproducibles at the end of this chapter are invitations and recipes for a Weekful of Success Celebrations and for a collection of other celebrations. Children give the invitations to each other (except the invitations for parents and grandparents). The Weekful of Success Celebrations are:

- Magnificent Monday
- Tea Party Tuesday
- Wonderful Wednesday
- Thoughtful Thursday
- Fabulous Friday

The other special celebrations are:

- Koala-Roo Can-Do's Birthday
- Grandparents' Day
- Parents' Career Day
- Fall Festival
- Book Bash
- Success in All Seasons
- Games Galore
- Spring Fling
- Summer Circus Celebration

You can have the children wear Can-Do Caps (page 58), Can-Do Ears (page 59), or Can-Do Blue Ribbons (page 113) to the Weekful of Success Celebrations or some of the other special celebrations.

Almost every celebration has an edible treat associated with it. The recipes at the end of the chapter contain directions that your students can follow easily. With supervision, the children can prepare the treats themselves.

Can-Do Recipe Book Cover

You can duplicate the recipes and make them into a **Chef Can-Do Cooks with You** cookbook for each student. The Can-Do Recipe Book Cover (page 200) has space for a student's name.

A Weekful of Success Celebrations The Weekful of Success Celebrations can be any week of the school year. In fact, you don't have to have the celebrations all in the same week. Adapt them to suit your needs.

Invitation for Magnificent Monday and Recipe for a Popcorn Picnic

Fill out the Invitation for Magnificent Monday (page 186), and make sure everyone gets a copy. Have the class choose in advance the kinds of seasonings that will flavor the popcorn (see the Recipe for a Popcorn Picnic, page 200). Gather supplies:

1. A popcorn popper
2. As many large bowls as there will be flavors of popcorn
3. A picnic-size tablecloth
4. Napkins
5. Paper cups
6. Ingredients listed on the Recipe for a Popcorn Picnic (page 200)

On Magnificent Monday, pop the popcorn and flavor it, one flavor per bowl. Serve the popcorn buffet-style on a large table covered with the picnic tablecloth. Let the children put their popcorn in paper cups.

Invitation for Tea Party Tuesday and Recipe for a Colossal Cookie

Fill out the Invitation for Tea Party Tuesday (page 187), and make sure everyone gets a copy. You will be serving Friendship Tea along with the Colossal Cookie, so have each child bring a teacup and any kind of tea bag.

Gather other supplies:

1. A teakettle and a teapot
2. A hot plate
3. Sugar or honey for the tea if you want (you can mix the sweetener into the hot water to simplify things)
4. Extra teacups and tea bags for those who neglect to bring them
5. Napkins
6. A knife to cut the cookie
7. A pizza pan
8. Kitchen equipment and an oven
9. Ingredients listed on the Recipe for a Colossal Cookie (page 201)

On Tea Party Tuesday, make the Colossal Cookie. Display all the teacups on a table with the Colossal Cookie. Make Friendship Tea by putting several kinds of tea bags together in the same pot.

You could use the variety of tea bags and teacups as the basis for a sorting, classifying, and graphing lesson.

Invitation for Wonderful Wednesday, Recipe for Bravo Garbanzo Dip, and Recipe for Terrific Tofu Dip

Fill out the Invitation for Wonderful Wednesday (page 188), and make sure each child gets a copy. The menu is chips and dips, so have the children bring things to dip: chips, crackers, pita bread to tear into small pieces, sliced carrots, green pepper, celery, cucumber, radishes, snow peas, zucchini. You can incorporate your discussion of the upcoming Wonderful Wednesday celebration into a unit on nutrition. Talk about unusual vegetables. Sort and classify vegetables. Discuss which portion of the plant each vegetable represents (root, stem, leaf, seeds, "fruit"). Discuss vitamins and healthy snacks. Many children don't like vegetables. Read *Green Eggs and Ham* by Dr. Seuss, and discuss what it's like to try new flavors or to try foods we think we don't like.

Gather supplies:

1. The things to dip brought by the children
2. Paper plates to serve from and paper plates for each child
3. Napkins
4. A food processor
5. A spatula
6. The ingredients listed on the Recipes for Bravo Garbanzo Dip (page 201) and Terrific Tofu Dip (page 202)

Prepare the dips. Serve the chips and dips buffet-style. Have each child try a little of everything.

Invitation for Thoughtful Thursday and Recipe for Koala-Roo Malted Milk

Fill out the Invitation for Thoughtful Thursday (page 189), and make sure each child gets a copy. Gather supplies:

1. A blender
2. Paper cups
3. Napkins
4. The ingredients listed on the Recipe for Koala-Roo Malted Milk (page 202)

On Thoughtful Thursday, make and serve the Koala-Roo Malted Milk. Being thoughtful is the theme. While the children enjoy their malted milk, they can be writing surprise compliment notes to others (see Can-Do Cards, pages 175–179, and Can-Do Awards, pages 106–112). Children can send notes to friends, teachers, school helpers, secretaries, parents, or Secret Pals (see below).

Secret Pals Secret Pals could be a week-long activity launched on Thoughtful Thursday and lasting until the next Thursday. Children could bring a small treasure from home that they no longer want and give it to their Secret Pal. Notes could be exchanged. Compliment notes could be mounted on the Tree for All Seasons (page 45). Call the finished display a Friendship Tree.

Invitation for Fabulous Friday and Recipe for Dessert Pizza

Fill out the Invitation for Fabulous Friday (page 190), and make sure each of your students gets a copy. Gather supplies:

1. A large pizza pan
2. Kitchen equipment and an oven
3. A knife to cut wedges of Dessert Pizza
4. Small paper plates
5. Napkins
6. The ingredients listed on the Recipe for Dessert Pizza (page 203)

Make and serve the Dessert Pizza, and have a Fabulous Friday!

Invitation for Koala-Roo Can-Do's Birthday and Recipe for Koala Cake

Read several birthday books, and discuss the experiences of the characters. Have the class write about the joys and anxieties of birthdays.

Fill out the Invitation for Koala-Roo Can-Do's Birthday (page 191), and make sure each student gets a copy. Plan a birthday celebration for Koala-Roo Can-Do. As a birthday favor, you can teach the students how to draw Koala-Roo Can-Do (see How to Draw Koala-Roo Can-Do, page 80), or you could give Koala-Roo Can-Do Pencil Tops (page 70). The children can make presents and cards for Can-Do. Everyone can make birthday hats (see Can-Do Caps, page 58) to wear to the party.

Gather supplies:

1. Two 9-inch round cake pans
2. Kitchen equipment and an oven
3. A large tray or pizza pan on which to serve the cake
4. Small plates
5. Plastic forks
6. Napkins
7. Birthday candles, if you wish
8. The ingredients listed on the Recipe for Koala Cake (pages 203–204)

Make the Koala Cake. Put a candle on the cake for each student in the class if you so desire. Serve the cake. Sing "Happy Birthday" and "There Was a Class That Had a Friend and Can-Do Was His Name-O" (to the tune of "B-I-N-G-O"). As a party game, play Can-Do Backpack Bingo (see the Can-Do Backpack Bingo Board, page 161, and the explanation on page 155).

Invitation for Grandparents' Day

From the school library, gather a collection of books about people, old and young. *Emma* by Wendy Kesselman (Doubleday & Co., 1980), for instance, is a story about an older woman who takes up a new hobby and becomes successful as a painter. Have your class discuss human relationships and personal success after they have done some reading.

Invite grandparents or older friends to visit the class by filling out the Invitation for Grandparents' Day (page 192) and making sure each student gets a copy for each grandparent. On Grandparents' Day, have the grandparents tell stories of when they were in school. Have them share the successes in their lives. Take pictures.

Invitation for Parents' Career Day

Invite parents to come share their careers or hobbies (see the Careers and Hobbies Letter Home, page 73). Fill out the Invitation for Parents' Career Day (page 193), and make sure each child gets a copy to take to each parent. On Parents' Career Day, encourage parents to share how some of their hobbies became jobs or careers.

Invitation for a Fall Festival and Recipe for Koala Apple Crispy

Prepare for an I Can Do It Talent Show (see below). Fill out the Invitation for a Fall Festival (page 194), and make sure each child gets a copy. Have each child bring an apple for the recipe. Gather supplies:

1. A cookie sheet
2. Aluminum foil
3. Kitchen equipment and an oven
4. A serving spoon
5. Paper plates
6. Plastic forks
7. Napkins
8. The apples from the children

9. The other ingredients listed on the Recipe for Koala Apple Crispy (page 204)

I Can Do It Talent Show Have each child share something he or she can do, and call the presentations an I Can Do It Talent Show. If some of the children say they have no talent, assure them that there are a lot of things they can do: make funny sounds, make amazing faces, do gymnastic feats, sing while standing on one foot, tell a joke, do a dance, or any of a number of other possibilities.

Invitation for a Book Bash and Recipe for Koala Frozen Yogurt

Have a success party when the class completes a reading text or finishes a read-a-thon (see Can-Do Reading Shoes, page 144, discussed on page 140). Fill out the Invitation for a Book Bash (page 195), and make sure each of your students gets a copy. You might have the students bring a favorite book from home to read to a friend; you could graph the kinds of books the students bring in. Or have a paperback book swap: each student brings a book to trade with another.

Gather supplies:

1. Muffin tins
2. A small knife
3. Napkins
4. The ingredients listed on the Recipe for Koala Frozen Yogurt (page 205)

Make and serve the Koala Frozen Yogurt. Have the students read their books to each other or swap their books, if you have included either of these activities in your plans. Otherwise, just celebrate your class's reading success.

Invitation for Success in All Seasons and Recipe for Chocolate Soup à la Can-Do

Fill out the Invitation for Success in All Seasons (page 196), and make sure each child gets a copy. Prepare Can-Do Blue Ribbons (page 113) for each child to wear. Gather supplies:

1. A pot
2. A hot plate
3. Cups or soup bowls
4. Spoons
5. Napkins
6. Ingredients listed on the Recipe for Chocolate Soup à la Can-Do (page 205)

Make the chocolate soup, and serve it. Have each child complete the phrase "I'm good at ———," and have a discussion about how we're all good at something.

Play Season Charades: Write the names of the seasons on slips of paper. Draw a slip. Two or three children act out some activity typical of the season drawn, and the other students try to guess the season.

Invitation for Games Galore and Recipe for Peanut Butter Hors d'Oeuvres

Fill out the Invitation for Games Galore (page 197), and make sure each child gets a copy. Have children bring their favorite board games from home.

Gather supplies:

1. A serving tray
2. Napkins
3. The ingredients listed on the Recipe for Peanut Butter Hors d'Oeuvres (page 206)

Prepare and serve the Peanut Butter Hors d'Oeuvres. When most of the peanut butter appears to have been consumed, have the children play the board games they brought in. Let play continue on each game for a given period of time. Or play games based on your curriculum. For instance, Can-Do Backpack Bingo (see the Can-Do Backpack Bingo Board, page 161, explained on page 155) has a math slant. Or play Rhyme in Time, a reading game (see below).

Rhyme in Time Write out the following nursery rhymes, line by line.

Humpty Dumpty sat on a wall,
Humpty Dumpty had a great fall;
All the King's horses and all the King's men
Couldn't put Humpty together again.

Peter, Peter, pumpkin eater,
Had a wife and couldn't keep her;
He put her in a pumpkin shell
and there he kept her very well.

Star light, star bright,
First star I see tonight,
I wish I may, I wish I might,
Have the wish I wish tonight.

Georgie Porgie, pudding and pie,
Kissed the girls and made them cry;
When the boys came out to play,
Georgie Porgie ran away.

A-tisket, a-tasket,
A green and yellow basket;
I sent a letter to my love
And on the way I lost it.

Hickory, dickory, dock,
The mouse ran up the clock.
The clock struck one, the mouse ran down,
Hickory, dickory, dock.

Bye, baby bunting,
Daddy's gone a-hunting,
Gone to get a rabbit skin
To wrap the baby bunting in.

Sing a song of sixpence,
A pocket full of rye;
Four and twenty blackbirds,
Baked in a pie.

Cut the rhymes into one-line strips. Tape the strips to the walls around your classroom. Have each child take a strip of paper at random. Then, without talking, each child looks for the three other people who have lines in the same rhyme. When the four children find each other, they sit in order of their lines, raise their hands, and read their lines in order (each child delivering his or her own line).

Invitation for a Spring Fling and Recipe for Koala Cooler

Fill out the Invitation for a Spring Fling (page 198), and make sure each child gets a copy. Have each child bring a favorite record. Gather supplies:

1. A blender
2. Cups
3. Napkins
4. The ingredients listed on the Recipe for Koala Cooler (page 206)

Make the Koala Cooler, and serve it. Play the records while doing a quiet activity.

Invitation for a Summer Circus Celebration

Have the children who are interested prepare circus acts to perform. The children can play the animals in the animal acts. The children can make a small prop or wear a costume if they like. Here are some suggestions for acts:

Seal Show
Clown Around
Magnificent Magician
Crazy Cat
Dog Act
Gymnasts

Fill out the Invitation for a Summer Circus Celebration (page 199), and make sure each student gets a copy. You can also invite another class to be the audience for the circus acts. You might choose to have balloons at the celebration. Use Can-Do Coins (page 162) for admission and for purchasing the popcorn. Your students could earn the coins like compliments prior to the celebration.

Those of your students who are not performing circus acts can be circus workers:

Ticket takers
Popcorn vendors
Balloon vendors
Ringmaster for the circus acts

Before the Summer Circus Celebration, gather supplies:

1. A popcorn popper
2. Oil, popcorn, salt, and butter if you like
3. Large bowls to hold the popcorn
4. Cups
5. Napkins

On the big day, pop the popcorn, blow up the balloons, and let the festivities begin!

We're having a

POPCORN PICNIC!

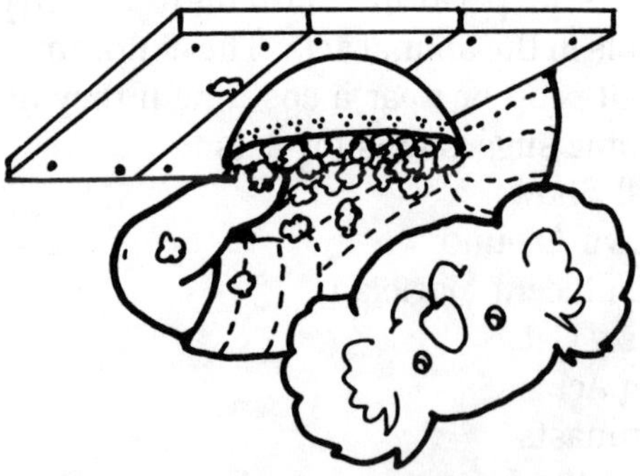

Date: ______________

Because: ______________

____

____

Chef Can-Do invites you to

MAGNIFICENT MONDAY

A celebration of success!

Menu:

FRIENDSHIP TEA
COLOSSAL COOKIE

Please bring: ____________________

____

Date: ____________________

WE DID IT!

Chef Can-Do
invites you to

TEA PARTY
TUESDAY

To celebrate
your success in

____

We worked hard for a

CHIP-N-DIP PARTY!

We'll celebrate on: ____________________

For: ____________________

Please bring: ____________________

____

Welcome to

WONDERFUL WEDNESDAY!

Our celebration of success

We'll be making

KOALA-ROO MALTED MILK

We'll send compliments to our friends, parents, and teacher!

Can-Do kids celebrate

THOUGHTFUL THURSDAY

On ______________________

A celebration of success

We worked hard to:

____

____

AND WE DID IT!

Menu:

DESSERT PIZZA

Please bring: ______________________

____

____

Can-Do invites you to

FABULOUS FRIDAY

Date ______________________

A celebration of our success

Koala-Roo Can-Do's birthday is on:

____

We'll make

KOALA CAKE!

Please bring: ______________________

____

____

We're celebrating success with a

KOALA-ROO CAN-DO BIRTHDAY PARTY!

Can-Do

Invites

____

Name

to celebrate on

____

Date

____

Place

Can-Do Invites

____
Name

to come to our class on

____

We're having an

I CAN DO IT
TALENT SHOW!

Date: ______________________

We'll make

KOALA APPLE CRISPY

Please bring: ______________________

____

____

Show us all
what you can do
at our

FALL FESTIVAL

We've accomplished our goal:

____

So we're having a

BOOK BASH!

Please bring: ____________________

____

____

____

Can-Do kids celebrate success with a

BOOK BASH

and Koala Frozen Yogurt

Date ____________________

Menu:

CHOCOLATE SOUP
À LA CAN-DO

Date: ____________________

We earned it by: ____________________

____

____

The Can-Do kids celebrate

SUCCESS IN ALL SEASONS

OUR GOAL WAS:

WE DID IT!

Please bring: __________

Date: __________

Celebrate success with

GAMES GALORE!

and Peanut Butter Hors d'Oeuvres

We'll make a
KOALA COOLER

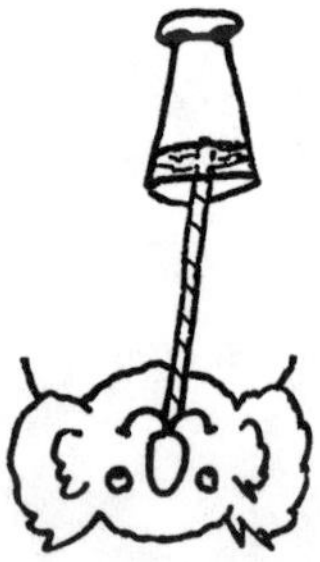

Date: ____________________

We tried ________________

____

AND WE DID IT!

Please bring a favorite record.

We're celebrating success with a

SPRING FLING

We'll celebrate

On: ____________________

Time: ____________________

CIRCUS ACTS:

Clown Can-Do invites you to a

SUMMER CIRCUS CELEBRATION

CHEF CAN~DO

COOKS WITH YOU

NAME ____________

Popcorn Picnic

Popcorn
Oil
Butter
Seasonings

Make popcorn, and put it in several bowls. Choose a seasoning to put on each bowlful. Suggested seasonings:

Dill weed and garlic salt
Grated cheddar or similar cheese
Celery salt
Grated parmesan with salt
Honey and cinnamon
Herb blend: ½ tsp each salt, thyme, basil, oregano, dill
Dry onion soup mixture

Melt the butter, and stir the seasoning into it. Pour the seasoned butter over the popcorn, and toss.

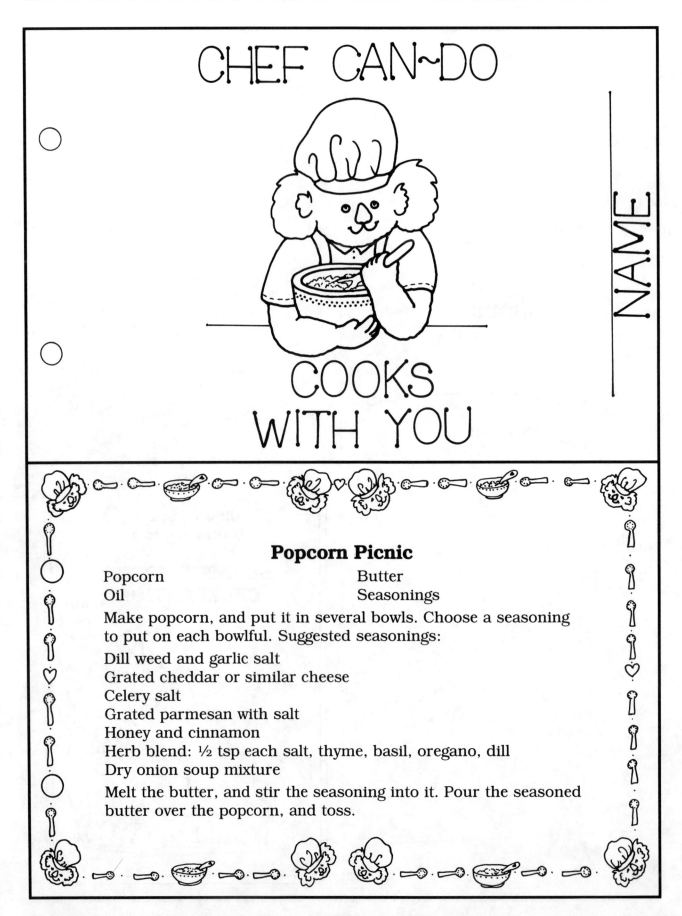

Colossal Cookie

1 cup margarine
½ cup white sugar
½ cup brown sugar
2 eggs
1 tsp vanilla
1 tsp baking soda
1 tsp salt
1 tsp cinnamon
½ tsp water
2¾ cups flour
1 cup oatmeal
1 pkg chocolate chips
½ cup nuts
Icing

Cream the margarine and sugar. Add the eggs, vanilla, soda, salt, cinnamon, and water. Slowly add the flour, oatmeal, chocolate chips, and nuts. Lightly grease a large pizza pan. Spread all the dough onto the pan. Use a wet table knife to smooth the edges. Use a spatula to smooth the top, forming one colossal cookie. Bake at 375 degrees for 20 minutes or until lightly brown. Frost the cookie by writing a slogan or saying on top. Store-bought icings in tubes can be used. Cut the cookie into pie slices to serve.

Bravo Garbanzo Dip

1 15- or 16-ounce can of garbanzo beans (chickpeas, ceci)
2 Tbsp mayonnaise
1 Tbsp plain yogurt
1 Tbsp tamari or soy sauce (optional)
1 tsp oil
½ tsp garlic powder
½ tsp dill weed
Salt to taste
Paprika to garnish

Whirl all the ingredients except the paprika in a food processor. Scrape the sides, and blend until smooth. Garnish with paprika.

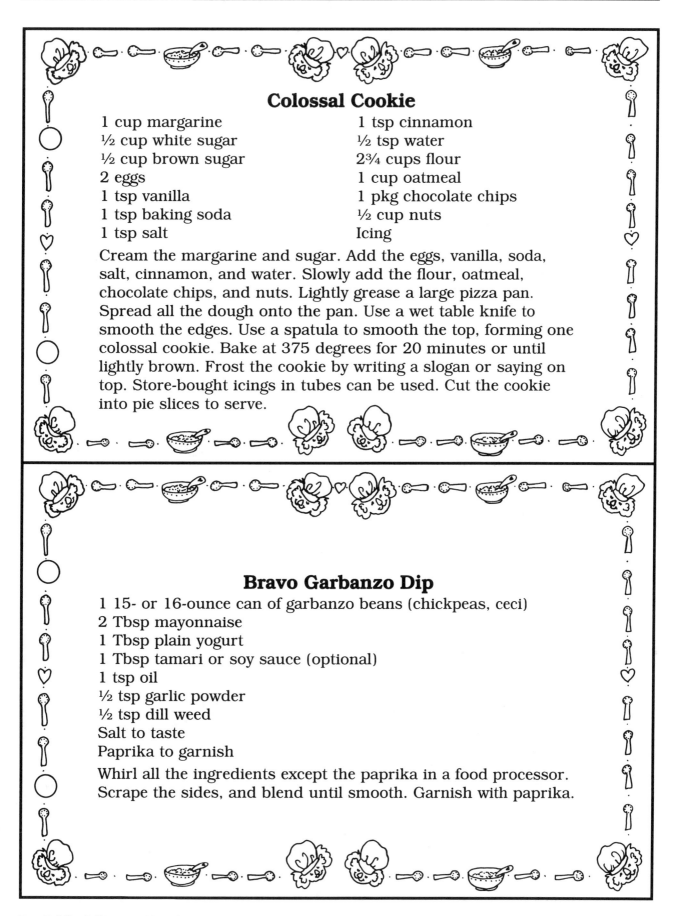

Terrific Tofu Dip

1 cake of firm tofu, broken into pieces
1 Tbsp mayonnaise
½ tsp garlic powder
1 tsp salt
½ tsp dill weed
1 Tbsp tamari or soy sauce (optional)
1 can of pitted olives

Blend all the ingredients except the olives. Cut the olives into small pieces, and add them to the creamy mixture.

Koala-Roo Malted Milk

2 cups milk
2 scoops of vanilla ice cream
¼ cup strawberries (fresh or frozen)
2 ice cubes
2 Tbsp vanilla malt (optional)

Blend all ingredients. One recipe makes enough Koala-Roo Malted Milk to fill twelve small cups.

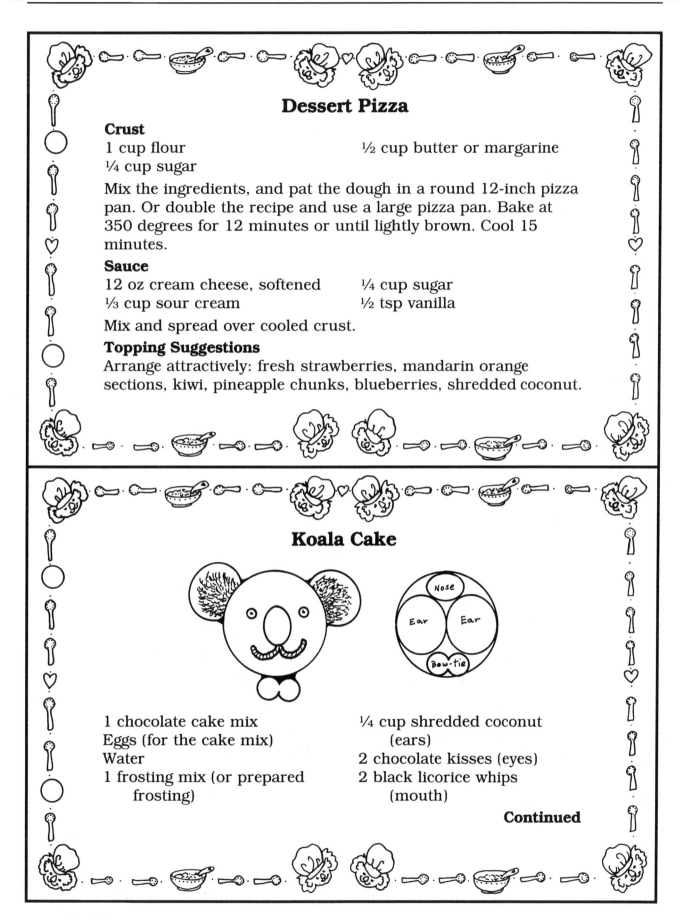

Dessert Pizza

Crust

1 cup flour
½ cup butter or margarine
¼ cup sugar

Mix the ingredients, and pat the dough in a round 12-inch pizza pan. Or double the recipe and use a large pizza pan. Bake at 350 degrees for 12 minutes or until lightly brown. Cool 15 minutes.

Sauce

12 oz cream cheese, softened
¼ cup sugar
⅓ cup sour cream
½ tsp vanilla

Mix and spread over cooled crust.

Topping Suggestions

Arrange attractively: fresh strawberries, mandarin orange sections, kiwi, pineapple chunks, blueberries, shredded coconut.

Koala Cake

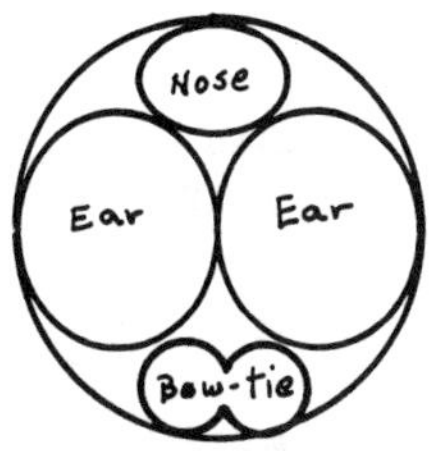

1 chocolate cake mix
Eggs (for the cake mix)
Water
1 frosting mix (or prepared frosting)

¼ cup shredded coconut (ears)
2 chocolate kisses (eyes)
2 black licorice whips (mouth)

Continued

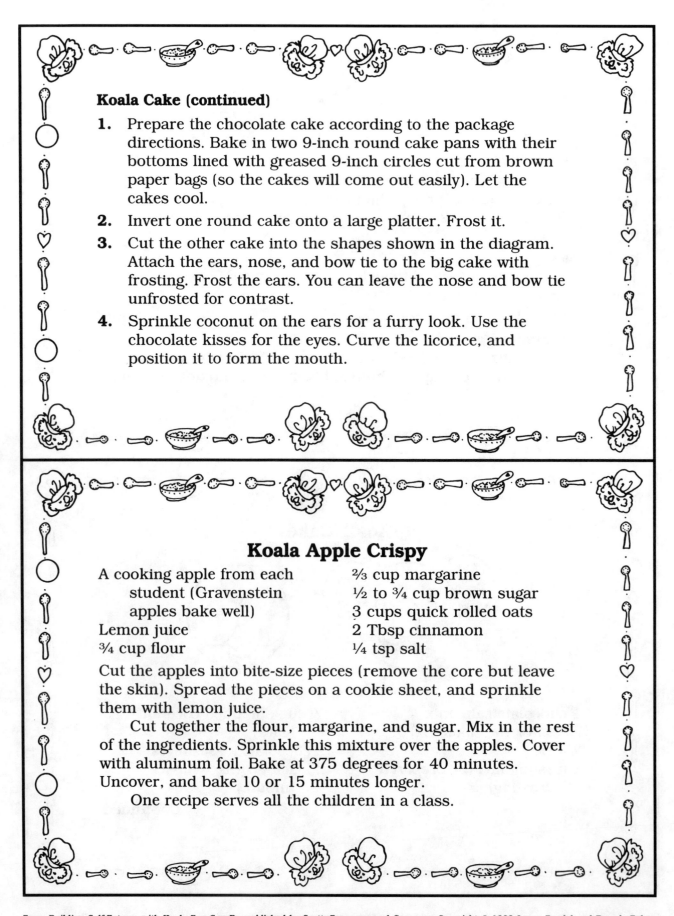

Koala Cake (continued)

1. Prepare the chocolate cake according to the package directions. Bake in two 9-inch round cake pans with their bottoms lined with greased 9-inch circles cut from brown paper bags (so the cakes will come out easily). Let the cakes cool.
2. Invert one round cake onto a large platter. Frost it.
3. Cut the other cake into the shapes shown in the diagram. Attach the ears, nose, and bow tie to the big cake with frosting. Frost the ears. You can leave the nose and bow tie unfrosted for contrast.
4. Sprinkle coconut on the ears for a furry look. Use the chocolate kisses for the eyes. Curve the licorice, and position it to form the mouth.

Koala Apple Crispy

A cooking apple from each student (Gravenstein apples bake well)
Lemon juice
¾ cup flour
⅔ cup margarine
½ to ¾ cup brown sugar
3 cups quick rolled oats
2 Tbsp cinnamon
¼ tsp salt

Cut the apples into bite-size pieces (remove the core but leave the skin). Spread the pieces on a cookie sheet, and sprinkle them with lemon juice.

Cut together the flour, margarine, and sugar. Mix in the rest of the ingredients. Sprinkle this mixture over the apples. Cover with aluminum foil. Bake at 375 degrees for 40 minutes. Uncover, and bake 10 or 15 minutes longer.

One recipe serves all the children in a class.

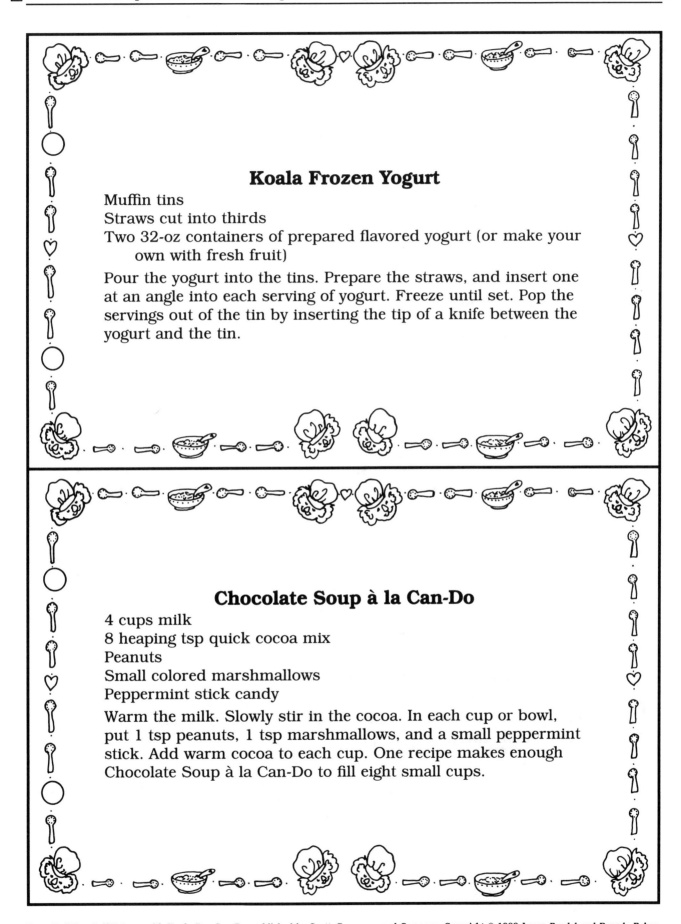

Koala Frozen Yogurt

Muffin tins
Straws cut into thirds
Two 32-oz containers of prepared flavored yogurt (or make your own with fresh fruit)

Pour the yogurt into the tins. Prepare the straws, and insert one at an angle into each serving of yogurt. Freeze until set. Pop the servings out of the tin by inserting the tip of a knife between the yogurt and the tin.

Chocolate Soup à la Can-Do

4 cups milk
8 heaping tsp quick cocoa mix
Peanuts
Small colored marshmallows
Peppermint stick candy

Warm the milk. Slowly stir in the cocoa. In each cup or bowl, put 1 tsp peanuts, 1 tsp marshmallows, and a small peppermint stick. Add warm cocoa to each cup. One recipe makes enough Chocolate Soup à la Can-Do to fill eight small cups.

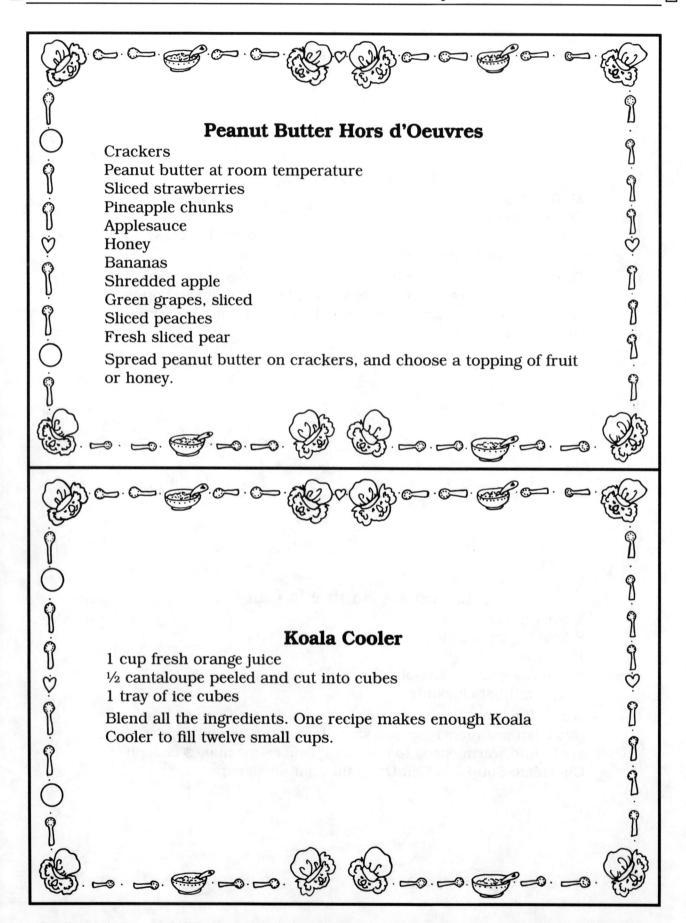

Peanut Butter Hors d'Oeuvres

Crackers
Peanut butter at room temperature
Sliced strawberries
Pineapple chunks
Applesauce
Honey
Bananas
Shredded apple
Green grapes, sliced
Sliced peaches
Fresh sliced pear

Spread peanut butter on crackers, and choose a topping of fruit or honey.

Koala Cooler

1 cup fresh orange juice
½ cantaloupe peeled and cut into cubes
1 tray of ice cubes

Blend all the ingredients. One recipe makes enough Koala Cooler to fill twelve small cups.

Suggested Reading

There are three sections in this bibliography: Books about Self-Esteem, Cookbooks: Ideas for Themes, and Books for Teachers.

The sections Books about Self-Esteem and Cookbooks: Ideas for Themes list books suitable for children.

Books about Self-Esteem

The titles are listed according to these categories:

Wishing You Were Someone Else
Handicaps
Emotions
Family
Friendship
Changing Stages in Life
View of the World
Finding Acceptance
Believing in Oneself
Making Decisions
Cultural Diversity

The books are recommended for classroom or recreational reading. Below each summary is a suggestion for extending the topic. Some books lend themselves well to a writing activity, bringing in the students' experiences. Other books may be good discussion starters, while some stories can be dramatized. You might use puppets or the children themselves to act out the story or to change the solution. Some books appear in different sections and are cross-referenced.

For your convenience an outline follows. (The entries themselves begin on page 209.)

Wishing You Were Someone Else

Alexander and the Windup Mouse
Dandelion
Donkey Donkey
Fish Is Fish
Freckle Juice
Jane, Wishing
The Luckiest One of All
Pezzettino

Handicaps

Apt. 3
A Button in Her Ear
Howie Helps Himself
My Brother Steven Is Retarded
Sally Can't See

Emotions

Adam Smith Goes to School
A Is for Angry
Being Adopted
Benjamin's 365 Birthdays
But Names Will Never Hurt Me
Eugene the Brave

The Fall of Freddie the Leaf
George and Martha
George and Martha Back in Town
Gilberto and the Wind
I Do Not Like It When My Friend Comes to Visit
I Don't Care
If I Were in Charge of the World and Other Worries
I Have Feelings
I'll Fix Anthony
It All Depends
It Could Always Be Worse
Lyle and the Birthday Party
Say It!
The Scared One
Sloppy Kisses
Whatever Happened to Beverly Bigler's Birthday?
Will It Be Okay?

Family
The Best Present Is Me
A Chair for My Mother
I'll Fix Anthony
My Uncle Nikos
Only the Best
The Relatives Came
Something Special for Me

Friendship
Amigo
A Bargain for Frances
George and Martha
I Do Not Like It When My Friend Comes to Visit
The New Friend
One Zillion Valentines
Rosie and Michael

Changing Stages in Life
Emma
The Fall of Freddie the Leaf
Ira Sleeps Over
Leo the Late Bloomer
Pig Pig Grows Up
The Quitting Deal
The Terrible Thing That Happened at Our House
When Will I Read?

View of the World
George and Martha Tons of Fun
Lazy Tommy Pumpkinhead
My Mother Is the Most Beautiful Woman in the World
The Shy Little Girl

Finding Acceptance
Crow Boy
Hector Penguin
The Hundred Dresses
Molly's Pilgrim
Sam
William's Doll
The Wonderful Little Boy

Believing in Oneself
Bodies
Chin Chiang and the Dragon's Dance
Daydreamers
Dumb Old Casey Is a Fat Tree
Eugene the Brave
The Fastest Quitter in Town
Fidelia
First Grade Takes a Test
Gilberto and the Wind
Gypsies' Magic Box
I Hate Red Rover
I'm Terrific
Land of Dreams
The Man Who Entered a Contest
Myra
Pumpernickel Tickle and Mean Green Cheese
The Quitting Deal
Swimmy
The 329th Friend
Try It Again, Sam

Making Decisions
The Bedspread
I Am a Big Help
I'll Tell on You
Lazy Tommy Pumpkinhead
The Quitting Deal
Something Special for Me
What Mary Jo Shared

Cultural Diversity

Amigo (Hispanic)
Being Adopted (interracial families)
But Names Will Never Hurt Me
The Butterflies Come
Chin Chiang and the Dragon's Dance (Chinese)
Cornrows (Black American)
Crow Boy (Japanese)
Daydreamers (Black American)
The Fastest Quitter in Town (Black American)
Fidelia (Hispanic)
Gilberto and the Wind (Hispanic)
Gypsies' Magic Box
How My Parents Learned to Eat (Japanese)
The Hundred Dresses (Polish)
It Could Always Be Worse (Jewish)
Molly's Pilgrim (Russian, Jewish)
Mr. Fong's Toy Shop (Chinese)
My Mother Is the Most Beautiful Woman in the World (Russian)
My Uncle Nikos (Greek)
Only the Best (Jewish)
Sam (Black American)
The Scared One (Native American)
What Mary Jo Shared (Black American)
Where The Buffaloes Begin (Native American)

Wishing You Were Someone Else

Alexander and the Windup Mouse

Leo Lionni (Pantheon, 1969)

Alexander wishes he could be like his friend Willy, the toy mouse, and be loved rather than be frightened away by the broom. He changes his mind when Willy is tossed in a box of discarded toys, and so Alexander goes into the forest and asks the lizard to change Willy into a real mouse. Be happy with who you are. "The grass is always greener."

- Acting
- Writing

Dandelion

Don Freeman (The Viking Press, 1964)

Dandelion is invited to a party. He has his mane coifed and buys new clothes that are very fancy but is not allowed into the party because the hostess doesn't recognize him. After a rainstorm messes his mane and he changes his clothes, he appears again at the party. Everyone is happy to see him, and he is happy to be himself. He says, "I'll always be just plain me."

- Discussion

Donkey Donkey

Roger Duvoisin (Parents' Magazine Press, 1968)

Donkey Donkey is not happy with how he looks. He asks the advice of other animals. They give him reasons why he should keep his ears to the side or in front of him instead of the way he keeps them naturally. When a little girl tells her father how beautiful the donkey's ears naturally are, he is happy.

- Discussion

Fish Is Fish

Leo Lionni (Pantheon, 1970)

Accept who you are.

- Discussion

Freckle Juice

Judy Blume, illustrated by Sonia O. Lisker (Four Winds Press, 1971)

Andrew really wants to have freckles like his friend. Sharon sells him the formula for getting freckles.

- Acting
- Discussion
- Writing

Jane, Wishing

Tobi Tobias, illustrated by Trina S. Hyman (Viking Press, 1977)

Jane wishes she looked different and had other experiences. Finally, she comes to the realization that these things won't happen, so she decides to accept herself just the way she is.

- Writing

The Luckiest One of All

Bill Peet (Houghton Mifflin, 1982)

A boy, animals, and inanimate objects all wish they were something or someone else. The theme is: Look at your positive side.

- Discussion
- Writing

Pezzettino
Leo Lionni (Pantheon, 1975)

In Italian, *pezzettino* means "little piece." Pezzettino doubts himself because he is so small. He tries to find out if he is part of something else—a larger whole. He discovers that he himself has smaller parts and so he himself is a larger whole: being small is okay.
- Discussion

Handicaps

Apt. 3
Ezra Jack Keats (The Macmillan Company, 1971)

Sam and his brother, Ben, observe the sounds and happenings in their apartment building. They are scared about Apt. 3 until they meet the blind tenant, who shares a secret and plays the harmonica for them. They love his music, and a friendship begins.
- Discussion

A Button in Her Ear
Ada B. Litchfield, illustrated by Eleanor Mill (Albert Whitman & Co., 1976)

Angela has trouble hearing what people say to her. Her parents take her to a doctor. She is fitted with a hearing aid. She is proud of what it does and shares it with the class at school.
- Discussion

Howie Helps Himself
Joan Fassler, illustrated by Joe Lasker (Albert Whitman & Co., 1975)

Howie has a handicap, and because of weak legs and arms, he must use a wheelchair. His wish is to be able to zoom around in his wheelchair without help. He tries hard and almost gives up but finally does it for his dad. He and his dad are so proud that it doesn't matter how weak or strong the boy's arms are. It's how he feels inside that counts. The themes are reaching your own goals and being proud.
- Discussion
- Writing

My Brother Steven Is Retarded
Harriet Langsam Sobol, photographs by Patricia Agre (Macmillan Publishing Co., 1977)

Beth has a retarded brother. She tells of her frustrations, hurts, fears, and embarrassments. She explains to a new friend, coming to her house to play, about Steven, so the friend will be prepared and will understand. (Follow up with a discussion of family honesty, patience, and loving each other no matter what.)
- Discussion
- Writing

Sally Can't See
Palle Peterson (The John Day Company, 1974)

The book describes Sally's life as a blind child, including what she learns in her special school, and touches on her feelings and frustrations.
- Discussion

Emotions

Adam Smith Goes to School
Bernard Wolf (Lippincott Jr. Books, 1978)

It's Adam's first day of school. The book follows the routine of the entire first day. (Follow up with a discussion after the children describe their first day of school. How is the first day of each school year the same or different? Have the children talk about impressions, feelings, and sensory perceptions.)
- Discussion
- Writing

A Is for Angry
Sandra Boynton (Workman Publishing, 1983)

Subtitled *An Animal and Adjective Alphabet*, this book presents emotion words that you could use to initiate discussions of anger, bashfulness, fear, grumpiness, kindness, outrage, playfulness, and vanity. Use the book in vocabulary development.
- Discussion

Being Adopted
Maxine B. Rosenberg, photographs by George Ancona (Lothrop, Lee & Shepard Books, 1984)

The book explores the frustrating emotions of being adopted, feelings about being a different nationality or race from the adopted family, and being proud of one's nationality. (Follow up with a discussion of families, sticking together, and loving each other. Love is not bound by physical appearance.)
- Discussion

Benjamin's 365 Birthdays
Judi Barrett, illustrated by Ron Barrett (Atheneum, 1974)

The book's subject is the possibility of recreating the excitement of one's birthday each day of the year, trying to capture every day the happiness found in birthdays. Benjamin discovers that he doesn't ever really need another birthday present, since everything around him is and always will be a gift.

- Discussion
- Writing

But Names Will Never Hurt Me
Bernard Waber (Houghton Mifflin Co., 1976)

Her name is Allison Wonderland. Her mother tells the story of how her name was chosen: such love went into it! In school, Allison gets a lot of teasing, but she grows in her sense of self-worth and is no longer affected by jeers.

- Discussion

Eugene the Brave
Ellen Conford, illustrated by John Larrecq (Little, Brown & Co., 1978)

Eugene, a possum, is afraid of the dark. Geraldine tries to help him overcome his fear, and he ends up saving her when she falls into a hole. By acting in this crisis, he overcomes his fear.

- Acting
- Writing

The Fall of Freddie the Leaf
Leo Buscaglia (Charles B. Slack, Inc., 1982)

Subtitled *A Story of Life for All Ages*, this book, with beautiful photographs of the seasons, tells a story about life, individual worth, fears, and death.

- Discussion

George and Martha
James Marshall (Houghton Mifflin, 1972)

The book's themes are being honest with friends and accepting the honesty of friends.

- Acting
- Discussion

George and Martha Back in Town
James Marshall (Houghton Mifflin, 1984)

In one story, George decides to jump from the high board. Martha easily convinces him not to do it: she says she herself couldn't do it. When she in fact jumps off, he is afraid. Another story deals with speaking of loneliness to another and then sharing time with that other person.

- Acting
- Writing

Gilberto and the Wind
Marie Hall Ets (Viking Press, 1963)

Gilberto plays with the wind. The story shows what a child can do. It focuses on discovery and feelings of laughter, fear, and joy.

- Discussion

I Do Not Like It When My Friend Comes to Visit
Ivan Sherman (Harcourt Brace, 1973)

A child talks about the negative emotions she feels when her friend comes over. She likes the friend but dislikes the experience of having the friend on her territory.

- Discussion
- Writing

I Don't Care
Marjorie Weinman Sharmat, illustrated by Lillian Hoban (Macmillan Publishing, 1977)

Jonathan's balloon blows into the sky. He tries to convince himself that he doesn't care. He tells his parents that repeatedly. Finally, he cries and cries and releases his emotion.

- Discussion
- Writing

If I Were in Charge of the World and Other Worries
Judith Viorst, illustrated by Lynne Cherry (Atheneum, 1982)

Subtitled *Poems for Children and Their Parents*, this book contains poems about personal worries.

- Discussion
- Writing

I Have Feelings
Terry Berger, photographs by Howard Spivak (Human Sciences Press, 1971)

This wonderful discussion starter deals with emotions and feelings in real life.

- Discussion

I'll Fix Anthony
Judith Viorst, illustrated by Arnold Lobel (Harper and Row, 1969)

The book's topic is sibling rivalry: what we might dislike about a brother or sister.

- Writing

It All Depends
Jane Yolen, illustrated by Don Bolognese (Funk and Wagnalls, 1969)

David asks his mother how big he is. She replies, "In relationship to what?" It all depends.

- Discussion

It Could Always Be Worse
Margot Zemach (Farrar, Straus, Giroux, 1976)

This book is about putting problems into perspective.

- Discussion
- Writing

Lyle and the Birthday Party
Bernard Waber (Houghton Mifflin, 1966)

Lyle the Crocodile is jealous of Joshua's birthday party. He tries to cover up his jealousy. The book touches on how to change one's own mood.

- Discussion

Say It!
Charlotte Zolotow, illustrated by James Stevenson (Greenwillow Books, 1980)

A little girl and her mother take a walk on an autumn day and share the beauty of fall. The child repeatedly asks her mother to "say it." Finally, the mother tells the child she loves her. (Follow up with a discussion of expressing feelings to people—telling them that we love them or that we need them to love us. We all need love.)

- Discussion
- Writing

The Scared One
Dennis Haseley, illustrated by Deborah Howland (Frederick Warne, 1983)

The story takes place in an Indian village. The protagonist is called the Scared One because he is afraid of many things. He discovers an injured bird, and what happens to the bird gives him courage.

This book is for older primary students.

- Acting

Sloppy Kisses
Elizabeth Winthrop, illustrated by Anne Burgess (Macmillan Publishing Co., 1980)

Why are kisses and hugs so important? How do people show love and affection? Emmy Lou, a lovable pig, is convinced by her friend that kissing is for babies. She stops kissing her family but finds that she misses the affection and can't sleep.

- Discussion
- Writing

Whatever Happened to Beverly Bigler's Birthday?
Barbara Williams, illustrated by Emily McCully (Harcourt, Brace, Jovanovich, 1979)

It is Beverly Bigler's birthday, but it is also her sister's wedding day. It seems that everyone has forgotten her birthday. Beverly Bigler gets into lots of mischief looking for her cake and presents. She is surprised by her teacher and friends.

- Writing

Will It Be Okay?
Crescent Dragonwagon, illustrated by Ben Shecter (Harper and Row, 1977)

A child has many fears, and her mother offers creative ways to cope with the fears. The theme is overcoming realistic and unrealistic fears.

- Discussion
- Writing

Family

The Best Present Is Me
Janet Wolf (Harper and Row, 1984)

A girl enjoys visiting her grandparents every Sunday. She makes a picture of herself to give her grandma as a birthday present, and then the girl can't find the picture when it's time to give the gift to her grandmother. Her grandmother understands, hugs her, and says, "The best present is you." The elevator man finds the picture and brings it to the girl. (Follow up with a discussion of families and the foods, sights, sounds, and smells associated with grandparents' or other relatives' homes.)

- Discussion
- Writing

A Chair for My Mother
Vera B. Williams (Greenwillow Books, 1982)

A fire destroys the home. Money is saved to buy a special chair. This is a story of love in a family and of overcoming tragedy.

- Discussion
- Writing

I'll Fix Anthony
See under Emotions, above.

My Uncle Nikos
Julie Delton, illustrated by Marc Simont (Thomas Y. Crowell, 1983)

Helena, a young girl, goes to visit her uncle in a small village in Greece. They form a close bond. The story describes a way of life.

- Discussion
- Writing

Only the Best
Meguido Zola, illustrated by Valerie Littlewood (Julia MacRae Books, 1981)

The father of a newborn girl wants to give her the very best gift of all. He makes inquiries with many local merchants. In the end, he gives her the best gift of all, his love.

- Discussion

The Relatives Came
Cynthia Rylant, illustrated by Stephen Gammell (Bradbury Press, 1985)

A warm, loving, hugging story about families visiting together. (Follow up with a discussion of what families need. What can families share? Tell about things your family likes to do together. Talk about favorite relatives.)

- Discussion
- Writing

Something Special for Me
Vera B. Williams (Greenwillow Books, 1983)

The subject is making choices about spending money on oneself. The story expresses the love in one family.

- Discussion
- Writing

Friendship

Amigo
Byrd Baylor Schweitzer, illustrated by Garth Williams (Macmillan Co., 1963)

Francisco, a Mexican boy, wants a pet, so he tames a prairie dog. Amigo, the prairie dog, wants to tame himself a boy. A special nonverbal communication builds trust and friendship between them.

- Discussion

A Bargain for Frances
Russel Hoban, illustrated by Lillian Hoban (Harper and Row, 1970)

The book's themes are understanding the motives of friends, solving the problem when a friend deceives, and remaining friends rather than holding a grudge.

- Acting
- Discussion

George and Martha
See under Emotions, above.

I Do Not Like It When My Friend Comes to Visit
See under Emotions, above.

The New Friend
Charlotte Zolotow, illustrated by Emily Arnold McCully (Thomas Y. Crowell, 1981)

A girl has a special friend. They share the wonders of the woods. She goes to find her friend another day and sees that her friend has someone else to play with. She cries and cries. She dreams she has a new friend. (Follow up with a discussion of the question of who her special friend was playing with: perhaps it was a relative. Why didn't she join in with the two other girls? Was the child making assumptions not based on reality? If your friend plays with someone else, does that mean your friendship is over? Can you have many friends?)

- Acting
- Discussion

One Zillion Valentines
Frank Modell (Greenwillow Books, 1981)

What is a zillion? Two boys make valentines to show friendship to lots of friends. One boy has a negative outlook, and the other uses his creativity and positive nature to good effect.

- Discussion

Rosie and Michael

Judith Viorst, illustrated by Lorna Tomei (Atheneum, 1974)

Friendship overcomes all problems. Friendship means being able to count on another person. (Follow up with a discussion of how Rosie and Michael stuck up for each other. Think of a time when you backed up your friend.)

- Discussion
- Writing

Changing Stages in Life

Emma

Wendy Kesselman, illustrated by Barbara Cooney (Doubleday & Co., 1980)

Emma is lonely. For her seventy-second birthday, her family gives her a painting of her hometown. She is then motivated to paint it the way it looks to her. She begins to paint. She turns her hobby into an avocation, and this brings friends and family to visit her successful gallery of paintings. She is no longer lonely.

- Discussion

The Fall of Freddie the Leaf

See under Emotions, above.

Ira Sleeps Over

Bernard Waber (Houghton Mifflin, 1972)

The book's themes are making decisions, changing decisions, and accepting the stage of development we are experiencing.

- Acting
- Discussion
- Writing

Leo the Late Bloomer

Robert Kraus, illustrated by Jose Aruego (Windmill Books, 1971)

Leo the tiger can't do anything. His parents are patient, knowing that one day soon he will be able to read, write, and eat neatly like his other animal friends. One day he blooms, and he's proud.

- Discussion

Pig Pig Grows Up

David McPhail (E.P. Dutton, 1980)

Pig Pig doesn't want to grow up. By stopping a runaway baby stroller, he comes to the rescue. He decides to grow. Changing stages are hard in our lives. Accepting new responsibility can be difficult.

- Acting

The Quitting Deal

Tobi Tobias, illustrated by Trina Schart Hyman (Viking Press, 1975)

The child needs to stop sucking her thumb, and the mother wants to stop smoking. They try various methods to solve their problem. They both decide that they can't give up their needs to have something in their mouths, so they compromise and try to cut down.

- Discussion

The Terrible Thing That Happened at Our House

Marge Blaine, illustrated by John C. Wallner (Four Winds Press, 1975)

Changes occur in a family when mom goes back to work. The book's themes are bearing the frustrations of a new situation that isn't "how it used to be" and learning to grow in new circumstances. The story tells how the family solves their problems and brainstorms to make compromises.

- Discussion
- Writing

When Will I Read?

Miriam Cohen, illustrated by Lillian Hoban (Greenwillow Books, 1977)

The theme is the joy of being able to read when you're ready.

- Discussion

View of the World

George and Martha Tons of Fun

James Marshall (Houghton Mifflin, 1980)

In one story, George tries to concentrate on practicing handstands. In another story, Martha discovers how to laugh at herself. The theme is one's view of oneself versus the view of others.

- Discussion
- Writing

Lazy Tommy Pumpkinhead
William Pène Du Bois (Harper & Row, 1966)

Lazy Tommy Pumpkinhead lives in an electric house. Everything is done for him. A storm hits one night, and the electricity goes out. Everything goes wrong. What will he do?

- Acting
- Discussion
- Writing

My Mother Is the Most Beautiful Woman in the World
Recky Reyher, illustrated by Ruth Gannett (Lothrop, 1945)

We do not love people because they are beautiful, but they seem beautiful to us because we love them, according to an old Russian proverb. What makes people beautiful to us? What is special about your mother or father?

- Acting
- Discussion

The Shy Little Girl
Phyllis Krasilovsky, illustrated by Trina Schart Hyman (Houghton Mifflin, 1970)

Anne is shy and doesn't like her own facial features. She has low self-esteem around other children until a new girl in school seeks her out and tells her what she admires in her. The theme is how other people's impressions of you can affect how you feel about yourself.

- Acting
- Discussion

Finding Acceptance

Crow Boy
Taro Yashima (The Viking Press, 1955)

Chibi goes to a village school in Japan. He has a hard time learning, and the children tease him until one day in a talent show he performs all kinds of crow sounds. The children are impressed and are ashamed that they misjudged him. Chibi is renamed Crow Boy, and he feels pride in his new name.

- Acting
- Discussion

Hector Penguin
Louise Fatio, illustrated by Roger Duvoisin (McGraw Hill, 1973)

Hector Penguin is lost in the forest. The other animals ridicule him and try to convince him he is not a bird. His feelings are hurt, and his pride is shattered. A crow finally puts the other animals in their place, and Hector proves his abilities. (Follow up with a discussion about being proud of who you are and how to overcome ridicule and cruel teasing.)

- Acting
- Discussion

The Hundred Dresses
Eleanor Estes, illustrated by Louis Slobodkin (Harcourt, Brace & Co., 1944)

Wanda Petronski had been teased by the other children because she was Polish and poor. She always wore the same blue dress. The other girls boasted about their new dresses, so Wanda told them she had one hundred dresses lined up in her closet. Wanda wins a coloring contest in school with her hundred dresses, which turn out to be one hundred drawings of dresses. She and her family move away. Peggy, a sort of friend to Wanda, feels remorse and writes to Wanda.

- Acting
- Discussion
- Writing

Molly's Pilgrim
Barbara Cohen, illustrated by Michael J. Deraney (Lothrop, Lee & Shepard Books, 1983)

Molly is a Russian Jewish immigrant child. She is teased in school and very much wants to be accepted. One day she brings a Pilgrim doll that her mother made for her Thanksgiving project and discovers that she is a pilgrim, too.

- Discussion
- Acting
- Writing

Sam
Ann Herbert Scott, illustrated by Symeon Shimin (McGraw-Hill, 1967)

Sam wants to help each person in the family. Each one tells him to find someone else. His feel-

ings are hurt until finally everyone understands, the air is cleared, and he helps his mom.
- Acting
- Discussion

William's Doll
Charlotte Zolotow, illustrated by William Pène Du Bois (Harper & Row, 1972)

William wants a doll. His brother says that wanting a doll is creepy and sissyish. His father bought him an electric train, but William wants to take care of a doll like a father would. His grandmother understands and buys him the doll so he'll practice being a father. (Follow up with a discussion: Should a boy have a doll? What can you say when kids tease you about being a sissy?)
- Discussion
- Writing

The Wonderful Little Boy
Helen E. Buckley, illustrated by Rob Howard (Lothrop, Lee & Shepard, 1970)

A little boy is the smallest and youngest in the family. He gets criticism from everyone except his grandmother, who praises the stage he's experiencing and the interests he has. The themes are dealing with criticism and finding acceptance from someone or enjoyment in what you can do well.
- Discussion

Believing in Oneself

Bodies
Barbara Brenner, photographs by George Ancona (E.P. Dutton, 1973)

The book's topics are the importance of accepting your physical appearance and the ways that all people are alike.
- Discussion

Chin Chiang and the Dragon's Dance
Ian Wallace (Atheneum, 1984)

Chin Chiang dreams of dancing the dragon's dance in the Chinese New Year parade. The time has come, but he feels clumsy. He finds a friend, an older woman who danced the dragon's dance as a young woman, and she teaches Chin Chiang.
- Acting
- Discussion
- Writing

Daydreamers
Eloise Greenfield, illustrated by Tom Feelings

The book's themes are daydreaming, wishing, planning, and growing into men and women.
- Writing

Dumb Old Casey Is a Fat Tree
Barbara Bottner (Harper & Row, 1979)

Casey's overwhelming desire to become a dancer indirectly helps her to lose weight, overcome teasing, and gain enormous self-esteem.
- Discussion
- Acting

Eugene the Brave
See under Emotions, above.

The Fastest Quitter in Town
Phyllis Green, illustrated by Lorenzo Lynch (Young Scott Books, 1972)

The powerful theme of not quitting on yourself underlies this story. Johnny Colmer often quits before the baseball game is over. He tries to control his anger but can't seem to change his behavior. He helps great-grandfather find a lost ring and discovers that he does have patience and determination.
- Discussion
- Acting

Fidelia
Ruth Adams, illustrated by Ati Forberg (Lothrop, Lee & Shepard Co., 1970)

Fidelia Ortega wants to play the violin in the school orchestra, but everyone thinks she is too young. She proves her readiness by her strong desire to play and her determination.
- Acting
- Discussion

First Grade Takes a Test
Miriam Cohen, illustrated by Lillian Hoban (Greenwillow Books, 1980)

The elements of tests are not always logical to children. This story is about a first grade class that takes a test and then discusses the things tests don't measure.
- Discussion

Gilberto and the Wind
See under Emotions, above.

Gypsies' Magic Box

Christopher Neal, illustrated by Marion Keen (New Paradigm, 1982)

Norman Anthony wants to be a success, but he doesn't know how. He meets King Gypsy. They strike a deal, and for Norman's money, King Gypsy gives him a carved wooden box that is sealed. Inside is the secret to success. Norman is not to open it until King Gypsy dies. Norman takes the box everywhere. He makes good grades in school, works hard at his job, and graduates from high school. He hears that King Gypsy has died, and although he knows he's a success, he opens the box. What is in the box? How did Norman become a success?

- Discussion

I Hate Red Rover

Joan M. Lexau, illustrated by Gail Owens (E.P. Dutton, 1979)

Jill hates to play Red Rover because she is not good at the game and the other children laugh at her. She and her grandfather share their problems. Jill overcomes her fears and becomes good at Red Rover. She and her grandfather learn to laugh at themselves.

- Acting
- Discussion

I'm Terrific

Marjorie Weinman Sharmat, illustrated by Kay Chorao (Holiday House, 1977)

Jason Everett Bear thinks he's terrific. He gives himself compliments and stars. But he also boasts to his friends. They tease him. He tries behaving another way, and that also sends his friends away. In the end, he decides who he is.

- Acting
- Discussion
- Writing

Land of Dreams

Michael Foreman (Holt, Rinehart and Winston, 1982)

An old man and a boy find pieces of dreams and put them together. A giant comes along and helps. The giant finds a dream that takes him back into the world again. What is your dream that you will follow?

- Discussion
- Writing

The Man Who Entered a Contest

Phyllis Krasilovsky, illustrated by Yuri Salzman (Doubleday & Co., 1980)

A man liked to bake cakes. The more he baked, the more creative he became. His oven broke down. He entered a cake-baking contest to win a new stove. He made such a splendid batter that it covered all the things in his kitchen. He won the contest. How did he win? What was his success as a baker?

- Discussion

Myra

Barbara Bottner (MacMillan, 1979)

By trying too hard in her dance class, Myra becomes annoying to those around her.

- Writing

Pumpernickel Tickle and Mean Green Cheese

Nancy Patz (Franklin Watts, 1978)

Benjamin is supposed to go to the store to buy some food, and he's afraid he'll forget what to buy. He and his elephant get mixed up over the words but are very proud when they remember what they came to buy.

- Acting
- Discussion

The Quitting Deal

See under Changing Stages in Life, above.

Swimmy

Leo Lionni (Pantheon Books, 1963)

The book's topics are believing in oneself, solving problems to achieve what one desires, and choosing to make the best of a situation.

- Discussion

The 329th Friend

Marjorie Weinman Sharmat, illustrated by Cyndy Szekeres (Four Winds Press, 1979)

Emery the Raccoon thinks of himself as rotten. He is lonely, so he invites 328 guests to lunch, hoping he will make new friends. He finds a wonderful friend in himself. How can you find a friend in yourself?

- Discussion

Try It Again, Sam
Judith Viorst, illustrated by Paul Galdone (Lothrop, Lee & Shepard Co., 1970)

To walk safely across town, Sam had to follow his mother's rules. He kept trying and trying again.

- Discussion

Making Decisions

The Bedspread
Sylvia Fair (William Morrow and Co., 1982)

Two elderly women who live in bed become bored and begin to solve their problem by decorating their bedspread. They find happiness in their creativity.

- Acting
- Discussion
- Writing

I Am a Big Help
Martin Parry (Greenwillow Books, 1980)

Young mouse is a great help around the house. He can do lots of things to help out. The book helps children organize the task of cleaning their own rooms.

- Discussion

I'll Tell on You
Joan Lexau, illustrated by Gail Owens (E.P. Dutton, 1976)

Rose and Mark are good friends. Rose wants to make the baseball team, and Mark is helping her practice. Mark's dog bites the coach's daughter, and Rose and Mark face the dilemma of whether to tell the coach, fearing they won't make the team.

- Acting
- Discussion

Lazy Tommy Pumpkinhead
See under View of the World, above.

The Quitting Deal
See under Changing Stages in Life, above.

Something Special for Me
See under Family, above.

What Mary Jo Shared
Janice May Udry, illustrated by Eleanor Mill (Albert Whitman & Co., 1966)

Mary Jo doesn't know what to share in school. She ends up sharing her father. She is very proud.

- Acting
- Discussion

Cultural Diversity

Amigo
See under Friendship, above.

Being Adopted
See under Emotions, above.

But Names Will Never Hurt Me
See under Emotions, above.

The Butterflies Come
Leo Politi (Charles Scribner's Sons, 1957)

Stephen and Lucia live on the Monterey peninsula in California and await the return of the Monarch butterflies. They play-act the time when the Indians lived in the area.

- Acting
- Discussion

Chin Chiang and the Dragon's Dance
See under Believing in Oneself, above.

Cornrows
Camille Yarbrough, illustrated by Carole Byard (Coward McCann and Geoghegan, Inc., 1979)

While Great Grammaw and Mama braid hair in rows, they tell about the history of Africa and of modern-day black people. Shirley Ann glows with pride as she learns about her heritage and the art form of braiding cornrows that look like the rows of corn in the fields.

- Discussion

Crow Boy
See under Finding Acceptance, above.

Daydreamers
See under Believing in Oneself, above.

The Fastest Quitter in Town
See under Believing in Oneself, above.

Fidelia
See under Believing in Oneself, above.

Gilberto and the Wind
See under Emotions, above.

Gypsies' Magic Box
See under Believing in Oneself, above.

How My Parents Learned to Eat
Ina R. Friedman, illustrated by Allen Say (Houghton Mifflin Co., 1984)

A Japanese woman and an American serviceman court and learn each other's customs, including table manners. The story is told long after the fact by their daughter, who takes pride in sharing both cultures.

- Discussion

The Hundred Dresses
See under Finding Acceptance, above.

It Could Always Be Worse
See under Emotions, above.

Molly's Pilgrim
See under Finding Acceptance, above.

Mr. Fong's Toy Shop
Leo Politi (Charles Scribner's Sons, 1978)

Mr. Fong makes and sells toys in Chinatown in Los Angeles. He tells children stories of ancient China. They share friendship, cultural heritage, and holidays.

- Discussion

My Mother Is the Most Beautiful Woman in the World
See under View of the World, above.

My Uncle Nikos
See under Family, above.

Only the Best
See under Family, above.

Sam
See under Finding Acceptance, above.

The Scared One
See under Emotions, above.

What Mary Jo Shared
See under Making Decisions, above.

Where the Buffaloes Begin
Olaf Baker, illustrated by Stephen Gammell (Frederick Warne, 1981)

The story has the tone of legend or dream. Little Wolf finds the lake where the buffaloes begin. The buffaloes appear. Off into the night ride Little Wolf and the herd. In the end his people are saved. The description of the prairie allows the reader almost to be there.

- Discussion

Cookbooks: Ideas for Themes

The Little Witch's Black Magic Cookbook

Linda Glovach (Prentice-Hall Inc., 1972)

This book presents delightful, unusual recipes that children can make easily.

The Pooh Cook Book

Virginia H. Ellison, illustrated by Ernest H. Shepard (E.P. Dutton, 1969)

Inspired by the A. A. Milne books *Winnie-the-Pooh* and *The House at Pooh Corner*, this cookbook can provide recipes for special lunches or snacks.

Slumps, Grunts and Snickerdoodles: What Colonial America Ate and Why

Lila Perl, illustrated by Richard Cuffari (Seabury Press, 1975)

The book is inspired by the history of early America: the New England colonies, the middle Atlantic colonies, the southern Colonies, and the American Indians. The book can enhance your unit on Thanksgiving or your study of family heritage. By studying their history and partaking of culinary delights based on historical recipes, your students can appreciate qualities of their heritage and feel pride in their background.

Books for Teachers

Berne, Patricia H., and Louis M. Savary. *Building Self-Esteem in Children.* New York: Continuum, 1985.

Borba, Michele, and Craig Borba. *Self-Esteem: A Classroom Affair.* Minneapolis: Winston Press, 1978.

———. *Self-Esteem: A Classroom Affair.* Volume 2. Minneapolis: Winston Press, 1982.

Branden, Nathaniel. *How to Raise Your Self-Esteem.* Toronto: Bantam Books, 1987.

———. *The Psychology of Self-Esteem.* Toronto: Bantam Books, 1969.

Briggs, Dorothy Corkille. *Your Child's Self-Esteem.* New York: Doubleday, 1975.

Clemes, Harris, and Reynold Bean. *How To Raise Children's Self-Esteem.* Los Angeles: Price/Stern/Sloan, 1986.

Clarke, Jean Illsley. *Self-Esteem: A Family Affair.* Minneapolis: Winston Press, 1978.

McGinnis, Alan Loy. *Bringing Out the Best in People.* Minneapolis: Augsburg, 1985.

Miller, Maureen. *To Share with Your Children: Activities to Help Them Feel Worthwhile.* Niles, Ill.: Argus Communications, 1978.

Purkey, William W. *Self Concept and School Achievement.* Englewood Cliffs, N.J.: Prentice Hall, 1970.

Smith, Sally L. *No Easy Answers: The Learning Disabled Child at Home and at School.* Toronto: Bantam Books, 1980.

Index

Absentee Pouch, 44
use of, 21
Apple Compliment Grid, 120
use of, 115
on Can-Do reading pocket, 139
Apples, 146
use of, 140
with A Tree for All Seasons, 21
Assignment sheet. *See* Koala-Roo Assignment Sheet
Awards. *See* Can-Do Awards

Backpack bingo. *See* Can-Do Backpack Bingo Board
Backpack Compliment Grid, 121
use of, 115
on Can-Do reading pocket, 139
Balloon Compliment Grid, 122
use of, 115
Balloon Detailed Compliment Grids 1 and 2, 135–136
use of, 117
Be Proud Poster, 32
use of, 18
Bingo. *See* Can-Do Backpack Bingo Board
Birthday card. *See* Can-Do Birthday Card
Blue ribbons. *See* Can-Do Blue Ribbons
Book Bash. *See* Invitation for a Book Bash
Bookmark mobile. *See* Koala-Roo Can-Do Bookmark mobile
Bookmarks. *See* Koala-Roo Can-Do Bookmarks
Book Record Sheet, 142
use of, 140
Borders. *See* Can-Do Borders
Bouquet Detailed Compliment Grid, 137
use of, 117
Bravo Garbanzo Dip. *See* Recipe for Bravo Garbanzo Dip
Bucket Compliment Grid, 123
use of, 115
Bulletin boards
Can-Do Compliment bulletin board, 19
Compliment Grids, 120–138
Goal and Reward Sheet, 119
Can-Do Kid of the Week, 19
Kid of the Week Letter Home, 74
use of, 23
Can-Do Name Tags, 27
use of, 18
Fifty-Valentine Pattern Sheet, 167
use of, 156
Koala-Roo Reading Tree, 147
use of, 140
posters, 32–37
use of, 18
Super Reader Logo, 28
use of, 18
A Tree for All Seasons, 45
use of, 21
Valentine Graph (enlarge), 166
use of, 156
Buttons. *See* Can-Do Buttons

Can. *See* Can-Do Can
Can-Do Assignments Tally, 87
use of, 83–85
Can-Do Awards, 106–112. *See also* Can-Do Blue Ribbons
use of, 86
on Can-Do Compliment bulletin board, 20, 86
during Celebrations of Success, 86
during Thoughtful Thursday, 182

Can-Do Backpack Bingo Board, 161
use of, 155
during Games Galore, 184
during Koala-Roo Can-Do's birthday, 183
Can-Do Birthday Card, 175
use of, 171
Can-Do Blue Ribbons, 113
use of, 86
on Can-Do Compliment bulletin board, 20
during Celebrations of Success, 181
during Success in All Seasons, 184
Can-Do Borders, 63–69
use of, 23
Can-Do Buttons, 26
use of, 18
on Can-Do Compliment bulletin board, 19
Can-Do Can, 46–50
assembly and use of, 21–22
Can-Do Caps, 58
use of, 23
during Celebrations of Success, 181, 183
Can-Do Cards, 175–179
use of, 171
on Can-Do Compliment bulletin board, 20
during Thoughtful Thursday, 182
Can-Do Chances, 57
use of, 22–23
in drawing for finished Compliment Grid, 117
Can-Do Chronicle, 173
use of, 171
Can-Do Clip Art, 60–62
use of, 23
on tally sheets, 84
Can-Do Coins, 162
use of, 155
during Summer Circus Celebration, 185
Can-Do Compliment bulletin board, 19
use of Compliment Grids on, 116, 117
Can-Do Compliment Slips, 25
use of, 17
in plan for math success, 153
Can-Do Contract, 97
use of, 85
in setting expectations, 96
Can-Do Curriculum Review, 79
use of, 24
Can-Do Deliveroo, 31
use of, 18
Can-Dollars, 162
use of, 155
Can-Do Door Decor, 51–56
assembly and use of, 22
use of head in Koala-Roo Can-Do Bookmark mobile, 141
Can-Do Ears, 59
use of, 23
Can-Do-Fly Detailed Compliment Grid, 138
use of, 117
Can-Do Giving Card, 176
use of, 171
Can-Do Gram, 114
use of, 86
Can-Do Group Tally Sheet, 158
use of, 153
Can-Do Habit Changer Tally, 89
use of, 83–85
Can-Do Hand Raiser Tally, 88
use of, 83–85
Can-Do Hop-a-roo Tally, 90
use of, 83–85
Can-Do Kid of the Week
bulletin board, 19
with Can-Do Name Tags forming border, 18
explained to parents in Kid of the Week Letter Home, 23
reported in Can-Do Chronicle, 171
Can-Do Name Tags, 27
use of, 18
Can-Do Note Card, 177
use of, 171
Can-Do 1-2-3 Tally, 88
use of, 83–85
Can-Do Placard Holder, 36
use of, 18
on Can-Do Kid of the Week bulletin board, 19
Can-Do Postal Worker cap. *See* Can-Do Caps
Can-Do reading pocket, 139
use of Dear Can-Do Book Report with, 140
use of Pouch Book Report with, 140
Can-Do Reading Shoes, 144
use of, 140
on Can-Do reading pocket, 139
Can-Do Reading Tickets, 151
use of, 140–141
with Koala-Roo Can-Do Bookmarks, 141
Can-Do Recipe Book Cover, 200
use of, 181
Can-Do Tallies, 87–90
designing your own, 84–85
use of, 83–85
in setting expectations, 96
Can-Do Thanksgiving Card, 178
use of, 171
Can-Do Triangle Card, 179
use of, 171
Caps. *See* Can-Do Caps
Cards. *See* Can-Do Cards

Careers and Hobbies Letter Home, 73
use of, 23
with Parents' Career Day, 183
Celebrations of Success, 181–185
after color-coded reading activity, 141
as group reinforcer, 118
in plan for math success, 153
after read-a-thon, 140–141
Chance slips. *See* Can-Do Chances
Chef Can-Do Cooks with You. *See* Can-Do Recipe Book Cover
Child's Self-Evaluations, 102–105
use of, 86
Child's Success Record, 98
use of, 85
Chips and dips, 182. *See also* Recipe for Bravo Garbanzo Dip, Recipe for Terrific Tofu Dip
Chocolate Soup à la Can-Do. *See* Recipe for Chocolate Soup à la Can-Do
Classroom organization
Absentee Pouch, 44
Can-Do Compliment bulletin board, 19–20
Can-Do Curriculum Review, 79
use of, 24
Can-Do Door Decor, 51
use of, 22
Can-Do Name Tags, 27
use of, 18
class rules chart, 19
Getting Started Checklist, 81
use of, 24
Koala-Roo Assignment Sheet, 30
use of, 18
Questionnaire Letter Home, 76
use of, 23
Room Job Chart, 38
use of, 20
Class rules chart, 19
Class rules, duplicated with Introductory Letter Home, 23
Clip art. *See* Can-Do Clip Art
Coins. *See* Can-Do Coins
Color Code for Can-Do Reading, 150
use of, 140–141
Colossal Cookie. *See* Recipe for a Colossal Cookie
Colossal Kid Award, 105
use of, 86
Compliment bulletin board. *See* Can-Do Compliment bulletin board
Compliment Grids, 120–138
use of, 115–119
on Can-Do Compliment bulletin board, 19–20
Contract. *See* Can-Do Contract
Curriculum review. *See* Can-Do Curriculum Review

Dear Can-Do Book Report, 149
use of, 140
Dessert Pizza. *See* Recipe for Dessert Pizza
Detailed Compliment Grids, 135–138
use of, 117
Doing Your Best Poster, 33
use of, 18
Door decor. *See* Can-Do Door Decor
Door logo. *See* Can-Do Door Logo

Emma, 183, 214
Expectations
Can-Do Compliment Slips, 17
Can-Do Compliment bulletin board, 19–20
Can-Do Contract, 97
use of, 85
Can-Do Tallies, 87–90
use of, 83–84
class rules chart, 19
Goal and Reward Sheet, 119
use of, 116
Introductory Letter Home, 71
use of, 23
math success program, 153–154
Reinforcing Your Expectations, 116
Setting Expectations, 96
use of, 85

Fabulous Friday. *See* Invitation for Fabulous Friday
Fall Festival. *See* Invitation for a Fall Festival
Family Tree, 21
Favorite Book Awards with Pouch, 143
use of, 140
Fifty-Valentine Pattern Sheet, 167
use of, 156–157
Finger puppets. *See* Koala-Roo Finger Puppets
Focus Sheet, 92
use of, 84
Friendship Tea, 182
Friendship Tree, 183

Games Galore. *See* Invitation for Games Galore
Getting Started Checklist, 81
use of, 24
Gingerbread House Compliment Grid, 124
use of, 115
Goal and Reward Sheet, 119
use of, 116
on Can-Do Compliment bulletin board, 19
in plan for math success, 153

Good News Note, 114
  use of, 86
Grandparents' Day. *See* Invitation for Grandparents' Day
Green Eggs and Ham, 182
Group Can-Do Counting, 160
  use of, 154

Happy Birthday Kid cap. *See* Can-Do Caps
Heart-Flower Compliment Grid, 125
  use of, 115
How Koala-Roo Can-Do Got His Name, 7–16
  use of, 21
    with Koala-Roo Finger Puppets, 172
How to Draw Koala-Roo Can-Do, 80
  use of, 24
    as a favor for Koala-Roo Can-Do's birthday, 183

I Am Special, 43
  use of, 21
I Can Do It Talent Show, 183–184
Ice Cream Compliment Grid, 126
  use of, 115
I "Chews" You Valentine, 170
  use of, 157
Ideas for Group Reinforcers, 118
  use of, 115
Ideas for Individual Reinforcers, 94
  use of, 84
Ideas for Show-and-Tell, 174
  use of, 171
Igloo Compliment Grid, 127
  use of, 115
    on Can-Do reading pocket, 139
Individual Can-Do Counting, 159
  use of, 154
Introductory Letter Home, 71
  use of, 23
Invitation for a Book Bash, 195
  use of, 184
Invitation for a Fall Festival, 194
  use of, 183
Invitation for a Spring Fling, 198
  use of, 185
Invitation for a Summer Circus Celebration, 199
  use of, 185
Invitation for Fabulous Friday, 190
  use of, 183
Invitation for Games Galore, 197
  use of, 184
Invitation for Grandparents' Day, 192
  use of, 183
Invitation for Koala-Roo Can-Do's Birthday, 191
  use of, 183
Invitation for Magnificent Monday, 186
  use of, 182
Invitation for Parents' Career Day, 193
  use of, 183
Invitation for Success in All Seasons, 196
  use of, 184
Invitation for Tea Party Tuesday, 187
  use of, 182
Invitation for Thoughtful Thursday, 189
  use of, 182
Invitation for Wonderful Wednesday, 188
  use of, 182

Kid of the Week. *See* Can-Do Kid of the Week
Kid of the Week Letter Home, 74
  use of, 23
Kite Compliment Grid, 128
  use of, 115
Knapsack Compliment Grid, 129
  use of, 115
    on Can-Do reading pocket, 139
Koala Apple Crispy. *See* Recipe for Koala Apple Crispy
Koala Cake. *See* Recipe for Koala Cake
Koala Cooler. *See* Recipe for Koala Cooler
Koala Frozen Yogurt. *See* Recipe for Koala Frozen Yogurt
Koala-Roo Assignment Sheet, 30
  use of, 18
Koala-Roo Can-Do Bookmark mobile, 141
Koala-Roo Can-Do Bookmarks, 152
  use of, 141
    in Koala-Roo Can-Do Bookmark mobile, 141
Koala-Roo Can-Do Door Logo, 29
  use of, 18
Koala-Roo Can-Do Pencil Tops, 70
  use of, 23
    as a favor for Koala-Roo Can-Do's birthday, 183
Koala-Roo Can-Do Reader Poster, 35
  use of, 18
Koala-Roo Can-Do's birthday. *See* Invitation for Koala-Roo Can-Do's Birthday
Koala-Roo Finger Puppets, 180
  use of, 172
Koala-Roo Malted Milk. *See* Recipe for Koala-Roo Malted Milk
Koala-Roo Reading Tree, 147
  use of, 140

Language arts curriculum, Can-Do in, 171-172
Leaf Compliment Grid, 130
  use of, 115

Magnificent Monday. *See* Invitation for Magnificent Monday
Malted milk. *See* Recipe for Koala-Roo Malted Milk
Math curriculum, Can-Do in, 153–157
Math games and activities, 154–157
Math success program, 158–160
  use of, 153–154
Mobile. *See* Koala-Roo Can-Do Bookmark mobile
Mottoes, 19
My Mother Is the Most Beautiful Woman in the World, 172, 215
My Sticker Board, 78
  use of, 24
    explained to parents in Sticker Board Letter Home, 24

The Name Game, 42
  use of, 21
Name tags. *See* Can-Do Name Tags
Note cards. *See* Can-Do Cards

Observable Problem Behaviors, 91
  use of, 84
Overview Assessment, 99
  use of, 85

Parent Involvement Letter Home, 72
  use of, 23
Parents' Career Day. *See* Invitation for Parents' Career Day
Peanut Butter Hors d'Oeuvres. *See* Recipe for Peanut Butter Hors d'Oeuvres
Pencil tops. *See* Koala-Roo Can-Do Pencil Tops
Placard, 37
  use of, 18
    on Can-Do Kid of the Week bulletin board, 19
Place value game, 154
Plan for group success, 115–119
Plan for individual success, 83–86
Plan for math success, 153–154
Planning Sheet, 95
  use of, 84
Pocket pouch for compliment slips, 17, 153
Popcorn Picnic. *See* Recipe for a Popcorn Picnic
Posters, positive motivation, 32–35
  use of, 18
    on Can-Do Compliment bulletin board, 20
Post office project. *See* Valentine Post Office project
Pouch Book Report, 148
  use of, 140
Pouch Stories, 171–172
  use of Stand-up Can-Do with, 20
Problem behaviors. *See* Observable Problem Behaviors
Projects for students
  Book Record Sheet, 142
    use of, 140
  Can-Do Can, 46–50
    use of, 21–22
  Can-Do Caps and Ears, 58–59
    use of, 23, 181, 183
  Can-Do Chronicle, 173
    use of, 171
  Can-Do reading pocket, 139
  Can-Do Reading Shoes, 144
    use of, 140
  Can-Do Reading Tickets, 151
    use of, 140
  Color Code for Can-do Reading, 150
    use of, 140
  Favorite Book Awards with Pouch, 143
    use of, 140
  Koala-Roo Can-Do Bookmark mobile, 141
  Koala-Roo Can-Do Bookmarks, 152
    use of, 141
  Koala-Roo Finger Puppets, 180
    use of, 172
  Reading Apple Barrel and Apples, 145–146
    use of, 140
  Stand-up Can-Do, 39–41
    use of, 20
  Valentine Post Office project materials, 163–170
    use of, 155–157
Proud Person of the Day cap. *See* Can-Do Caps
Pumpkin Compliment Grid, 131
  use of, 115

Questionnaire Letter Home, 76
  use of, 23

Read-a-thon, 140
  Book Bash after, 184
Reading Apple Barrel, 145
  use of, 140
Reading curriculum, Can-Do in, 139–141
Reading Hut, 118
Reading pocket. *See* Can-Do reading pocket
Reading tickets. *See* Can-Do Reading Tickets
Reading tree. *See* Koala-Roo Reading Tree
Recipe book cover. *See* Can-Do Recipe Book Cover
Recipe for a Can-Do Classroom, 2

Recipe for a Colossal Cookie, 201
use of, 182
Recipe for a Popcorn Picnic, 200
use of, 182
Recipe for Bravo Garbanzo Dip, 201
use of, 182
Recipe for Chocolate Soup à la Can-Do, 205
use of, 184
Recipe for Dessert Pizza, 203
use of, 183
Recipe for Koala Apple Crispy, 204
use of, 183
Recipe for Koala Cake, 203–204
use of, 183
Recipe for Koala Cooler, 206
use of, 185
Recipe for Koala Frozen Yogurt, 205
use of, 184
Recipe for Koala-Roo Malted Milk, 202
use of, 182
Recipe for Peanut Butter Hors d'Oeuvres, 206
use of, 184
Recipe for Terrific Tofu Dip, 202
use of, 182
Reinforcement
awards, 105–114
Can-Do Blue Ribbons, 113
use of, 86
Can-Do Buttons, 26
use of, 18
Can-Do Chances, 57
use of, 22
holding a drawing with, 117
Can-Do Coins and Can-Dollars, 162
use of, 155
Can-Do Compliment Slips, 25
use of, 17
Can-Do Group Tally (math), 158
use of, 153
Can-Do Placard Holder and Placard, 36–37
use of, 18
Can-Do Reading Shoes, 144
use of, 140
Can-Do Tallies, 87–90
use of, 83
Child's Self-Evaluations, 102–105
use of, 86
competition, 117
Compliment Grids, 120–138
use of, 115
Ideas for Group Reinforcers, 118
use of, 115
Ideas for Individual Reinforcers, 94
Koala-Roo Can-Do Pencil Tops, 70
use of, 23
Reinforcement *(cont.)*
My Sticker Board, 78
Sticker Board Letter Home, 77
use of, 24
Reinforce with a Purpose, 5
Reinforcing Your Expectations, 116
Ways to Say or Write "Good Job," 5
Rhyme in Time, 184–185
Room Job Chart, 38
use of, 20

Say "I Can" Poster, 34
use of, 18
Season Charades, 184
Seasons Tree, 21
Secret Pals, 182–183
Setting Expectations, 96
use of, 85
Show-and-Tell
Ideas for, 174
use of, 171
Letter Home, 75
use of, 23
Slogans. *See* Mottoes
Song, 183
Spaceship Compliment Grid, 132
use of, 115
on Can-Do reading pocket, 139
Spring Fling. *See* Invitation for a Spring Fling
Stand-up Can-Do, 39–41
assembly of, 20–21
with flat pouch, 143
use of, 20–21
on Can-do reading pocket, 139
with Favorite Book Awards, 140
in place value game, 154–155
with Pouch Stories, 171
Sticker Board, My, 78
use of, 24
Sticker Board Letter Home, 77
use of, 24
Story starters. *See* Pouch Stories
Story writing, 171–172
Success in All Seasons. *See* Invitation for Success in All Seasons
Success management programs
Can-Do Compliment bulletin board, 19
Can-Do Coins and Can-Dollars, 162
use of, 155
Can-do Compliment Slips, 25
use of, 17
Can-Do Chances, 57
use of, 22
Can-Do Tallies, 87–90
use of, 83

Success management programs *(cont.)*
Compliment Grids, 120–138
use of, 115–119
math success program, 158–160
use of, 153–154
My Sticker Board, 78
Sticker Board Letter Home, 77
use of, 24
Observable Problem Behaviors, 91
use of, 84
Success Management for Individual Children, 83–86
Success Management for Small Groups, 115–138
Summer Circus Celebration. *See* Invitation for a Summer Circus Celebration
Super Reader Logo, 28
use of, 18

Tally sheets. *See* Can-Do Tallies
Teacher Effectiveness Checklist, 101
use of, 86
Teacher Effectiveness Sheet, 100
use of, 85
Tea Party Tuesday. *See* Invitation for Tea Party Tuesday
Terrific Tofu Dip. *See* Recipe for Terrific Tofu Dip
"There Was a Class That Had a Friend and Can-Do Was His Name-O," 183
Things I Like, 93
use of, 84
Thoughtful Thursday. *See* Invitation for Thoughtful Thursday
A Tree for All Seasons, 45
use of, 21
instead of Koala-Roo Reading Tree, 140
with Secret Pals, 183
A Treeful of Pigs, 21
Turkey Compliment Grid, 133
use of, 115

Umbrella Compliment Grid, 134
use of, 115

Valentine, I "Chews" You, 157
Valentine border, 68
Valentine Employment Form, 164
use of, 156
Valentine Graph, 166
use of, 156
Valentine Math Report, 169
use of, 157
Valentine Postal Worker Checks, 168
use of, 157
Valentine Postal Worker Schedule, 165
use of, 156
Valentine Post Office Flyer, 163
use of, 155
Valentine Post Office project, 155–157
Valentine Tree, 21

Ways to Promote Self-Esteem, 5
Ways to Say or Write "Good Job," 5
Weekful of Success Celebrations, 181–183
as group reinforcer, 118
Wishing Tree, 21
Wonderful Wednesday. *See* Invitation for Wonderful Wednesday
Writing ideas
Books about Self-Esteem, 207–219
Can-Do Borders, 63–69
use of, 23
Can-Do Can, 46–50
use of, 21–22
Can-Do Cards, 175–179
use of, 171
Can-Do Chronicle, 173
use of, 171
Dear Can-Do Book Report, 149
use of, 140
Mottoes, 19
Pouch Book Report, 148
use of, 140
Pouch Stories, 171–172
Stand-up Can-Do, 39–41
use of, 20–21

You Are Special, 82
use of, 24